SRA

Reading Mastery

Signature Edition

Language Arts Workbook

Siegfried Engelmann
Jean Osborn
Karen Lou Seitz Davis

Columbus, OH

SRAonline.com

Printed in the United States of America.

Send all inquiries to this address:
SRA/McGraw-Hill
4400 Easton Commons
Columbus, OH 43219

ISBN: 978-0-07-612486-2
MHID: 0-07-612486-X

1 2 3 4 5 6 7 8 9 DBH 13 12 11 10 09 08 07

The McGraw·Hill Companies

Name ________________________________

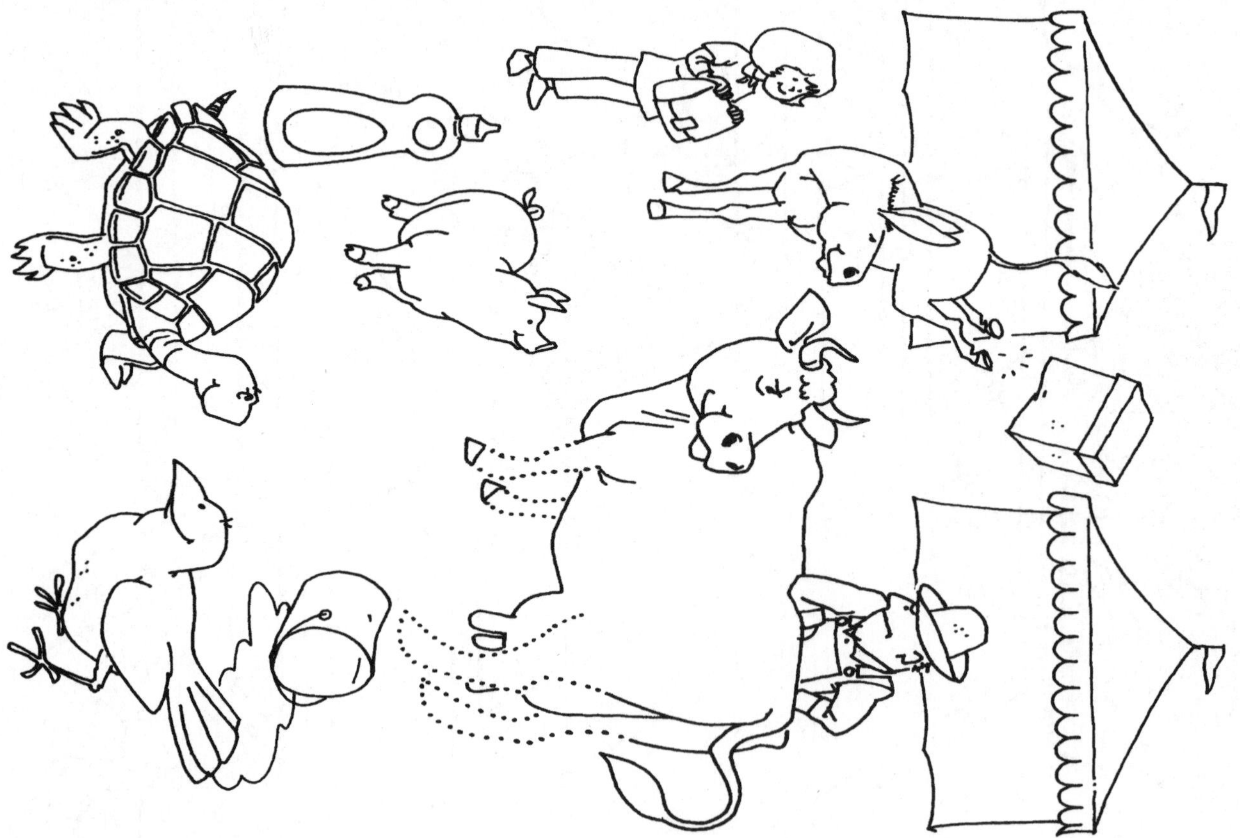

Name ______________________________

Name ______________________________

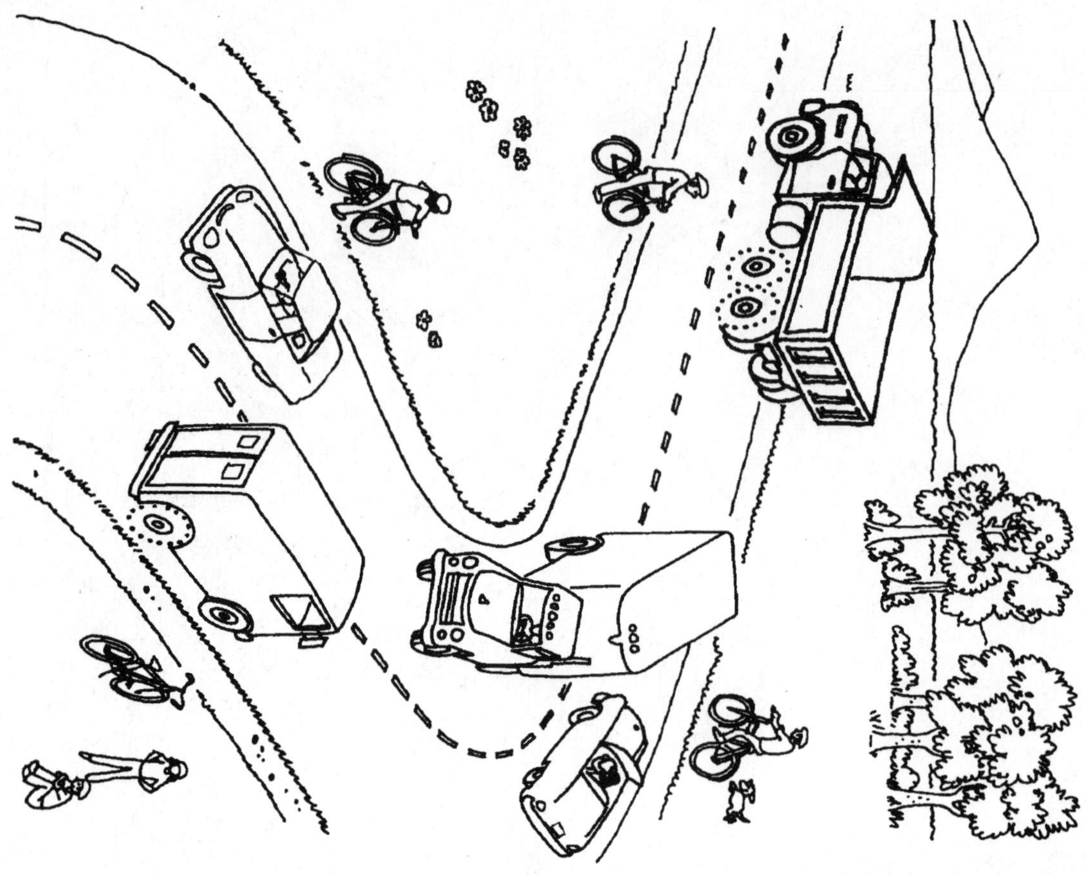

Name ___________________________

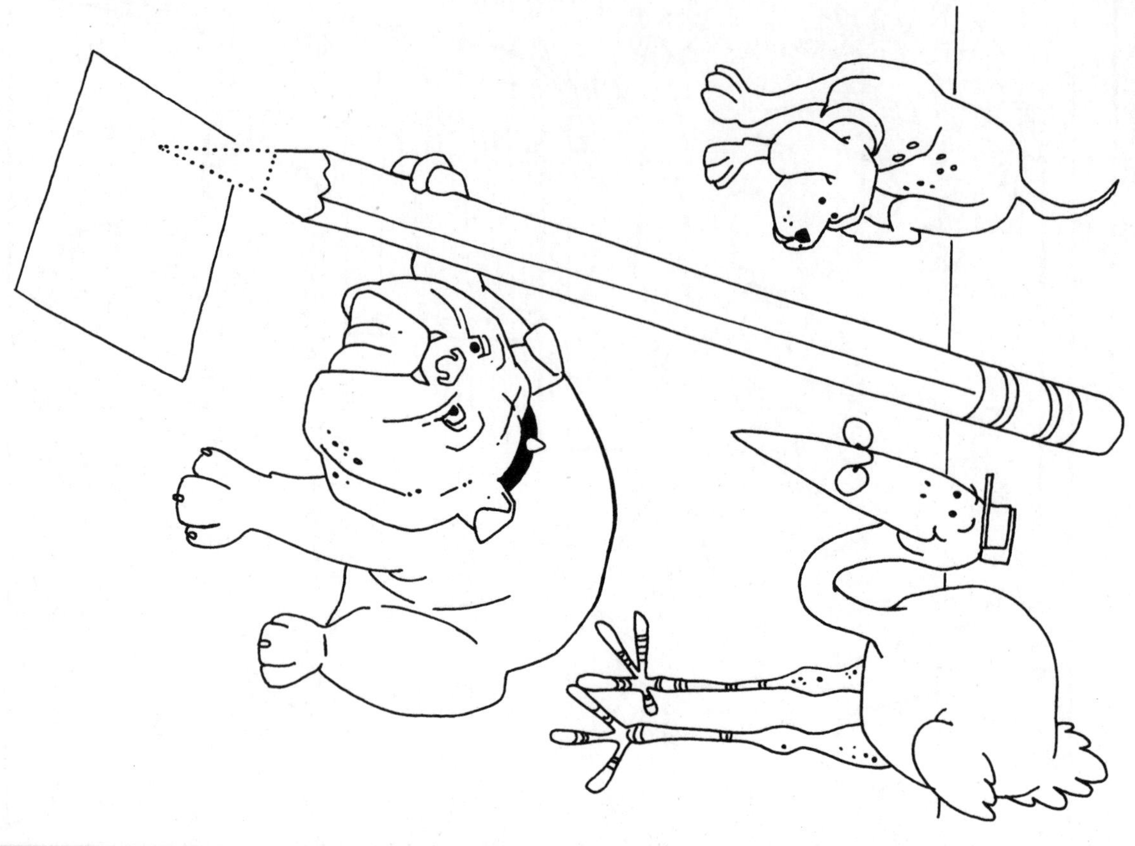

Name ________________________________

T

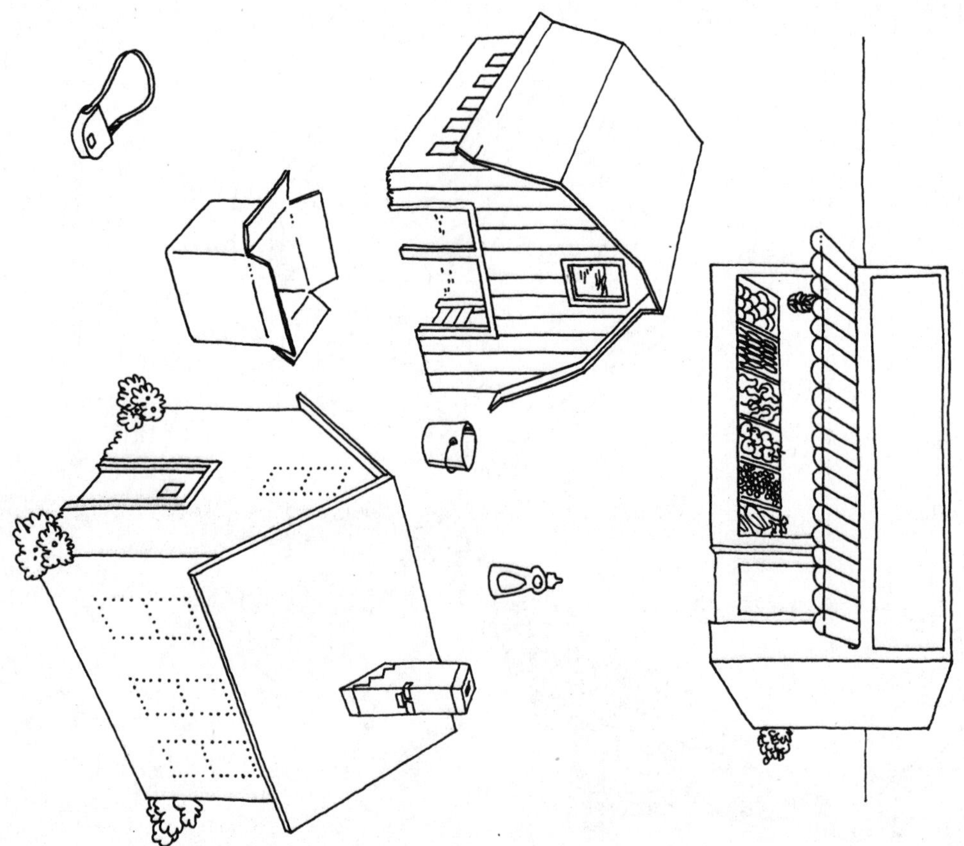

Name ___________________________________

Name ______________________________

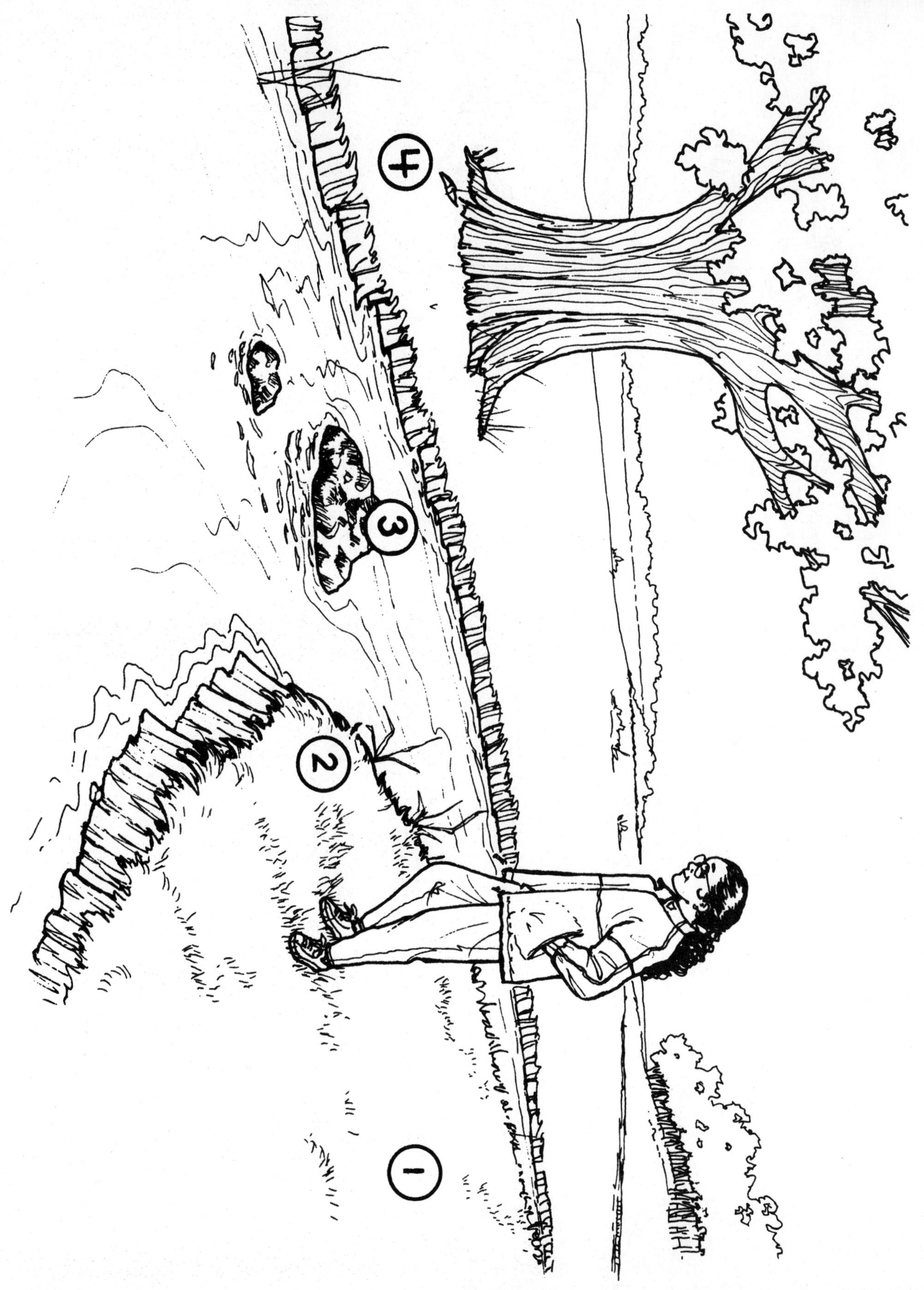

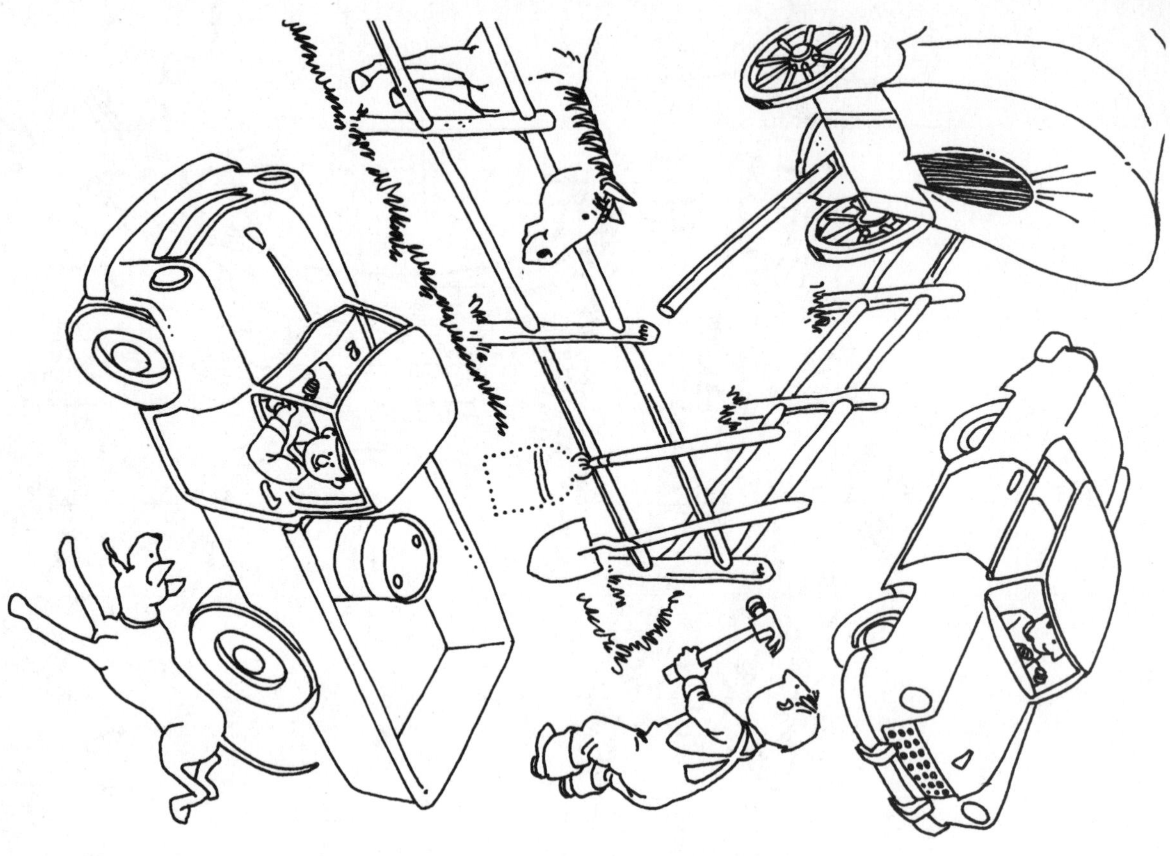

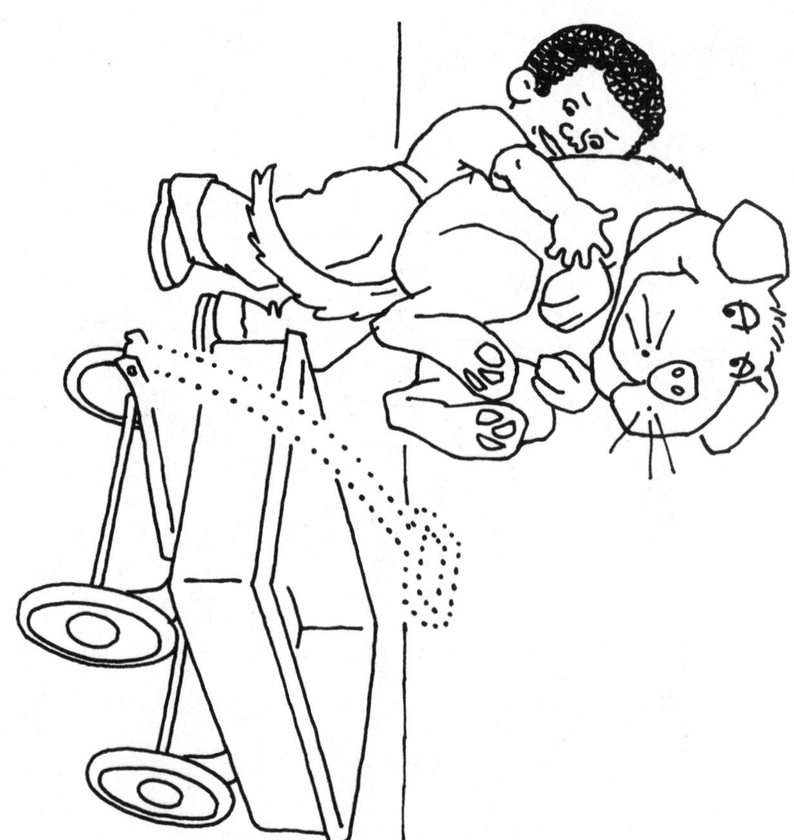

Name ________________________________

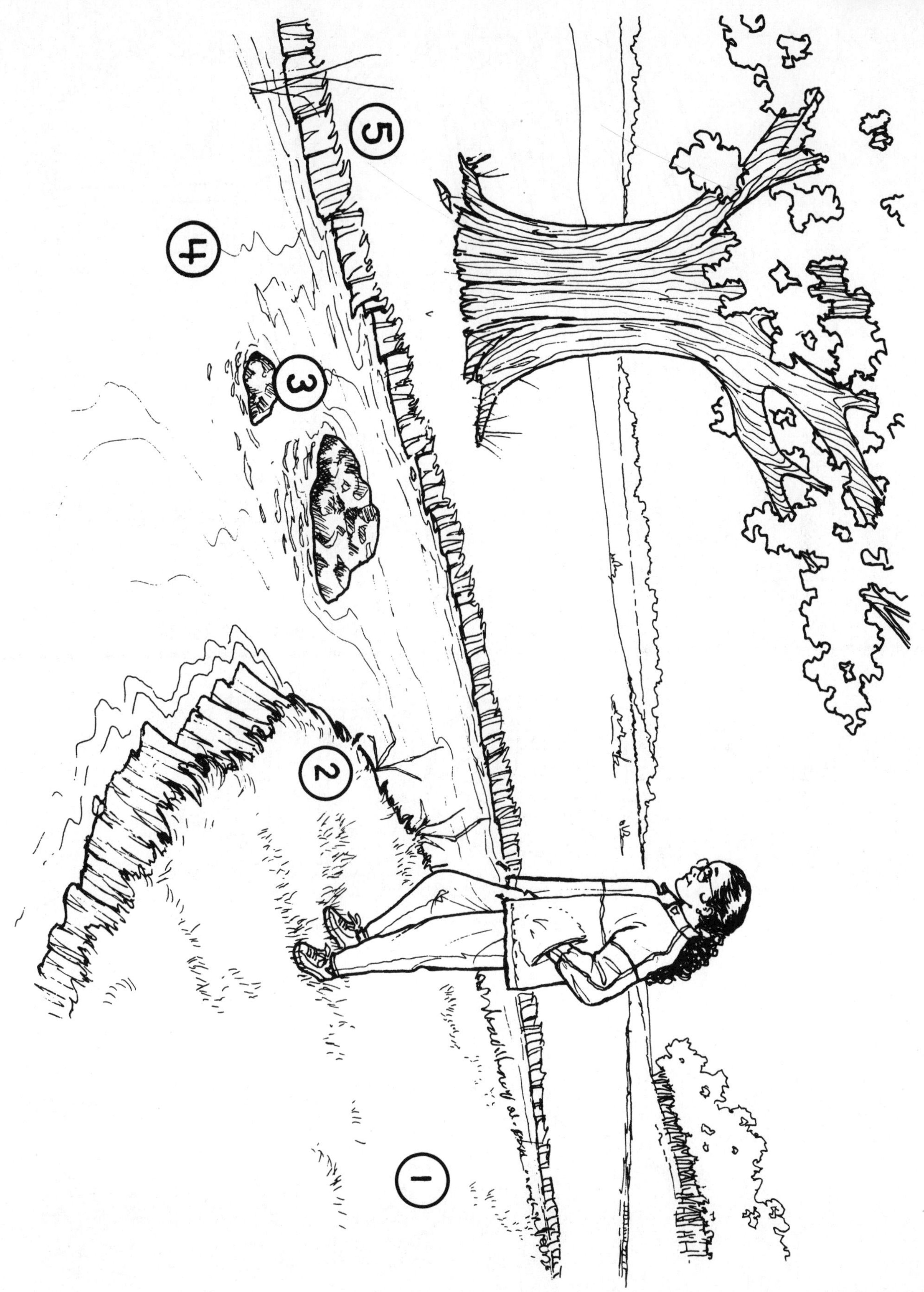

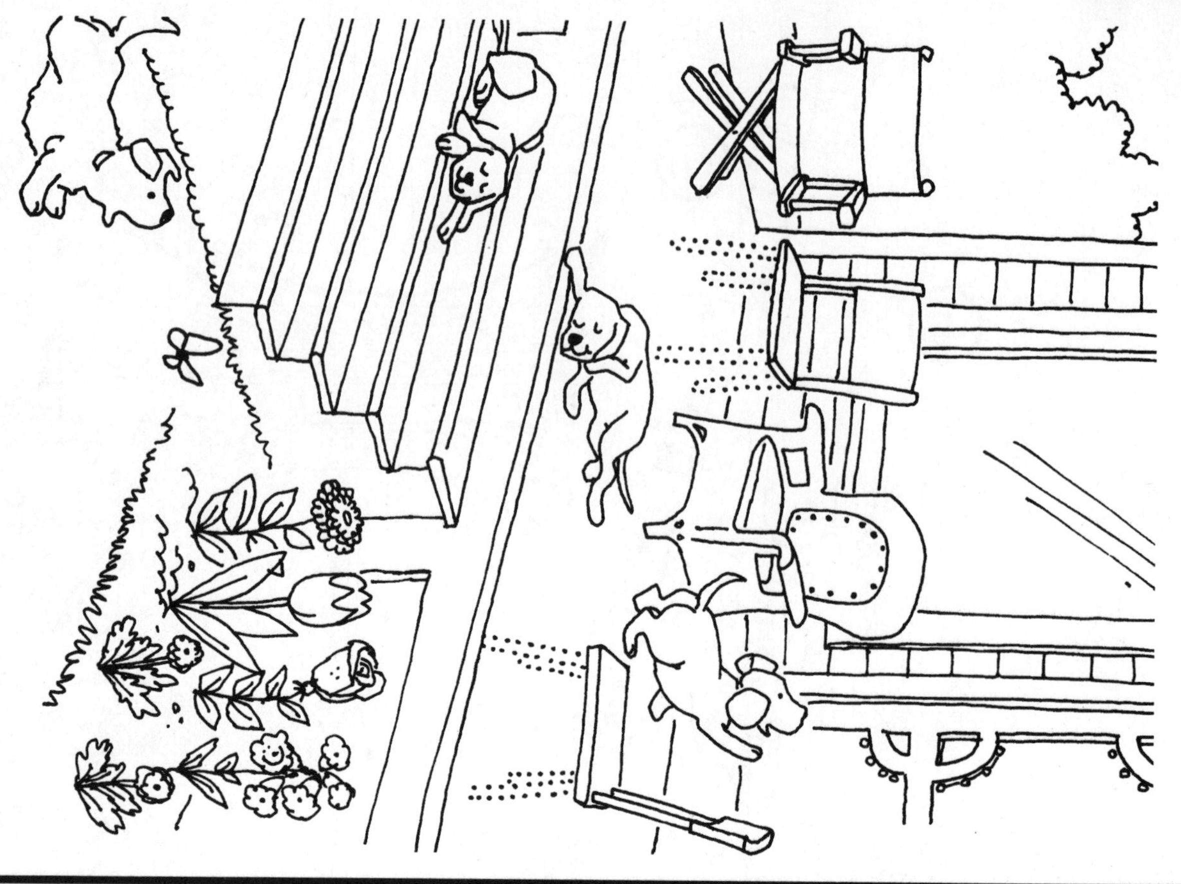

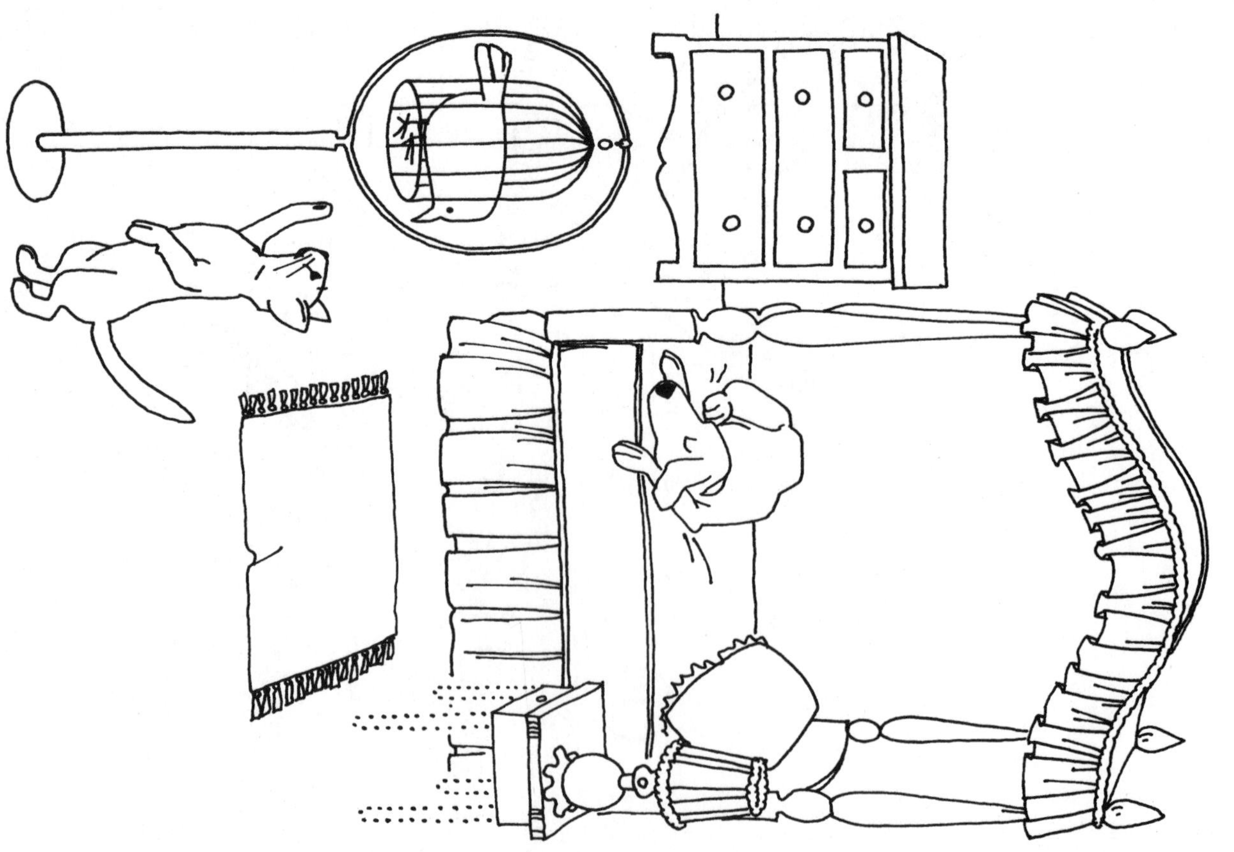

Name ___________________________________

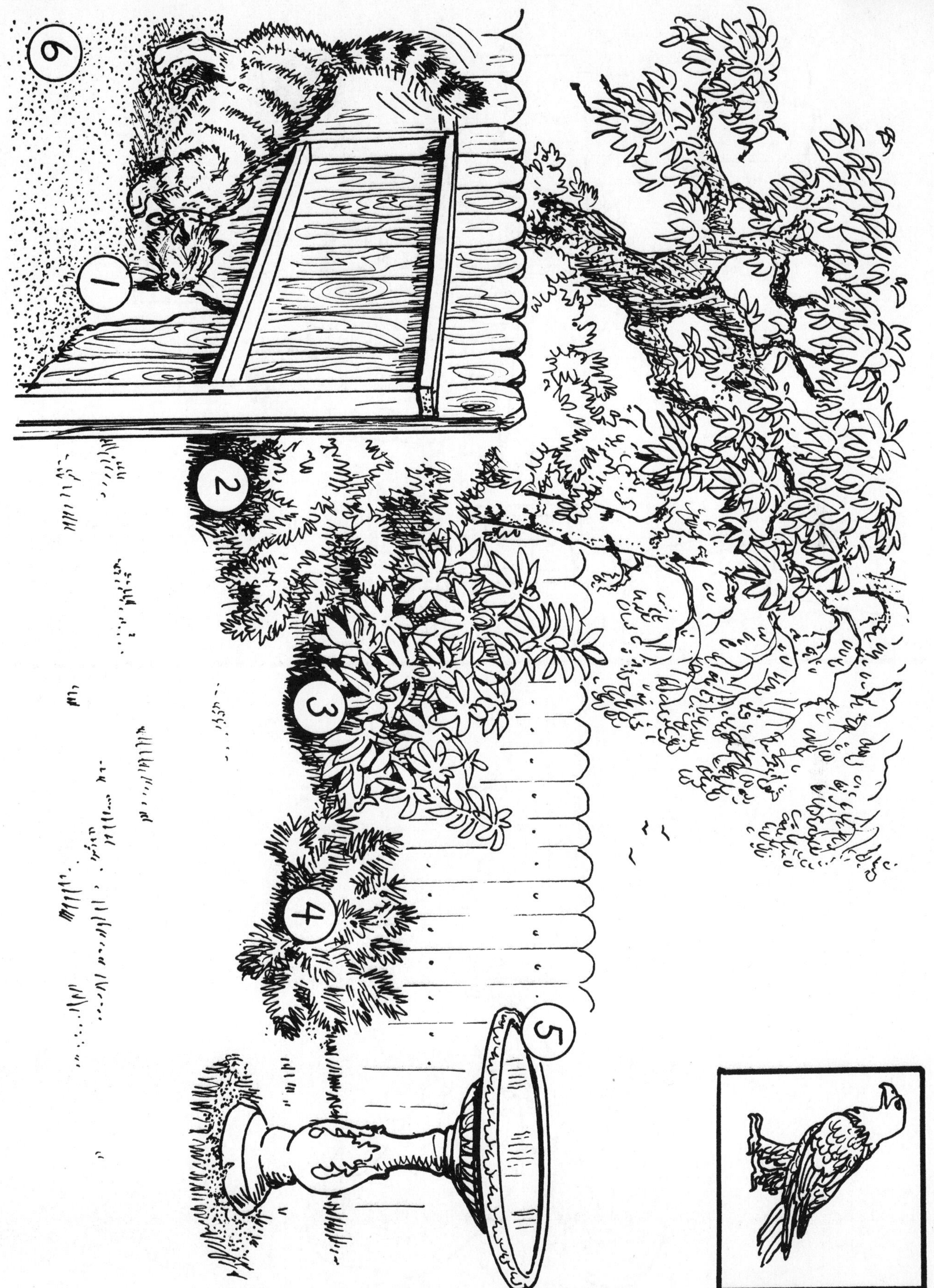

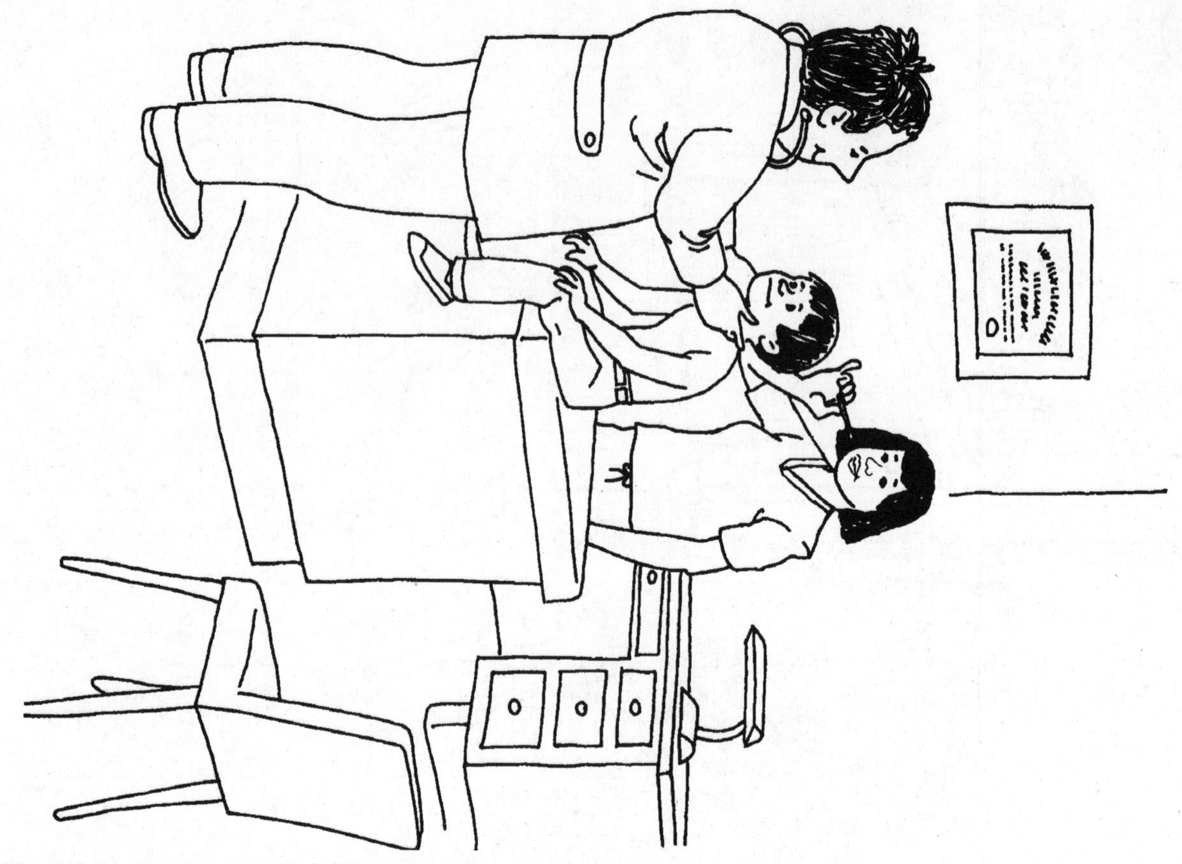

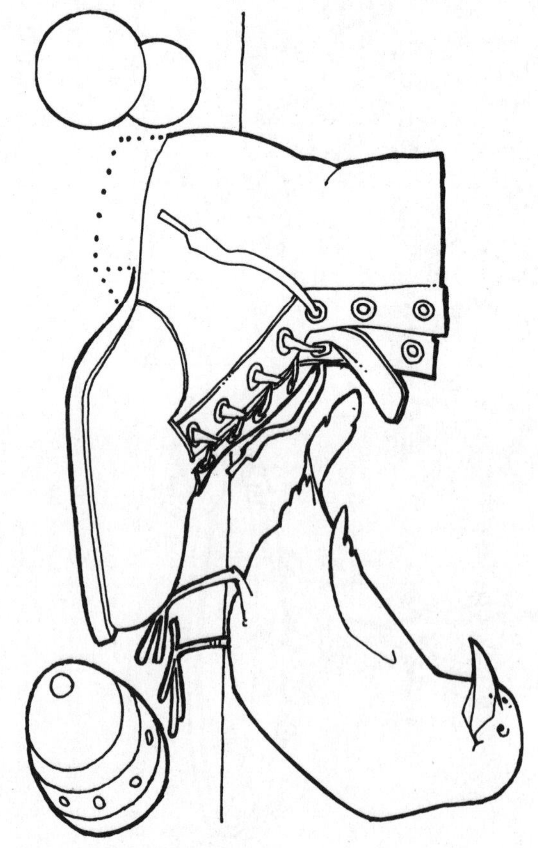

Name ___________________________

10

Name ________________________________

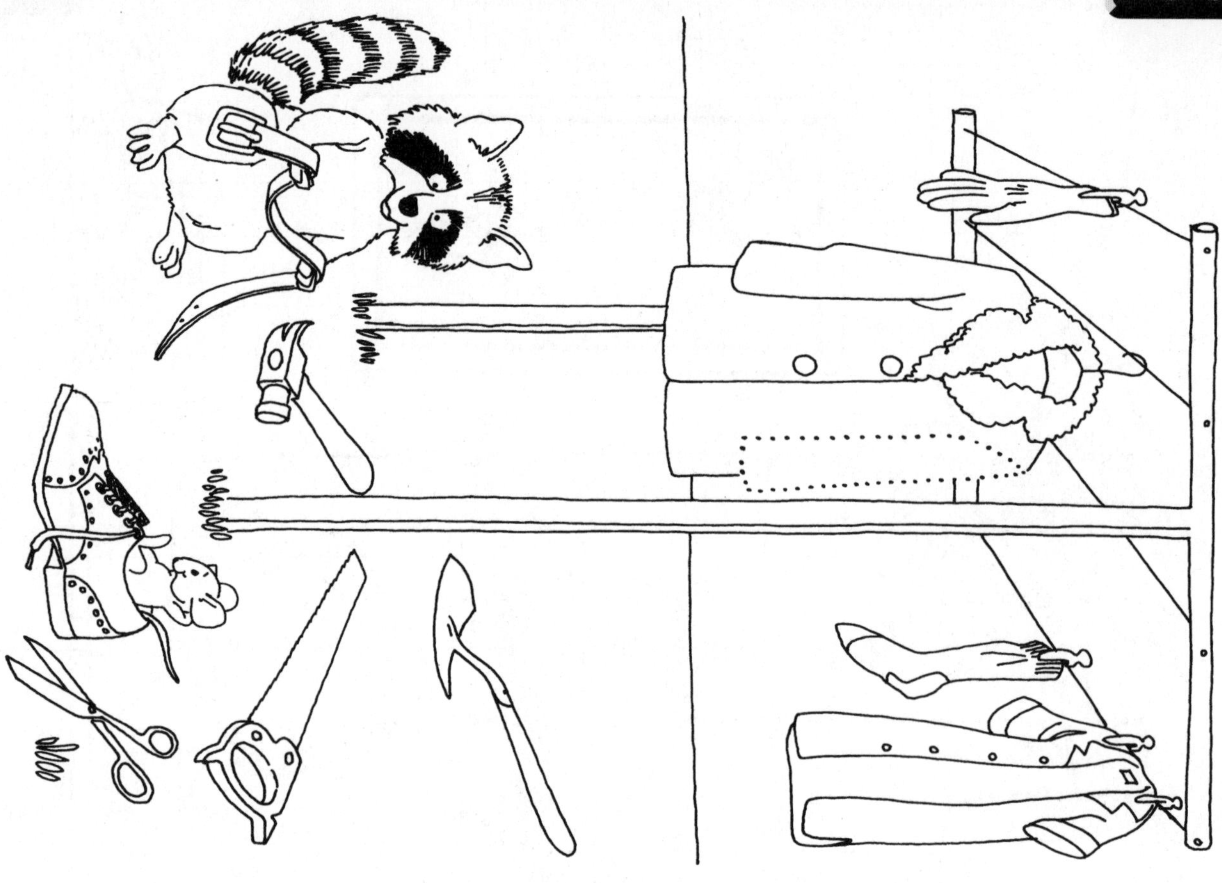

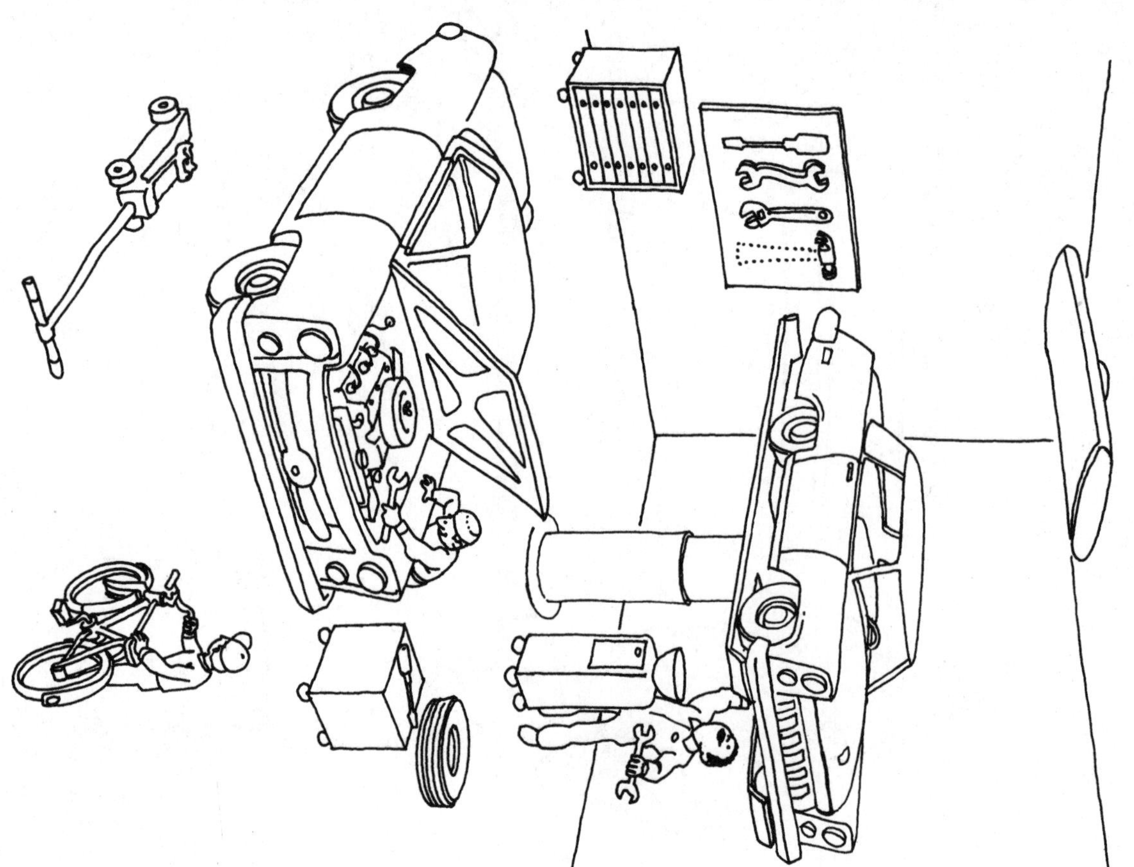

Name ______________________________

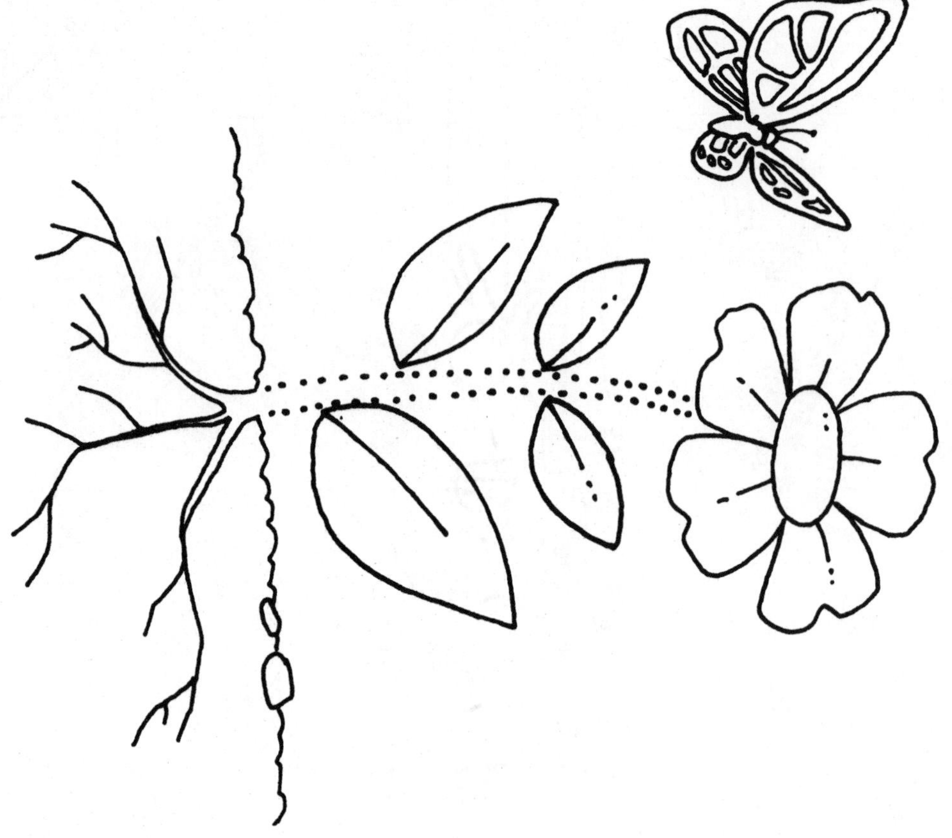

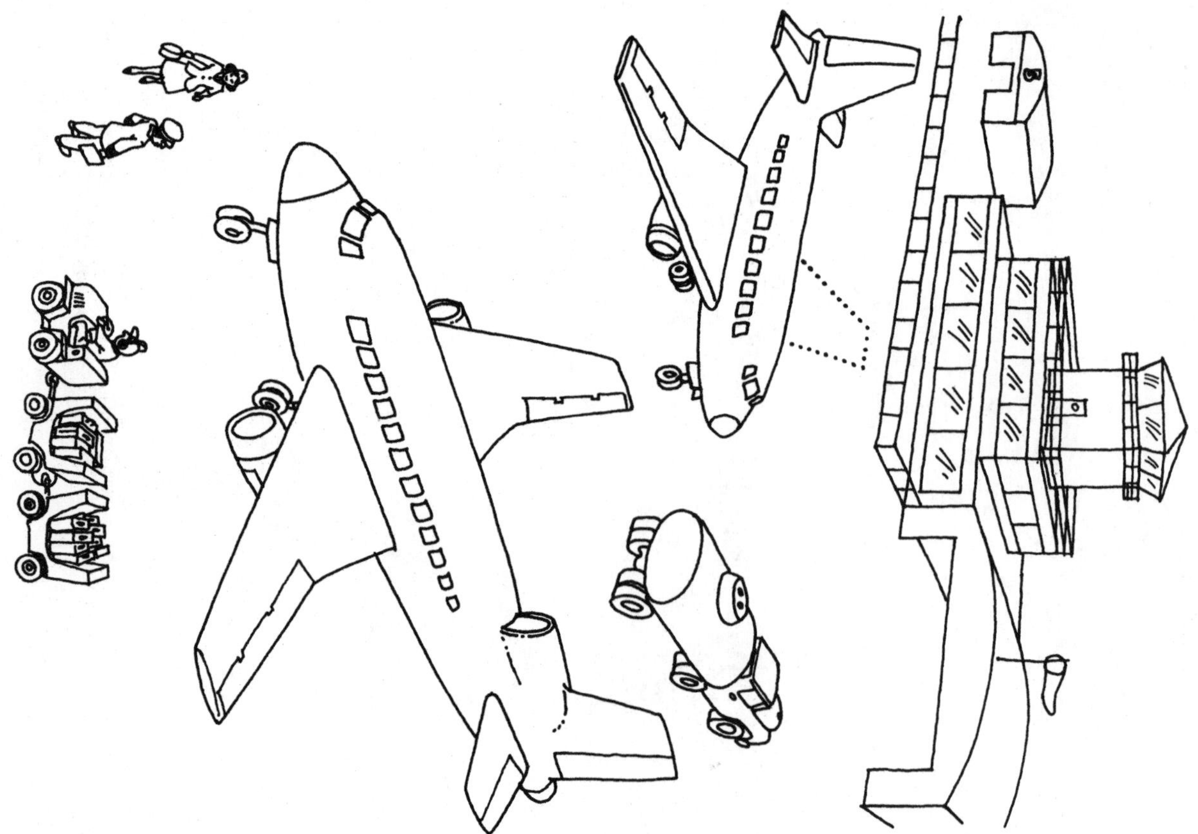

Name ___________________________________

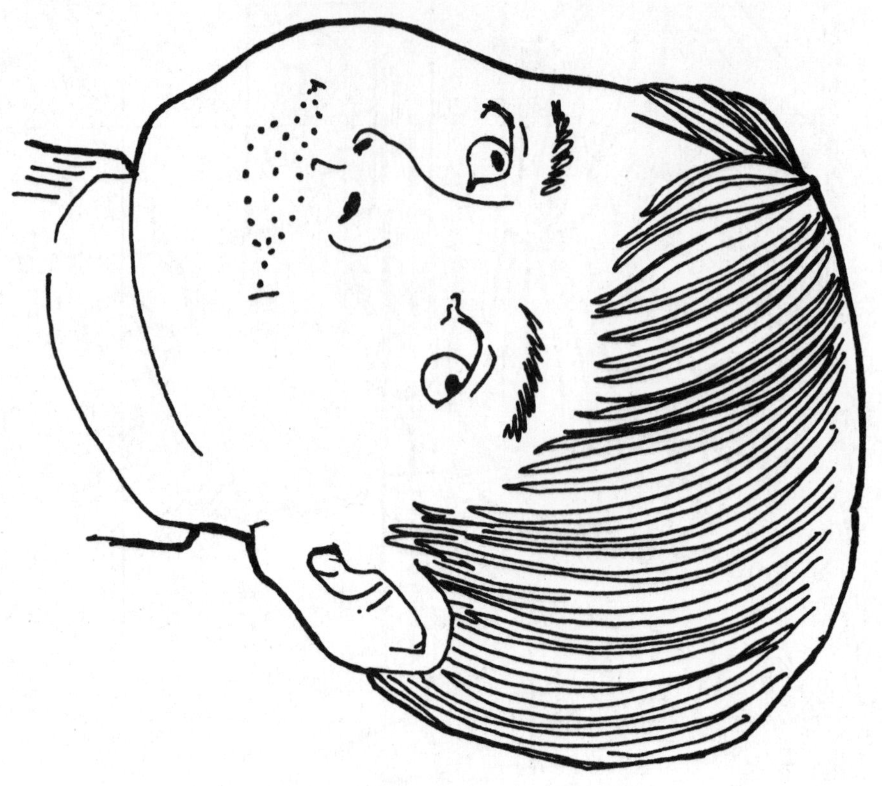

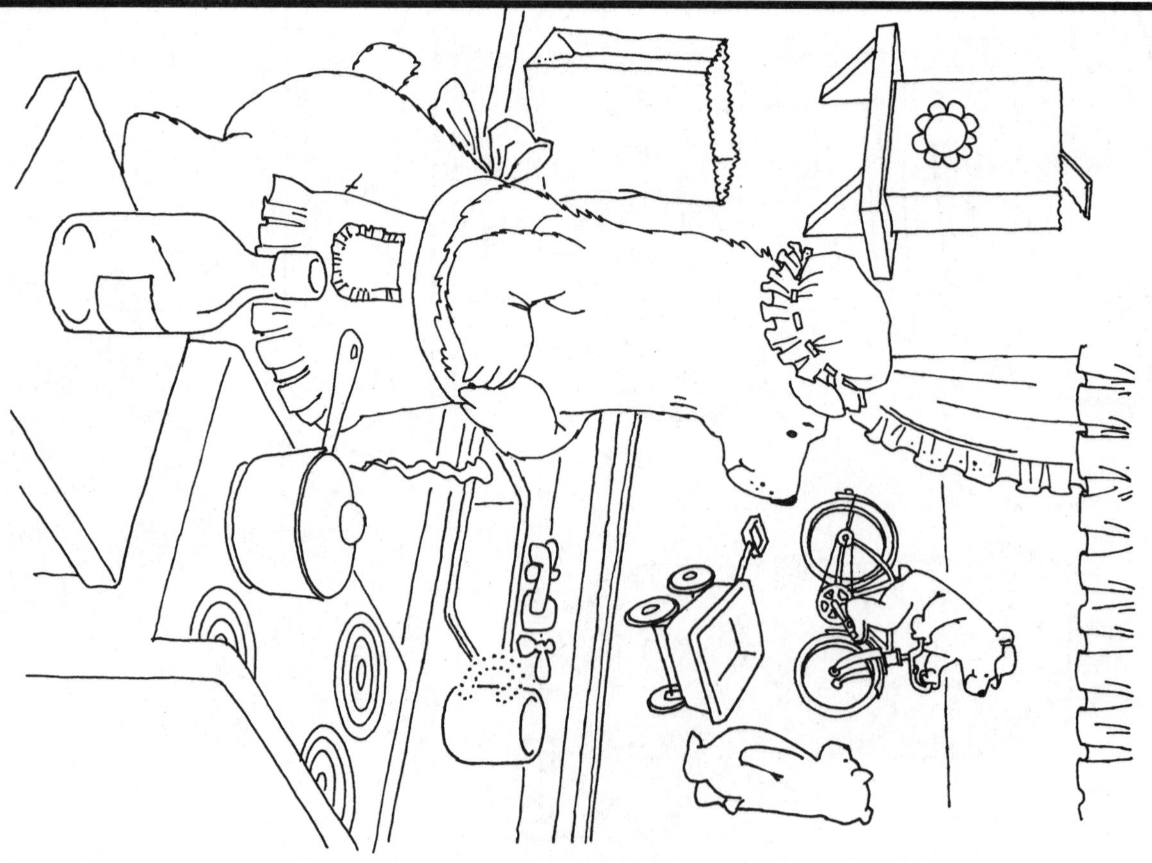

Name ______________________________

Name ________________________________

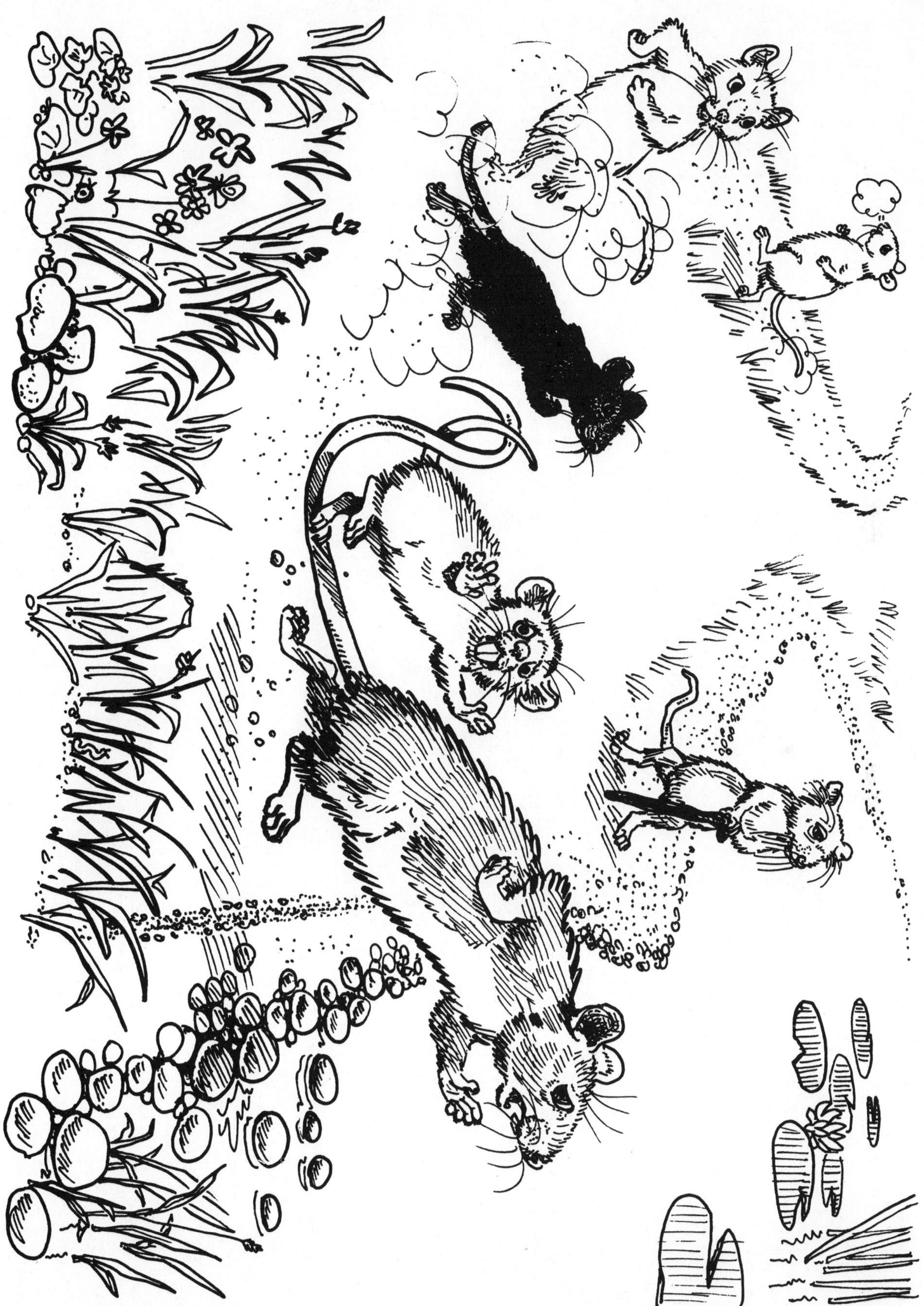

Name ______________________________

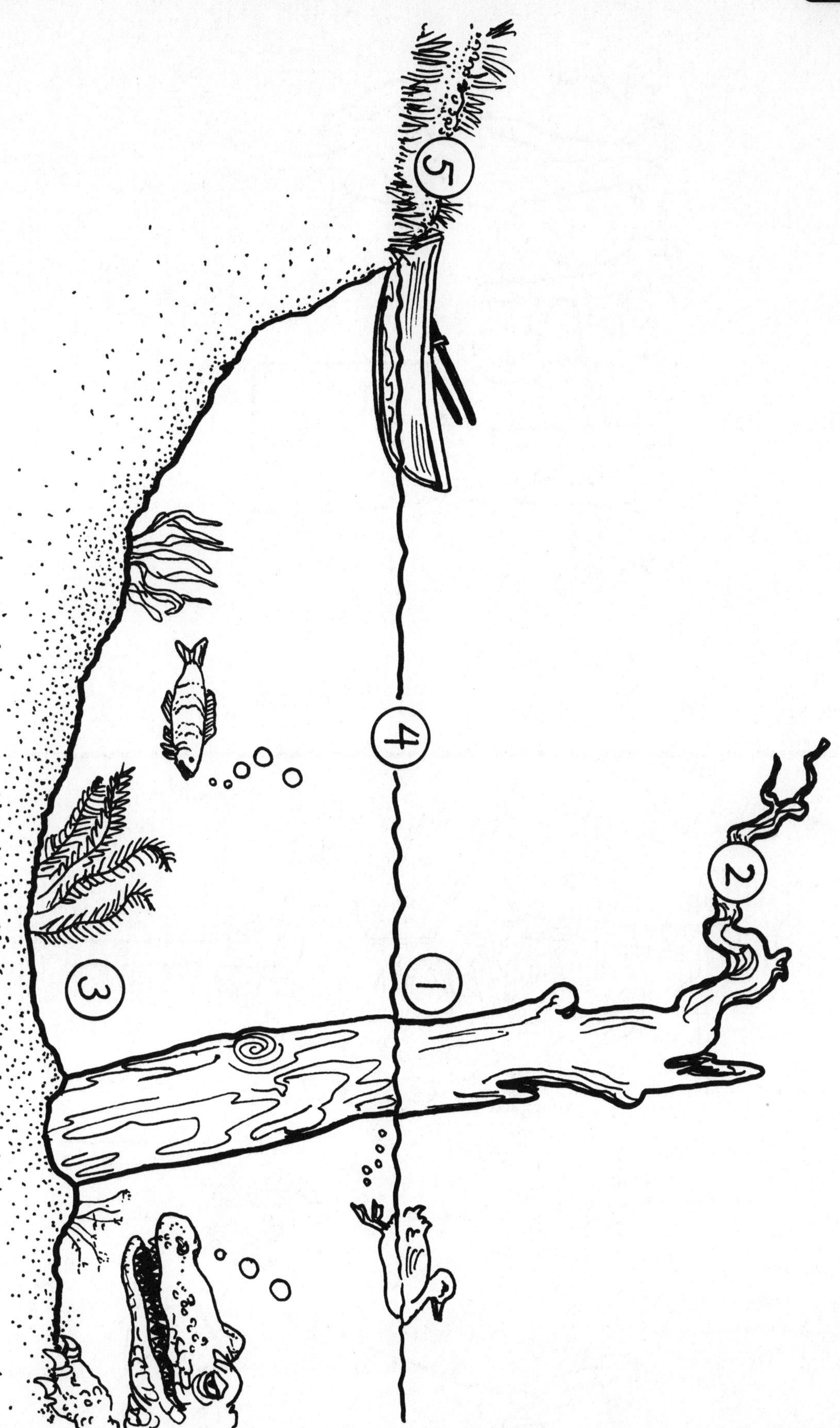

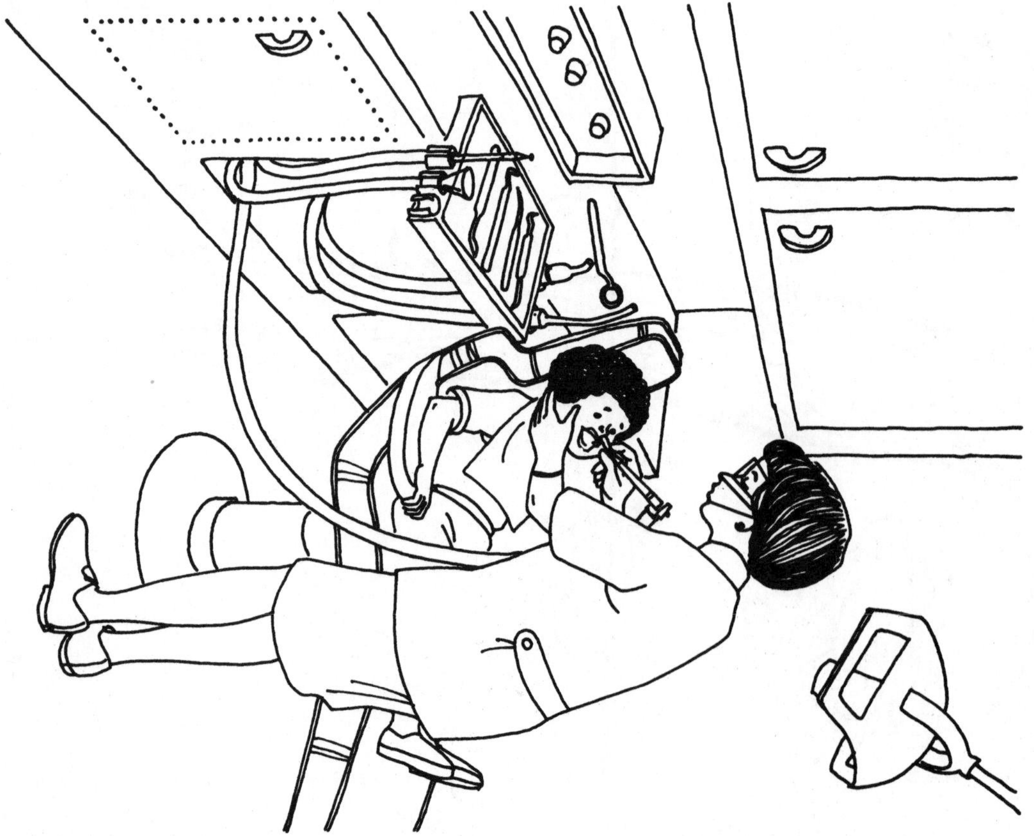

Name ______________________________

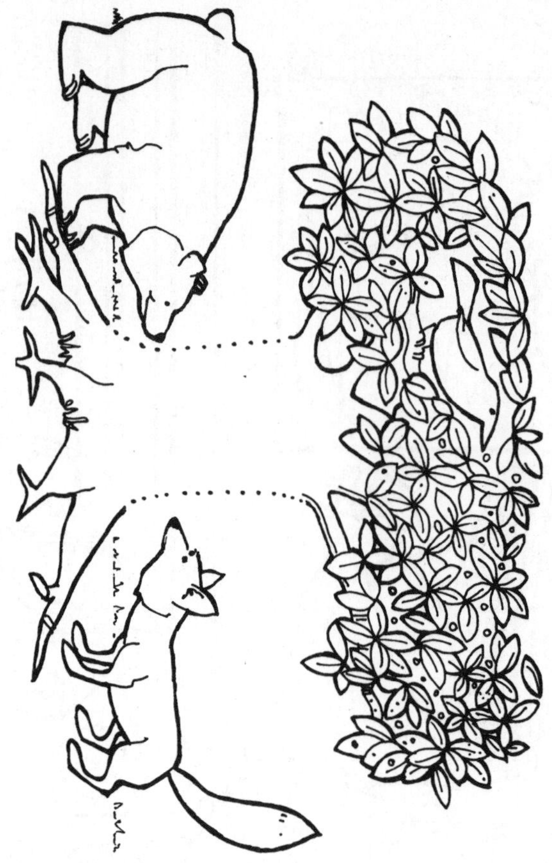

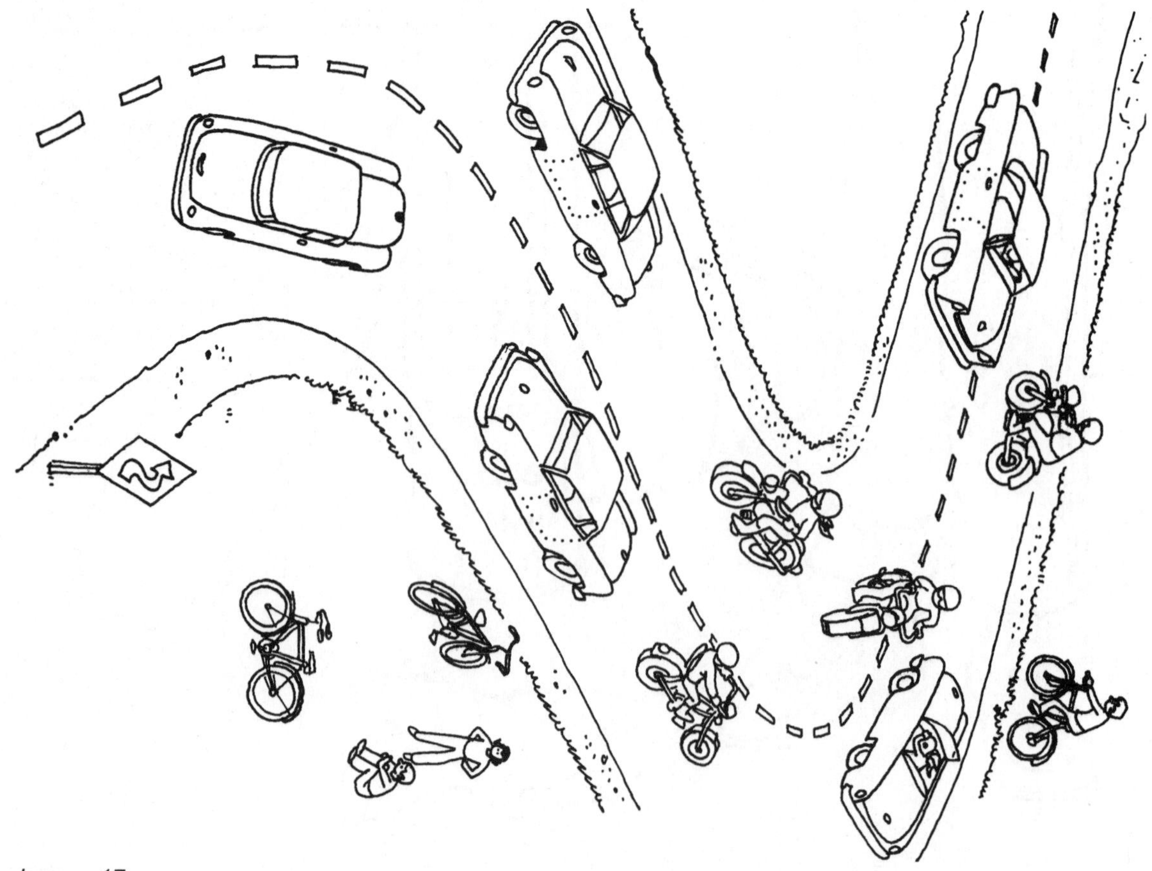

Name ______________________________

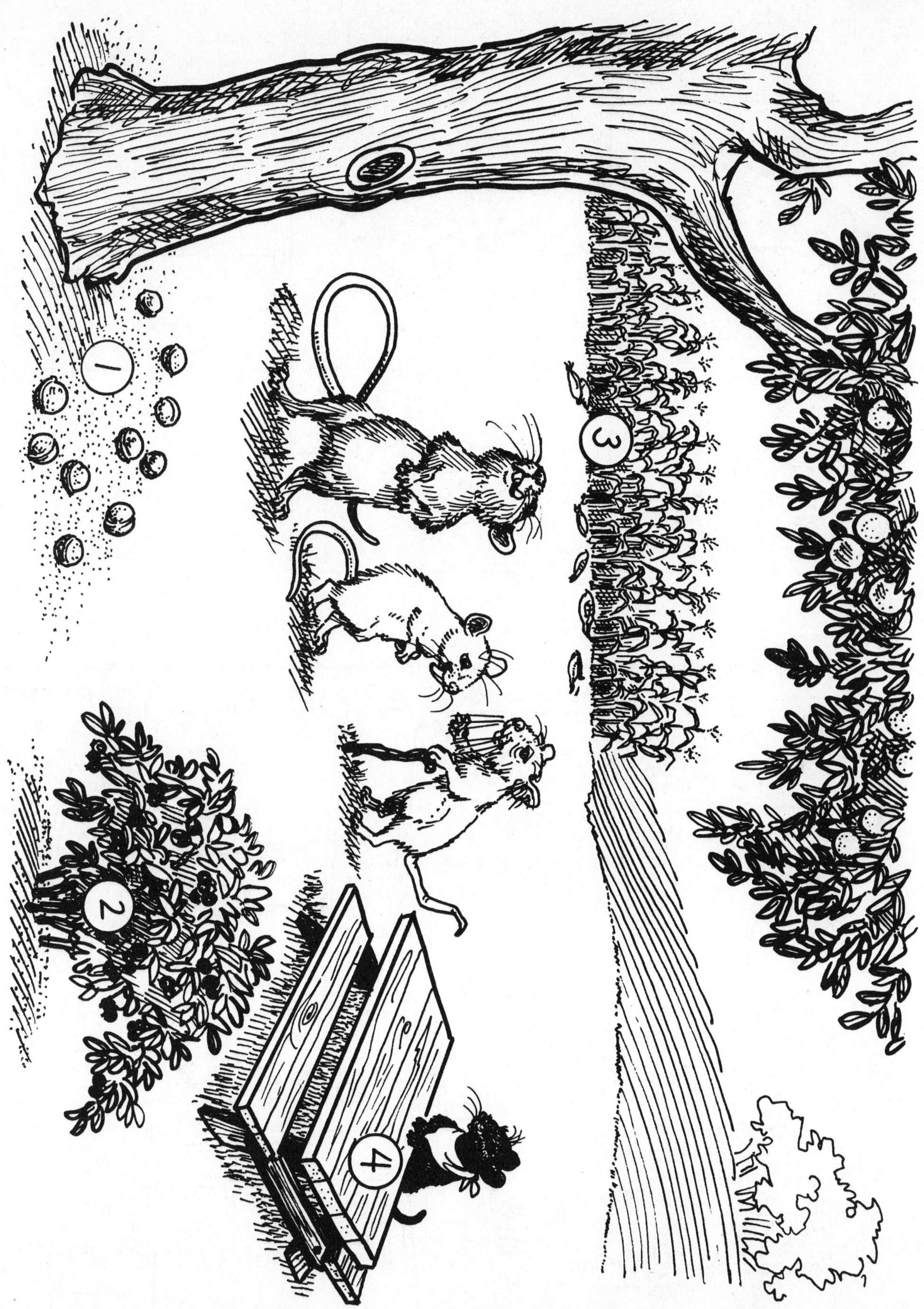

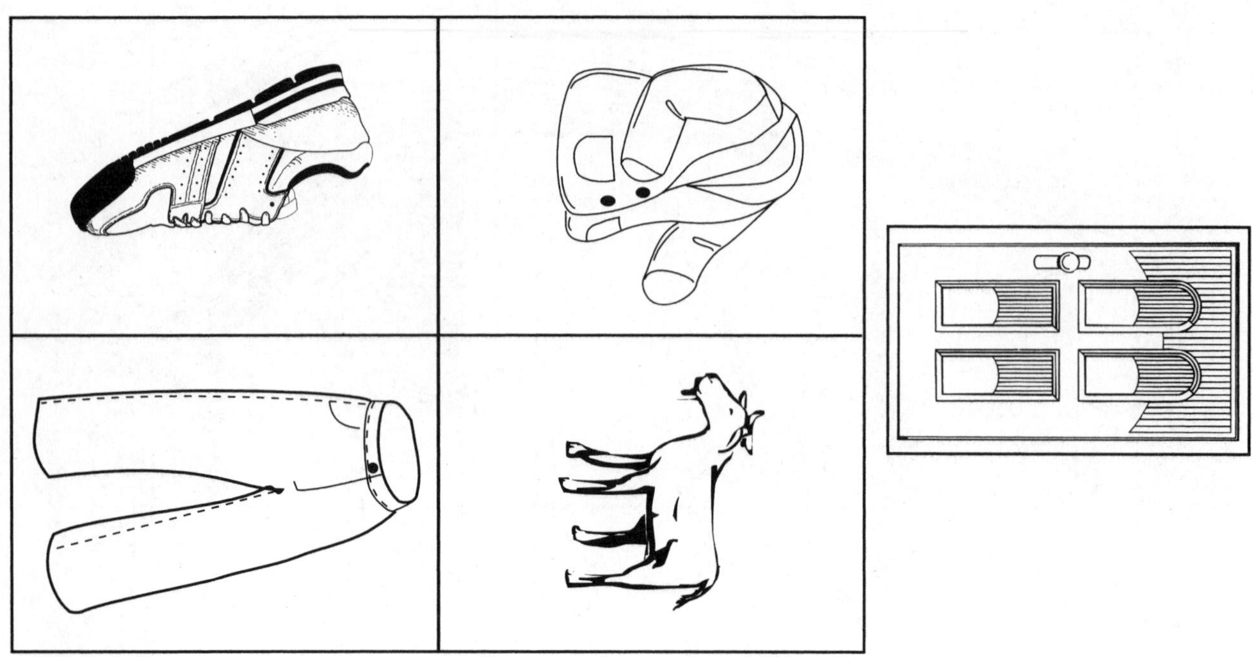

Name ________________________________

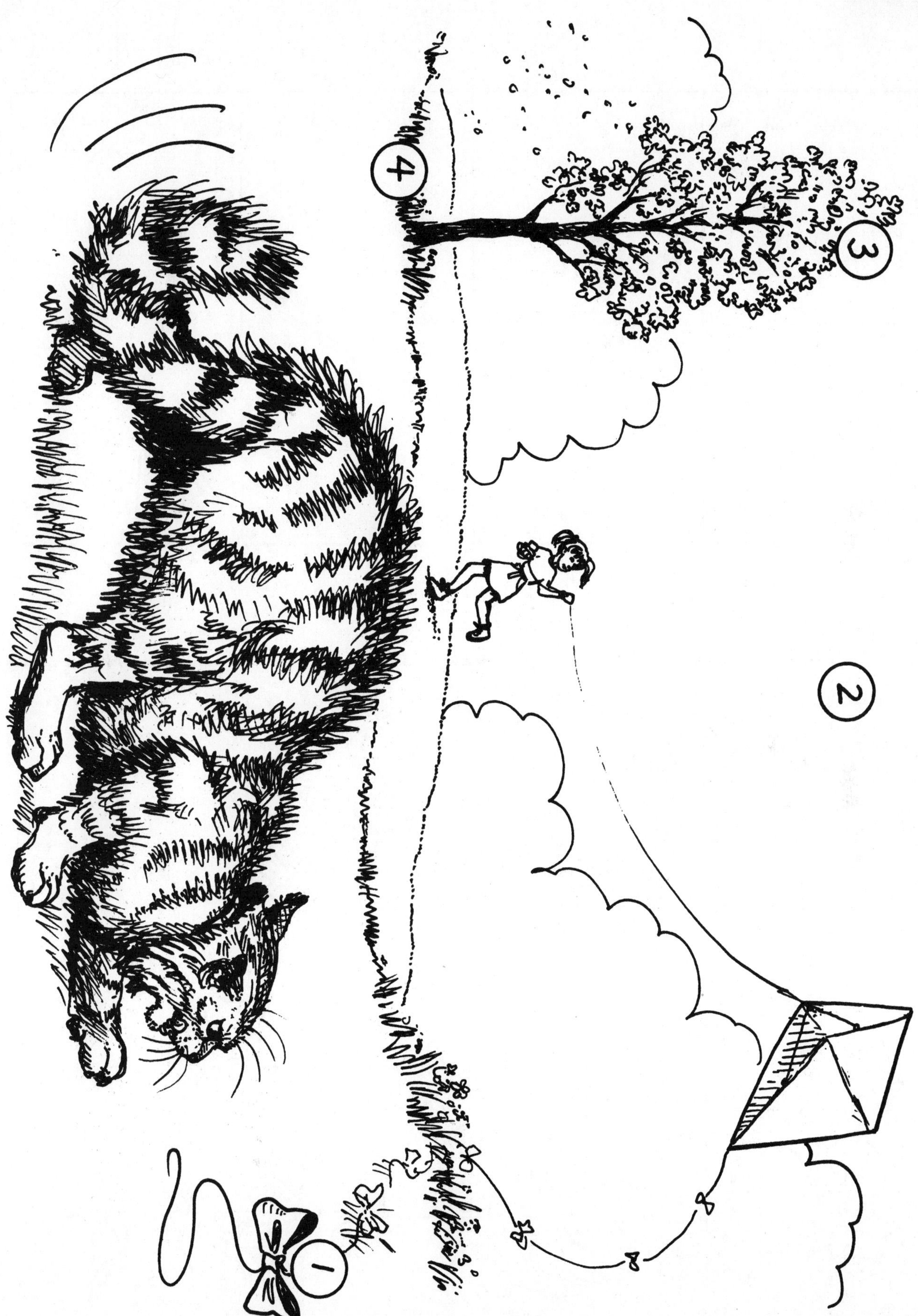

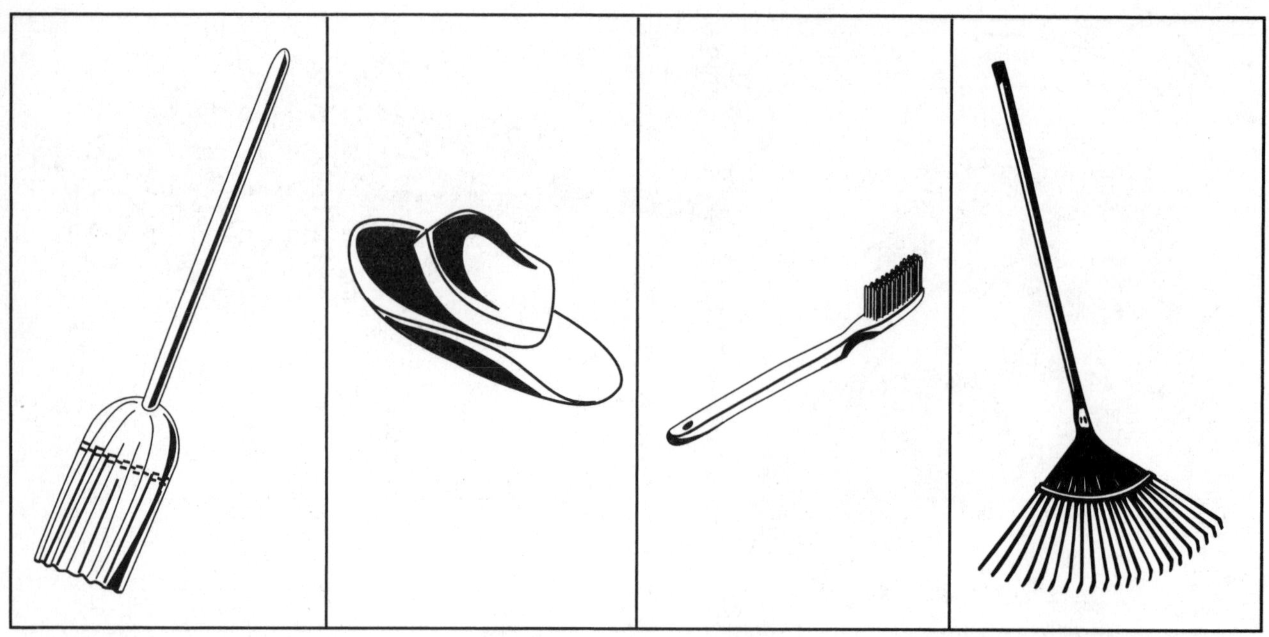

Name ____________________

Name ______________________________

Name ___________________________

Name ____________________

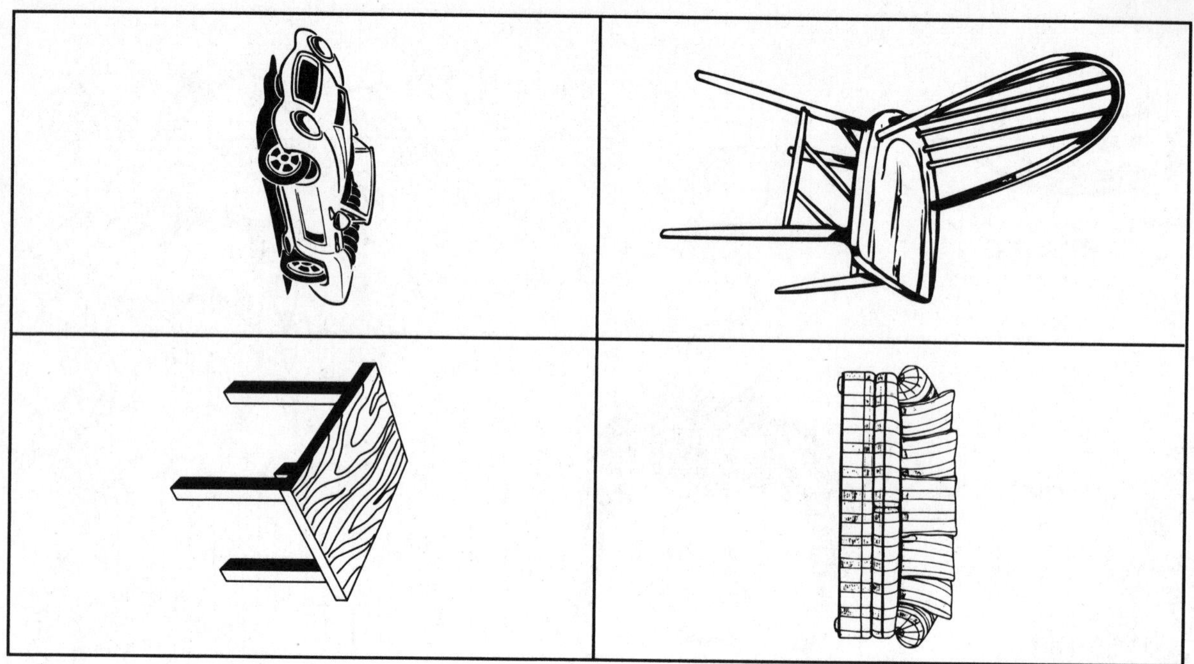

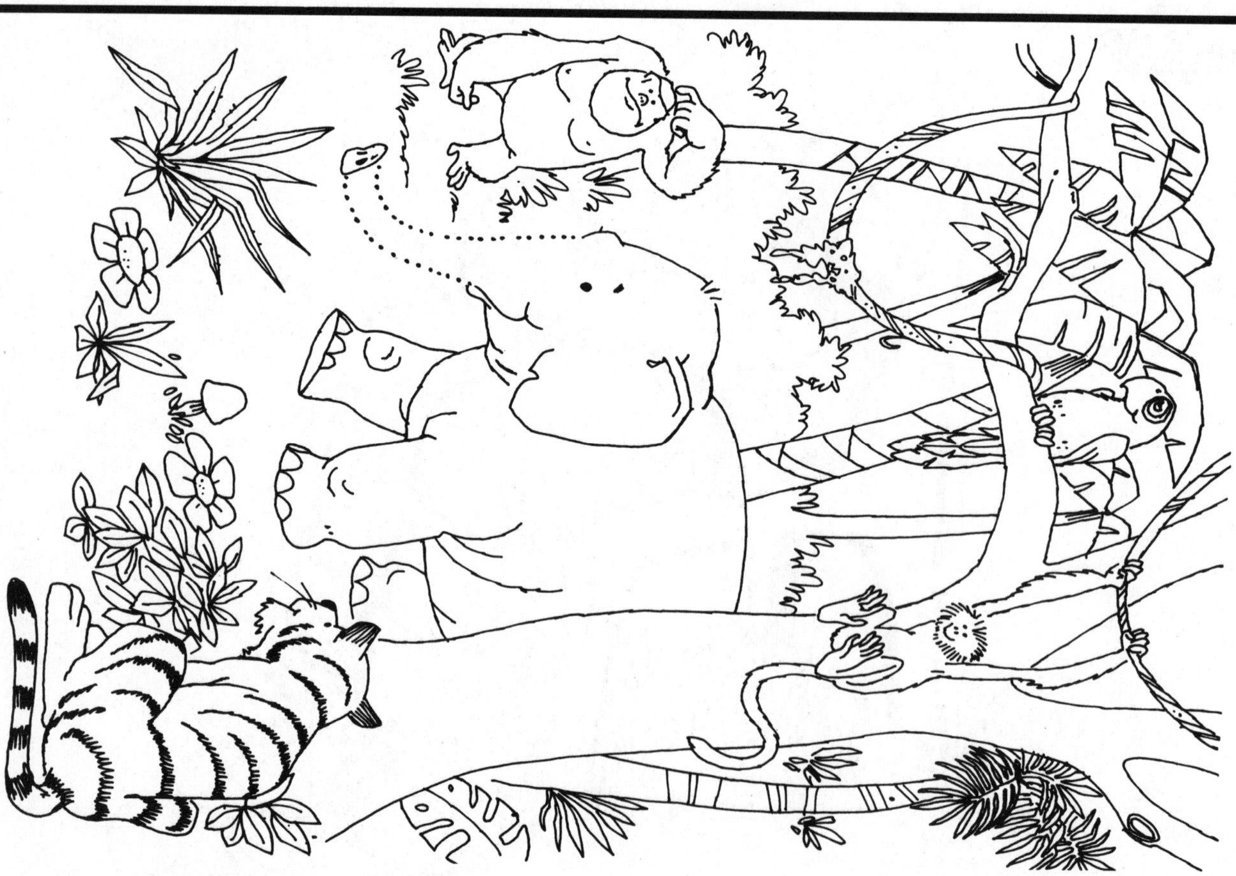

Name ______________________

Name ___________________________

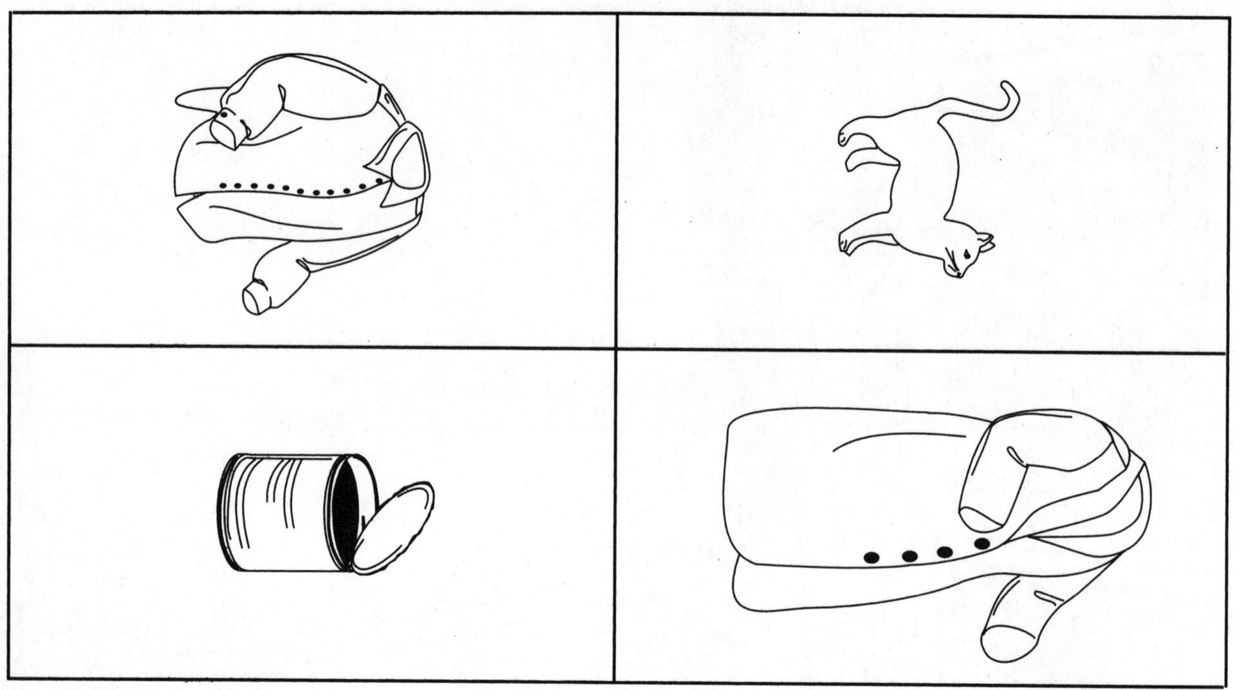

Name ______________________________

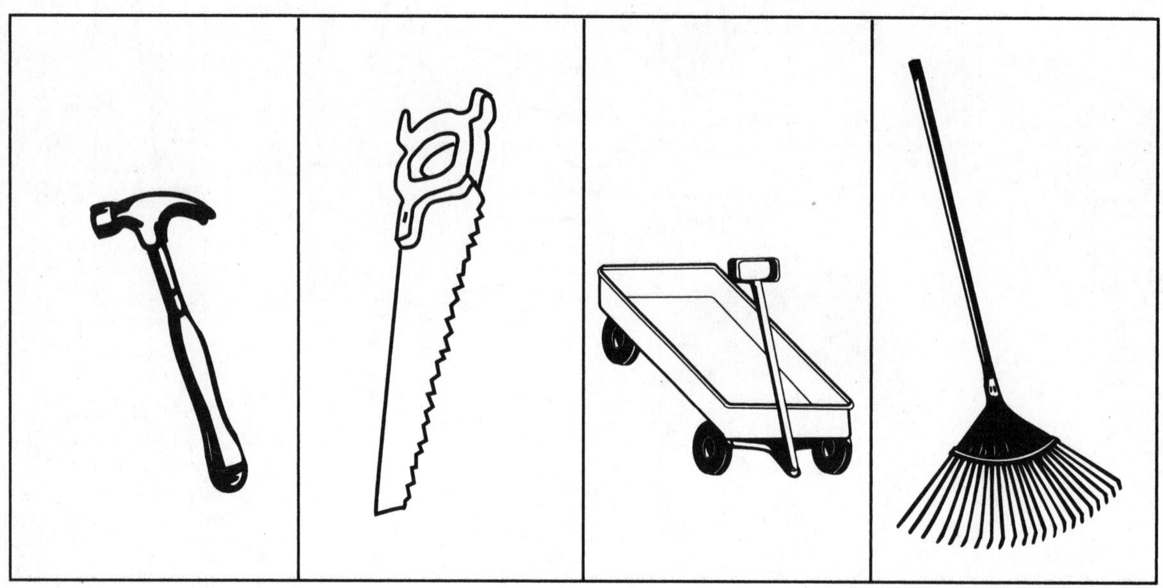

Name ______________________________

Menu

Name ______________________________

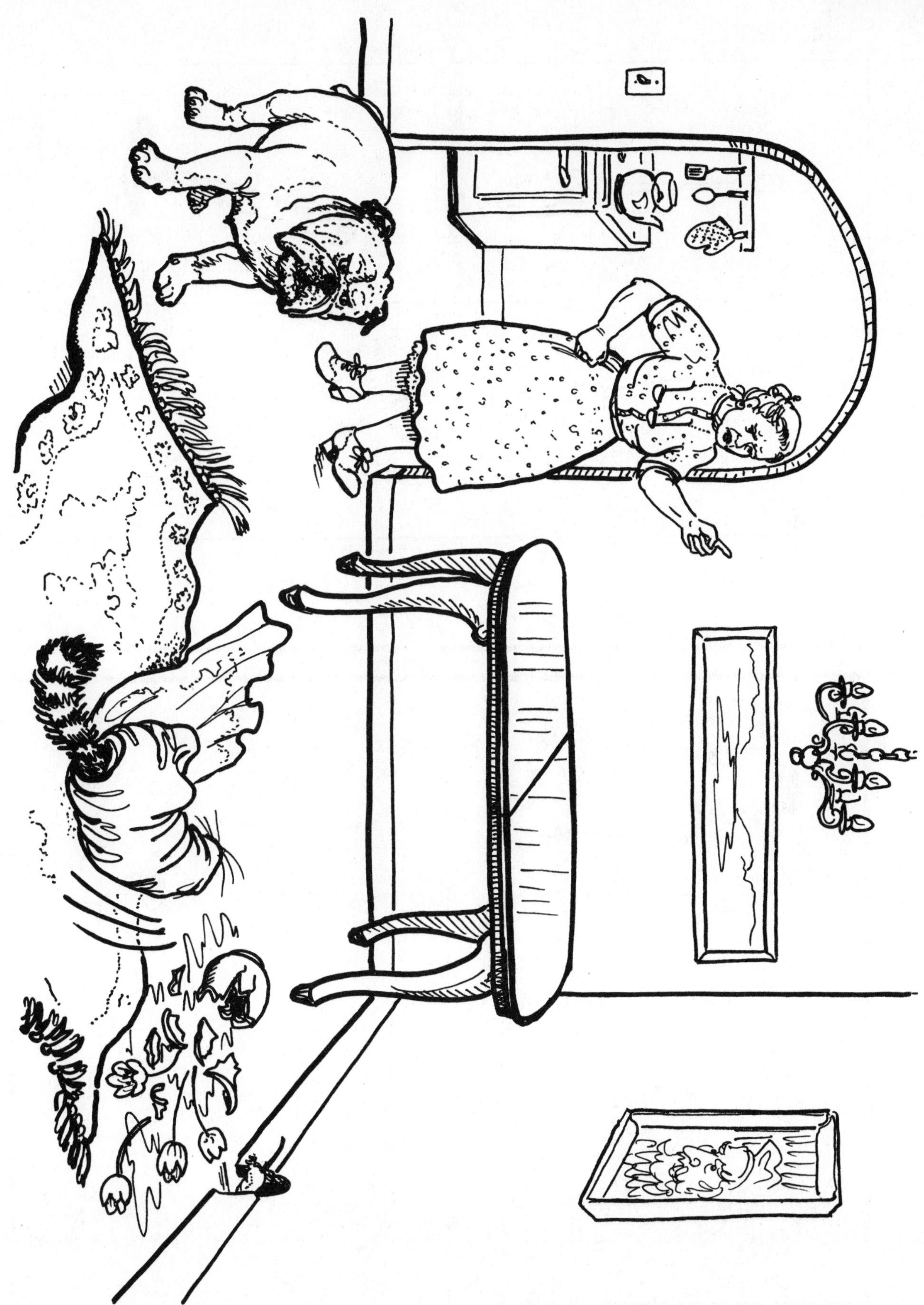

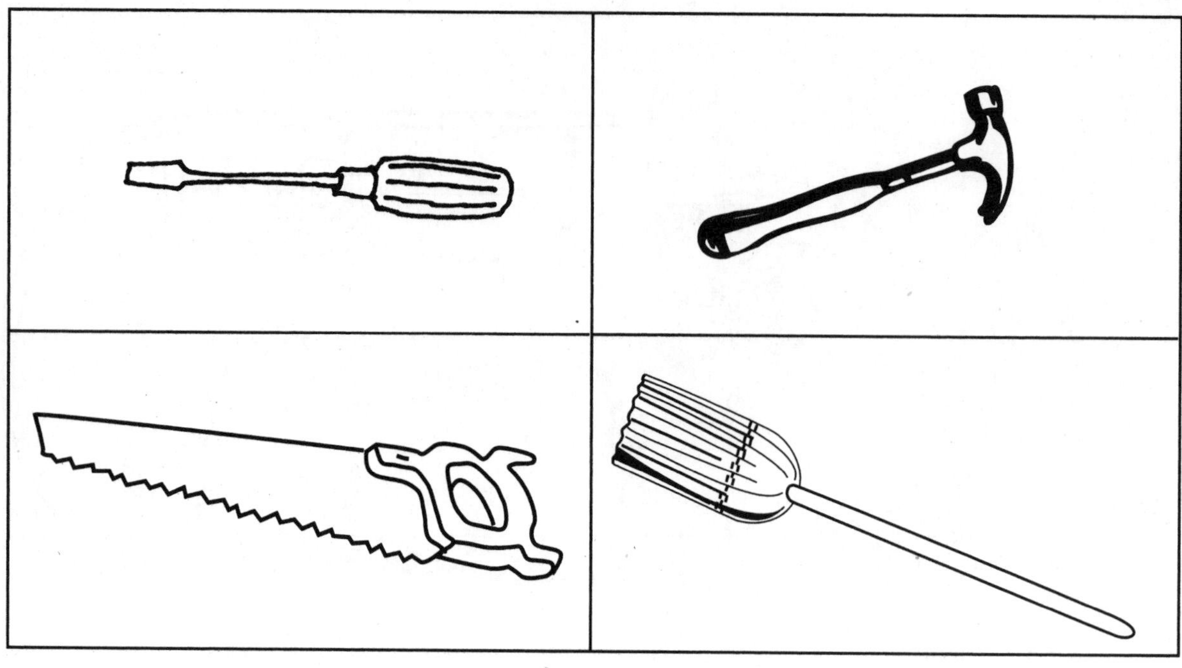

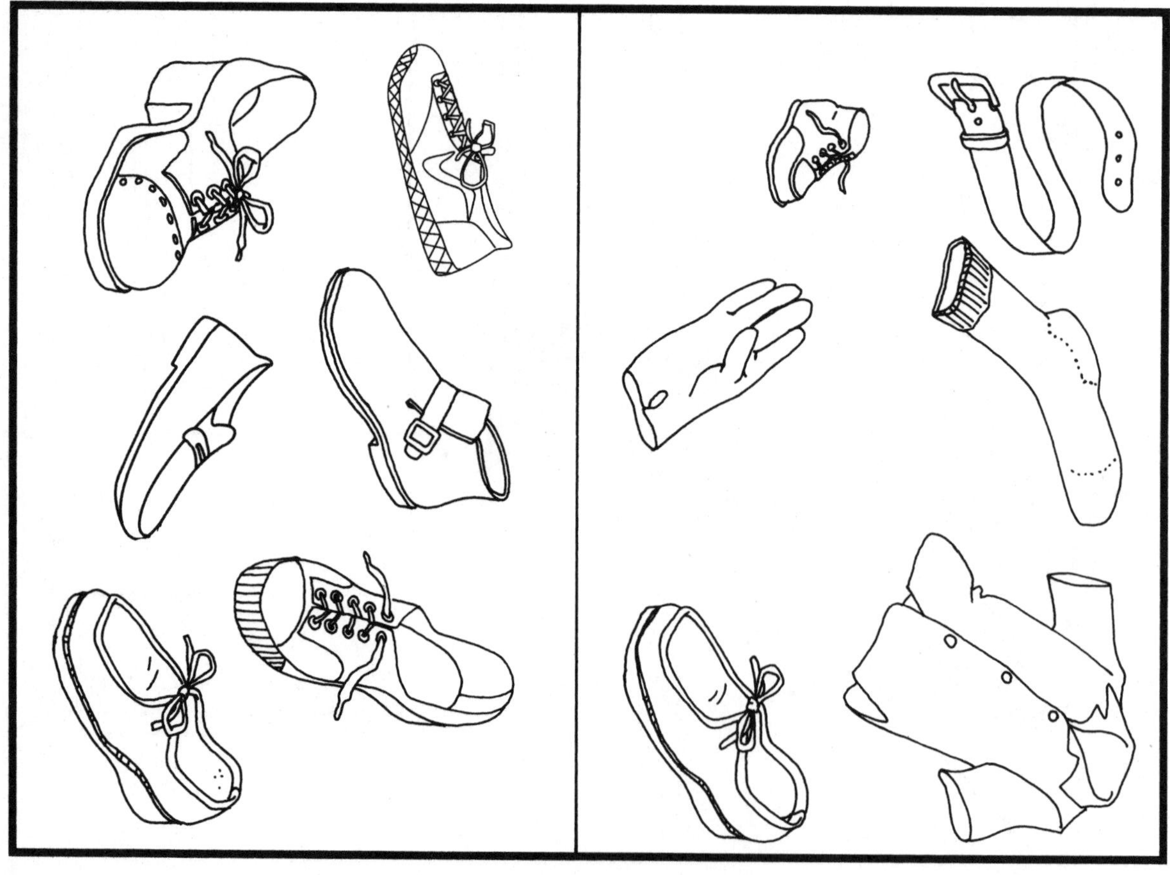

Name ________________________

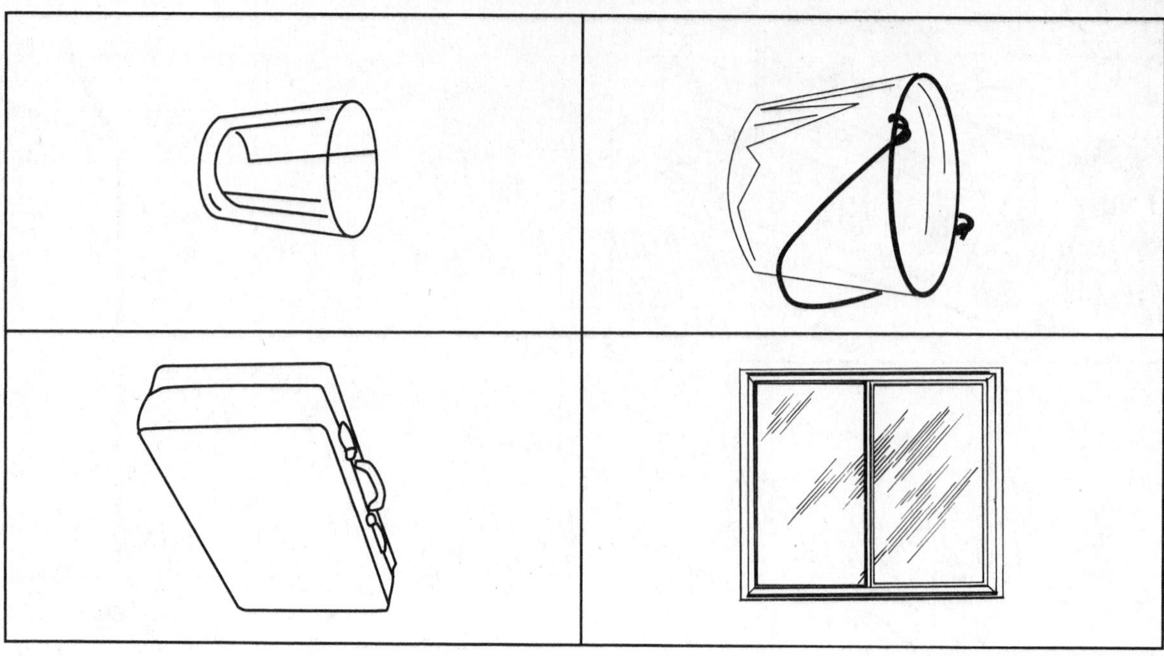

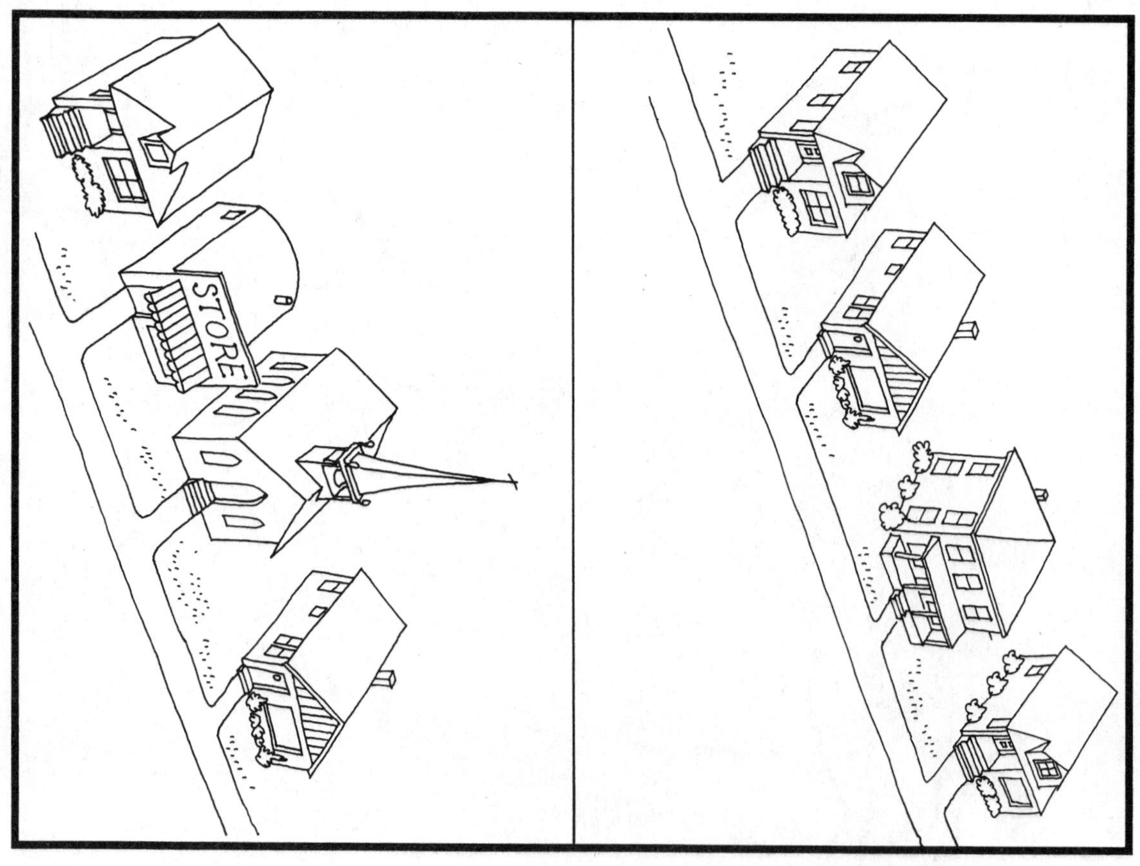
STORE

Name ______________________________

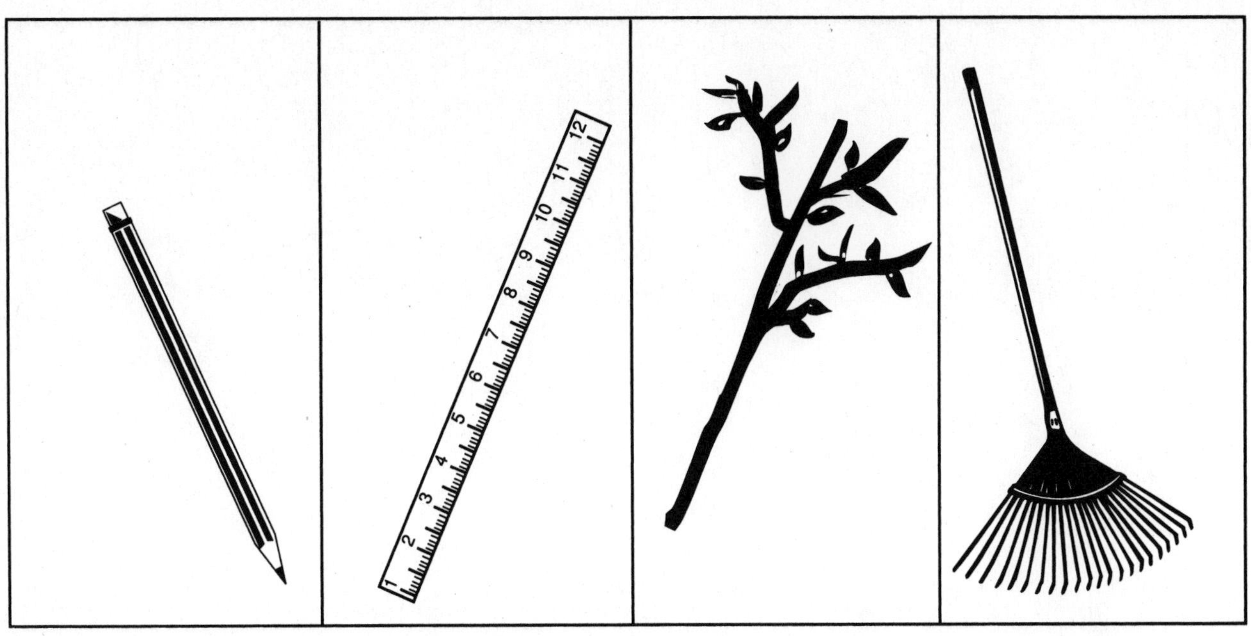

Name ___________________________

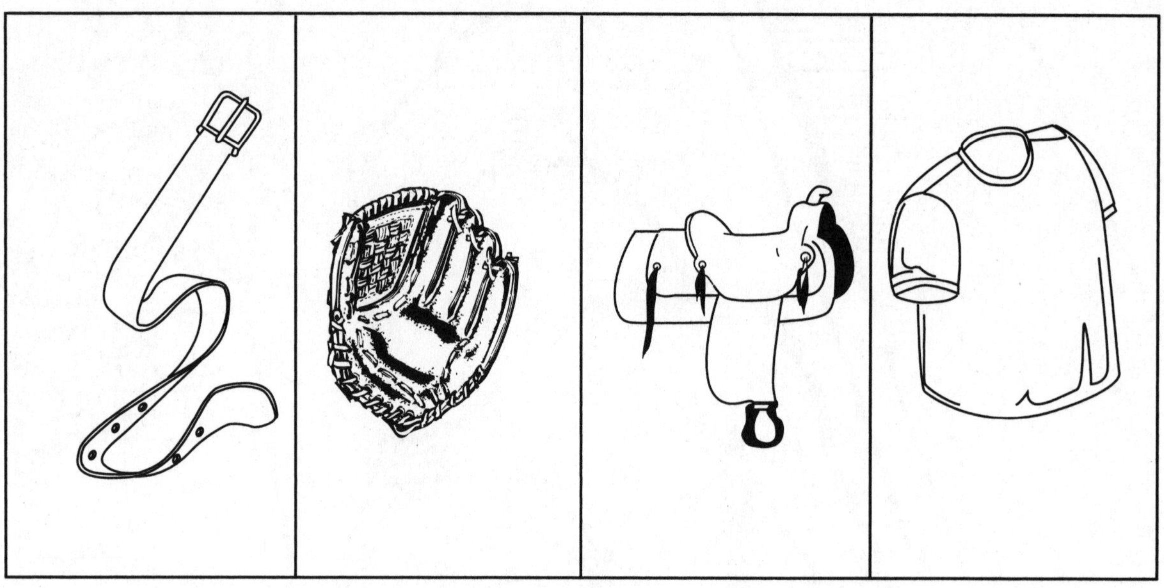

Name ______________________________

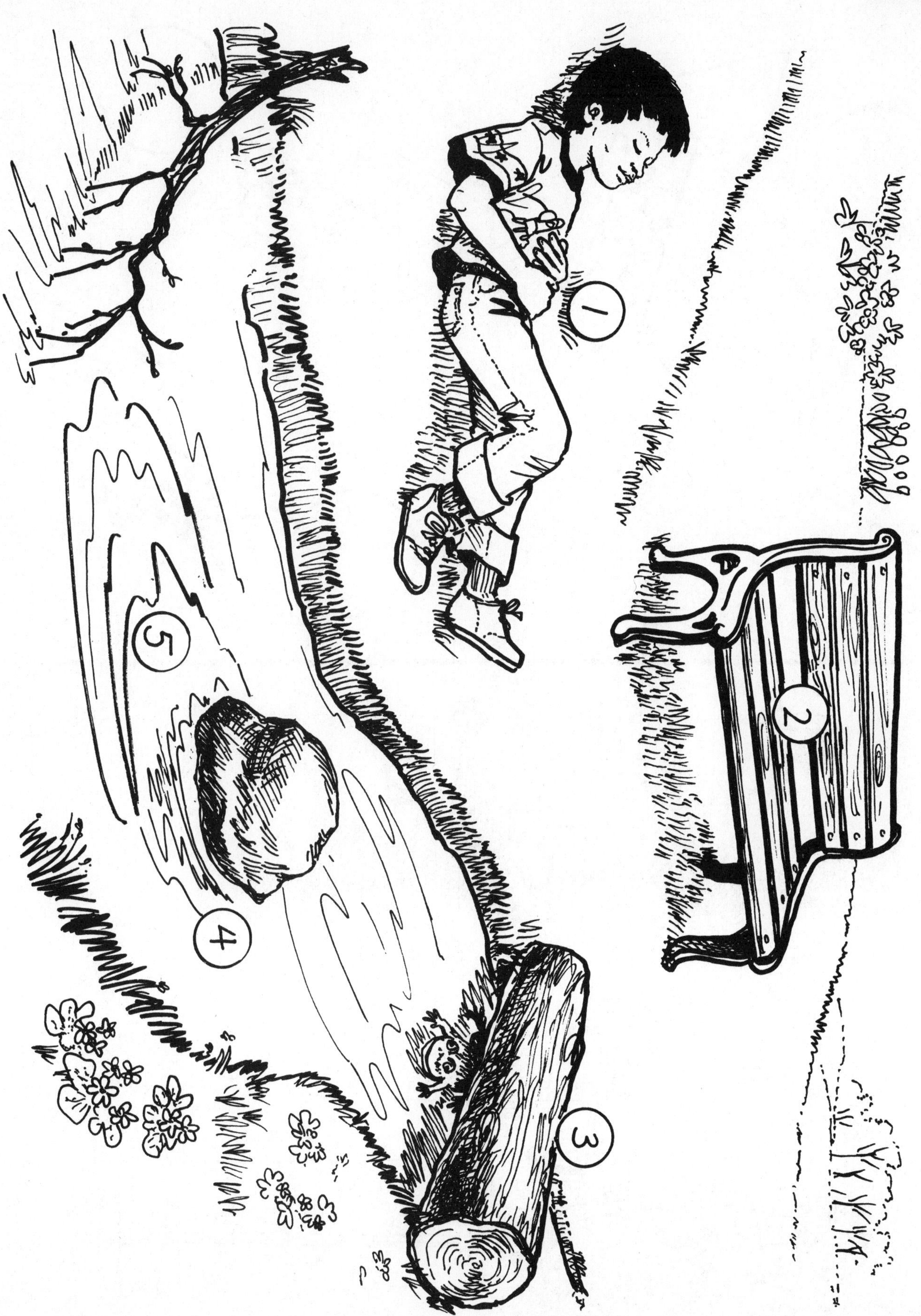

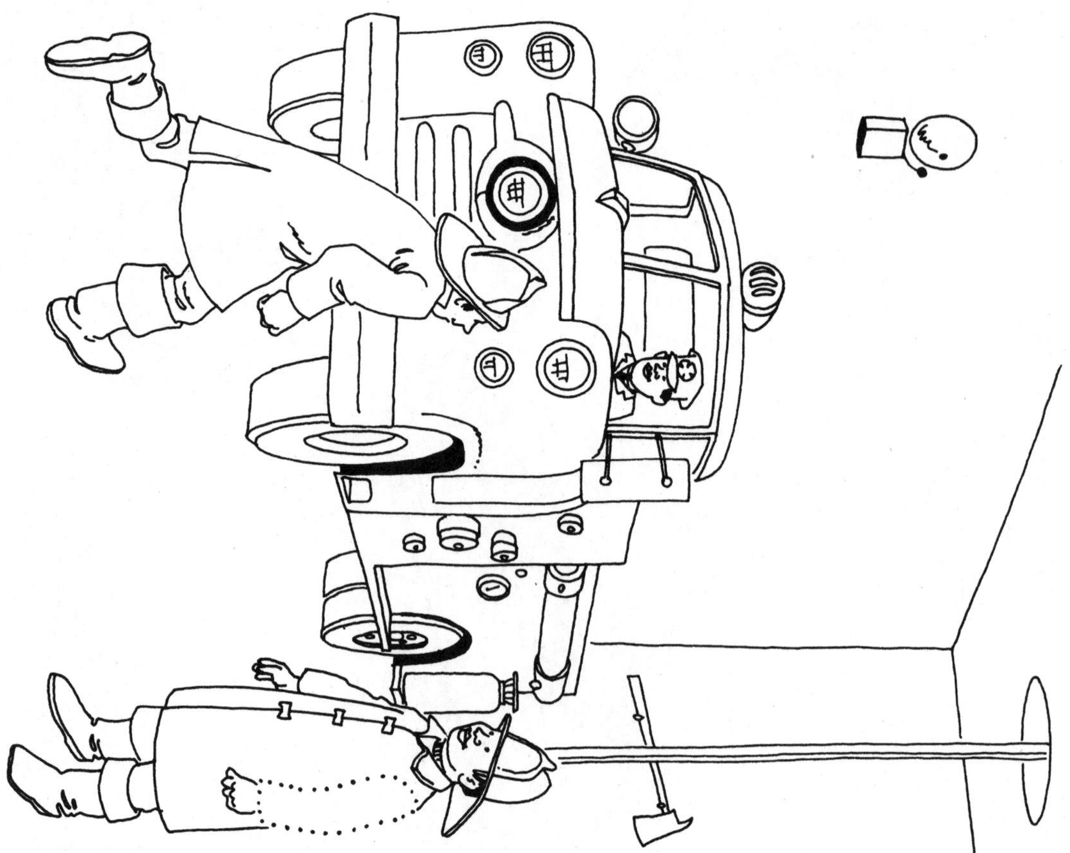

Name ______________________________

Name ___________________________

Name ______________________________

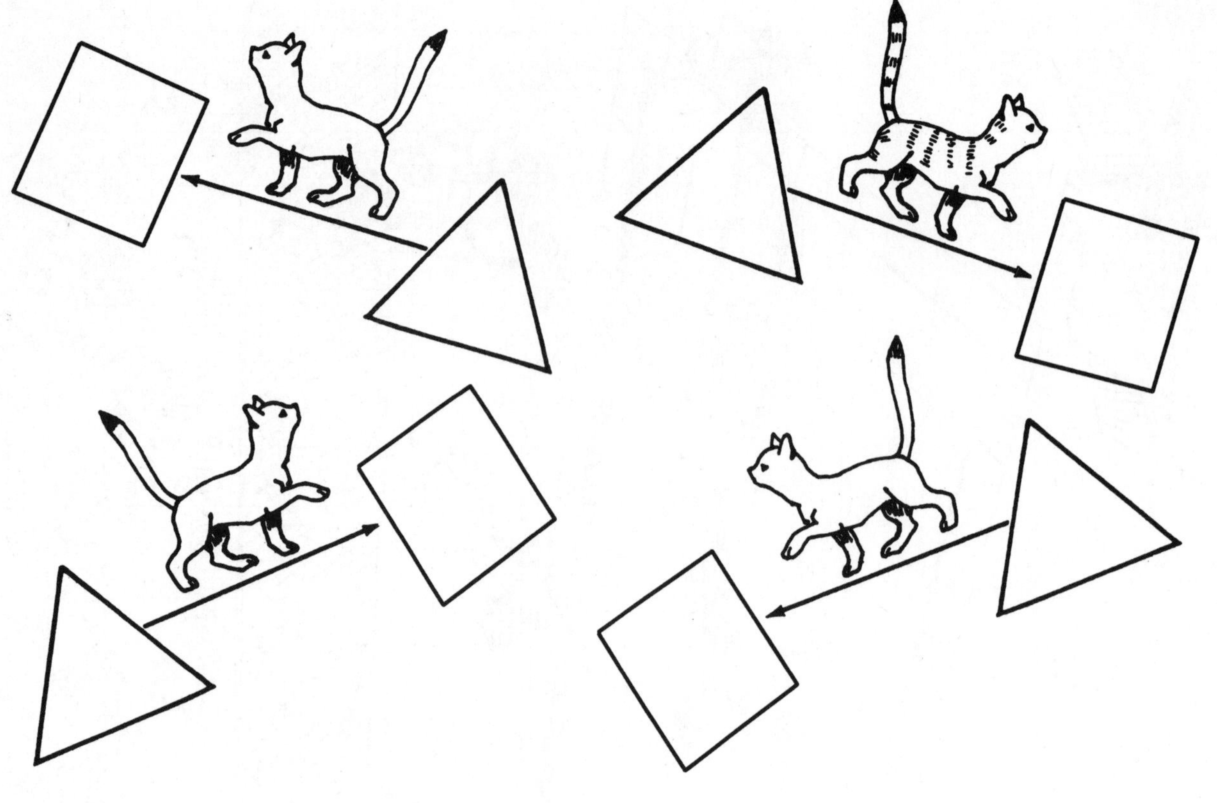

Name ______________________________

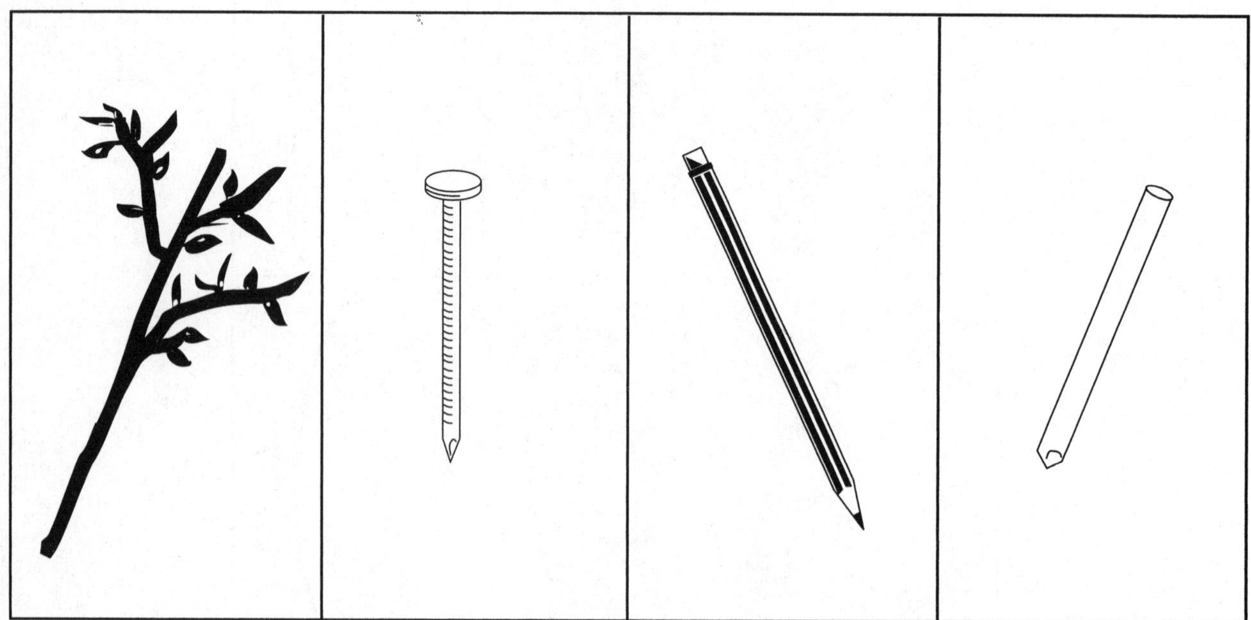

Name ______________________________

Name ______________________________

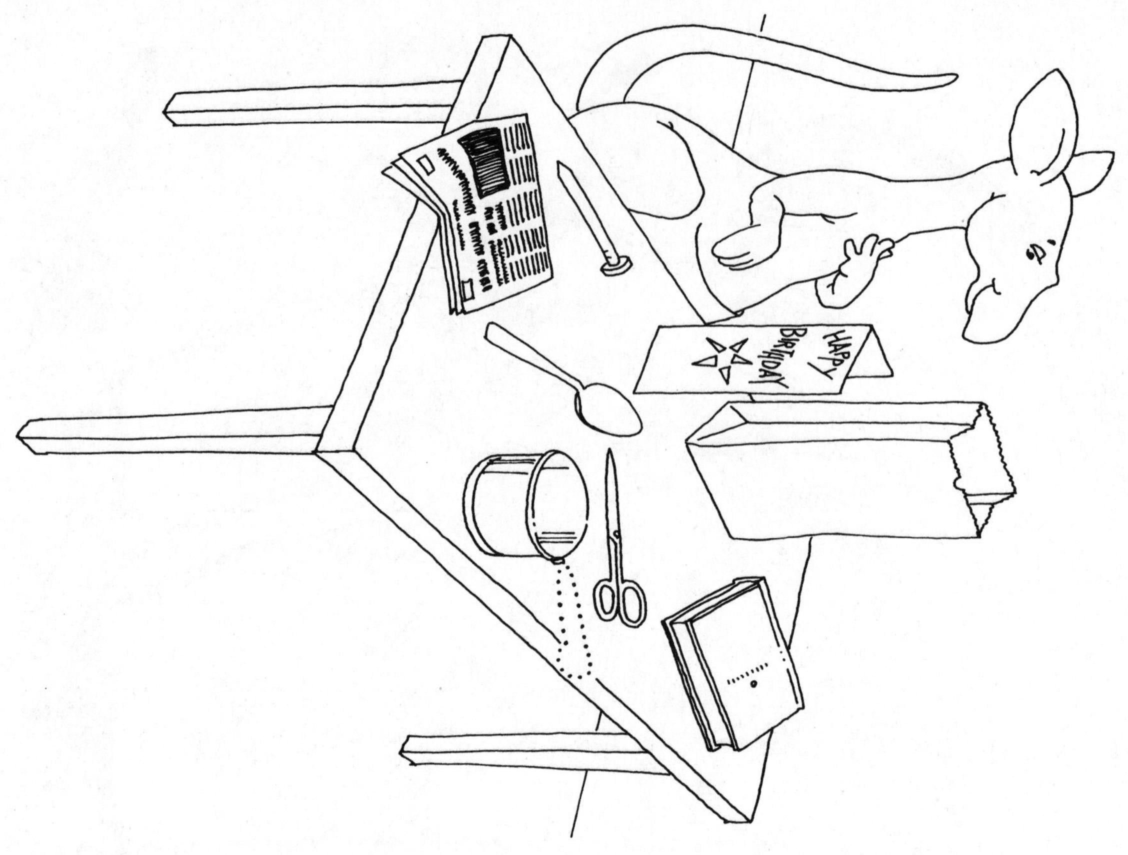
HAPPY
BIRTHDAY

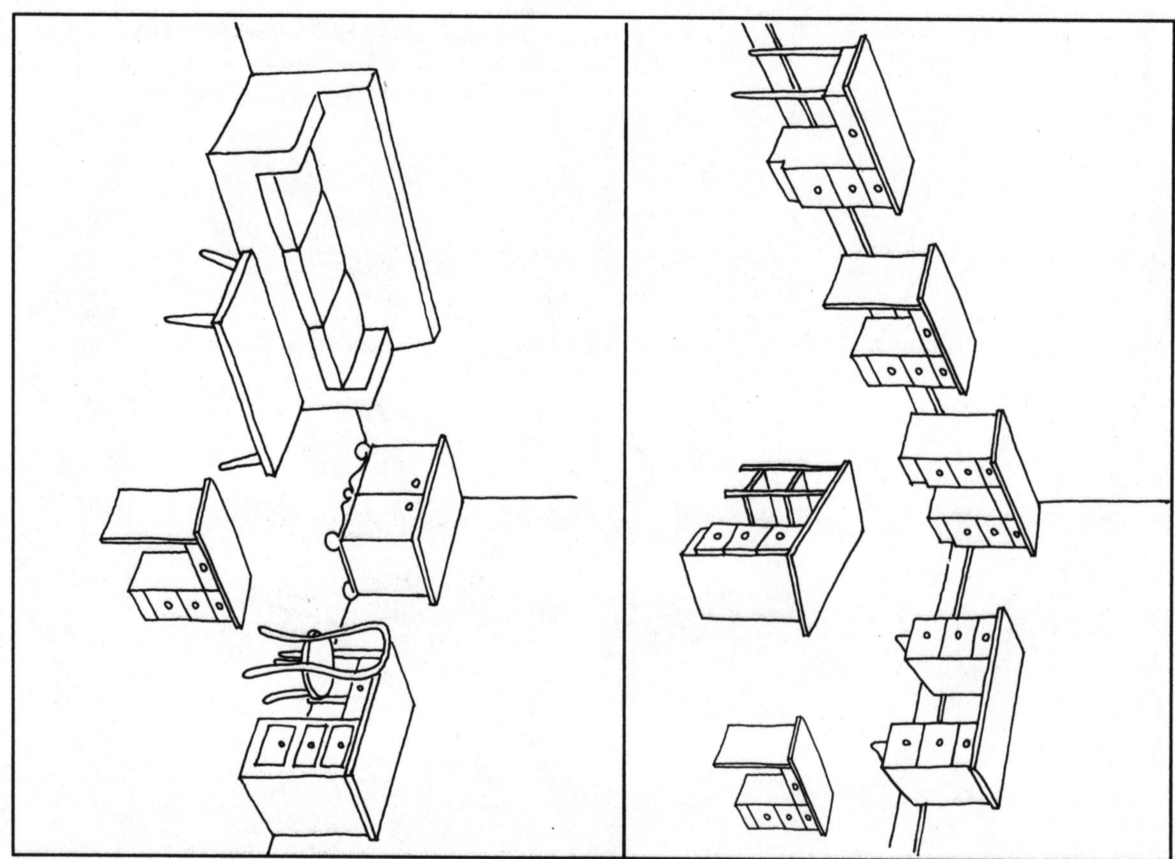

Name ______________________________

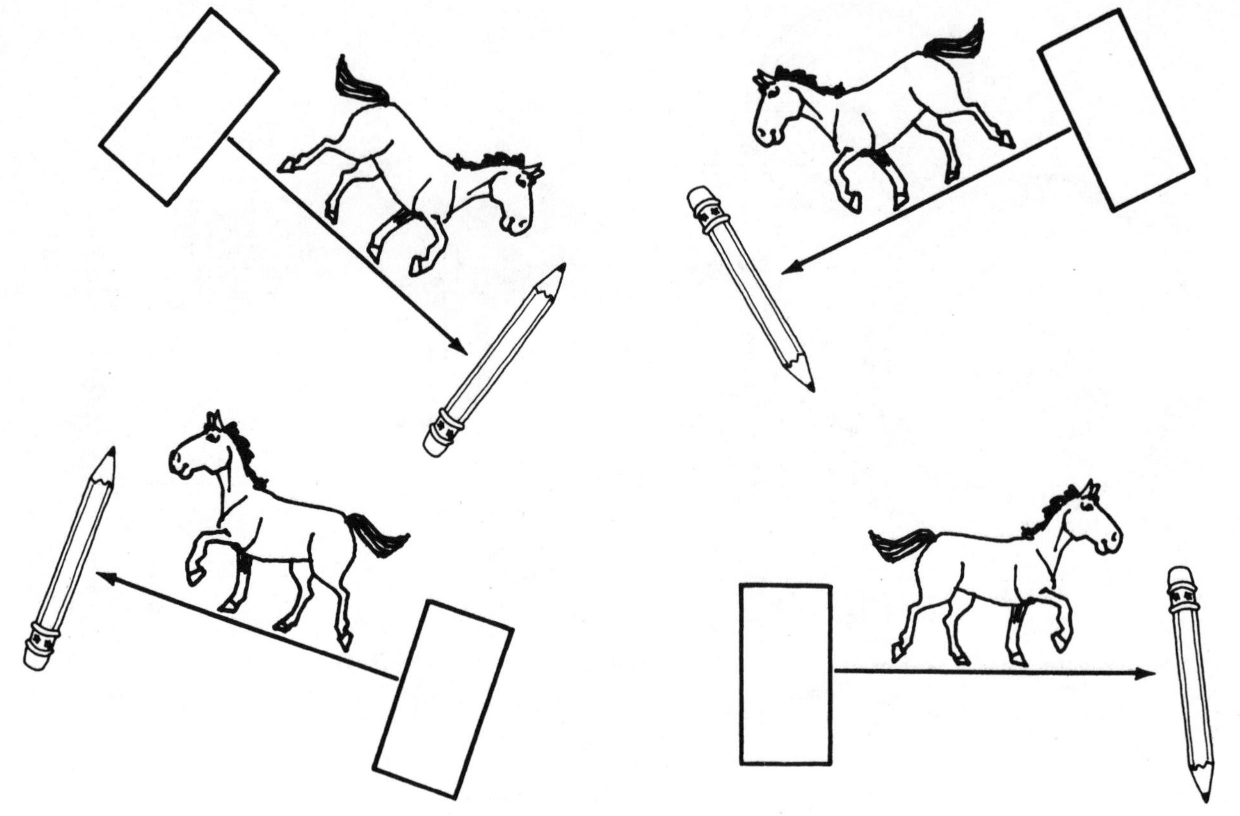

Name ____________________

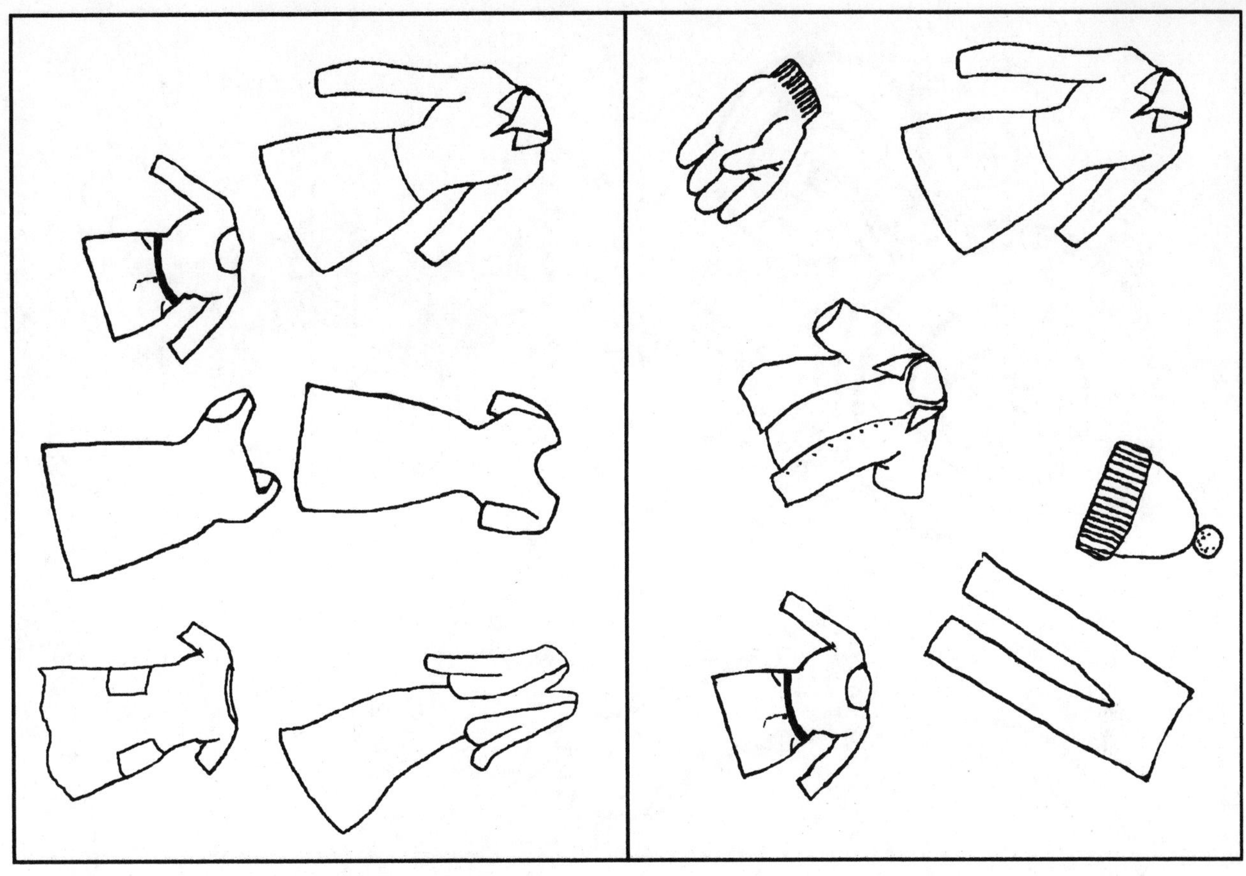

2
3
1

Name ______________________________

41

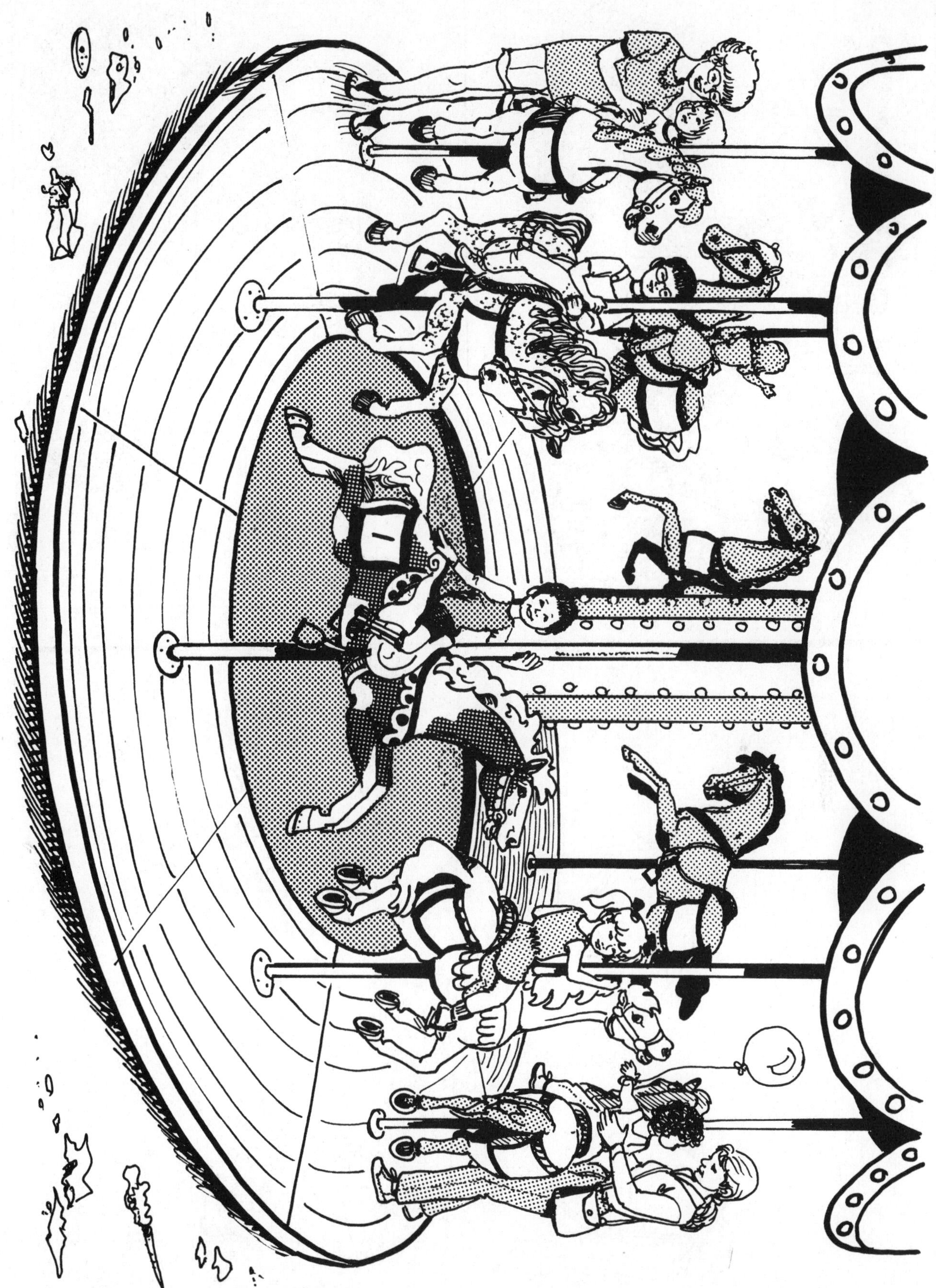

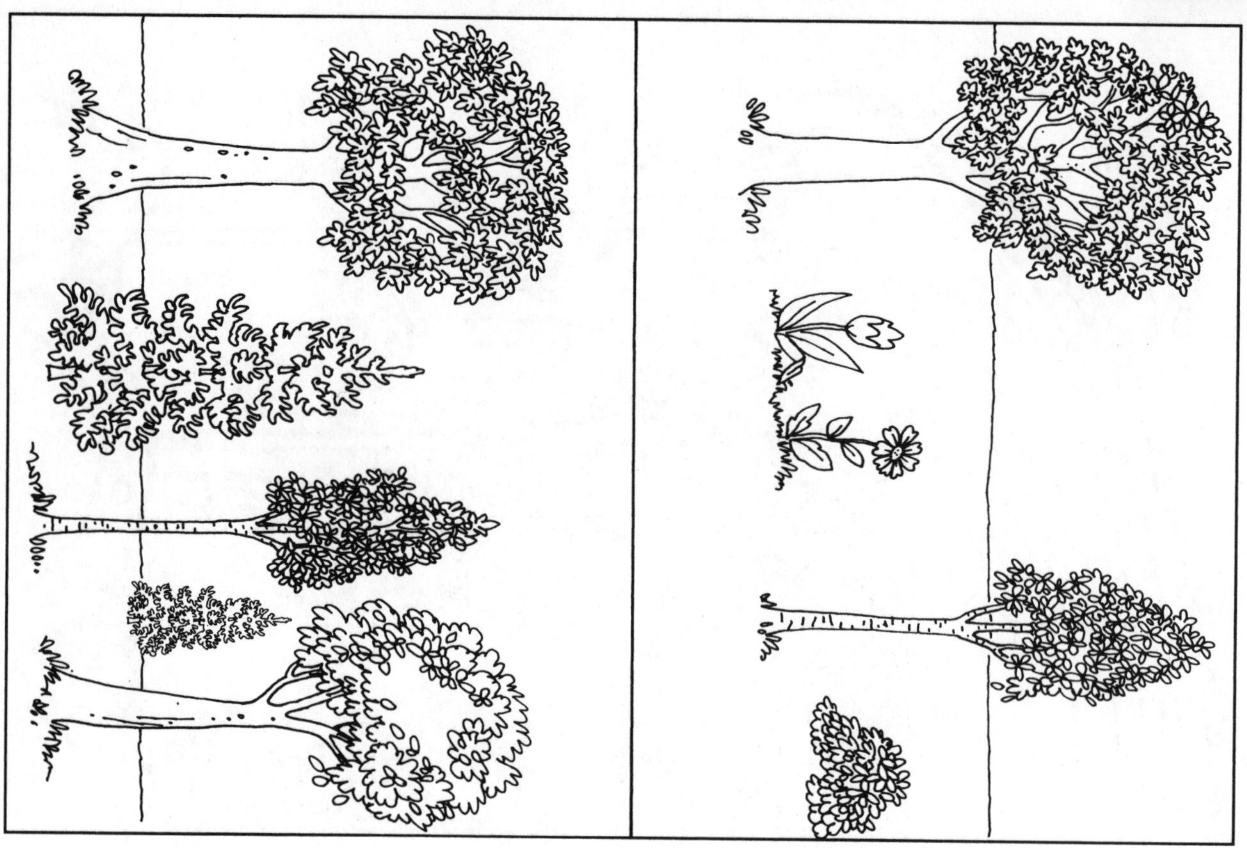

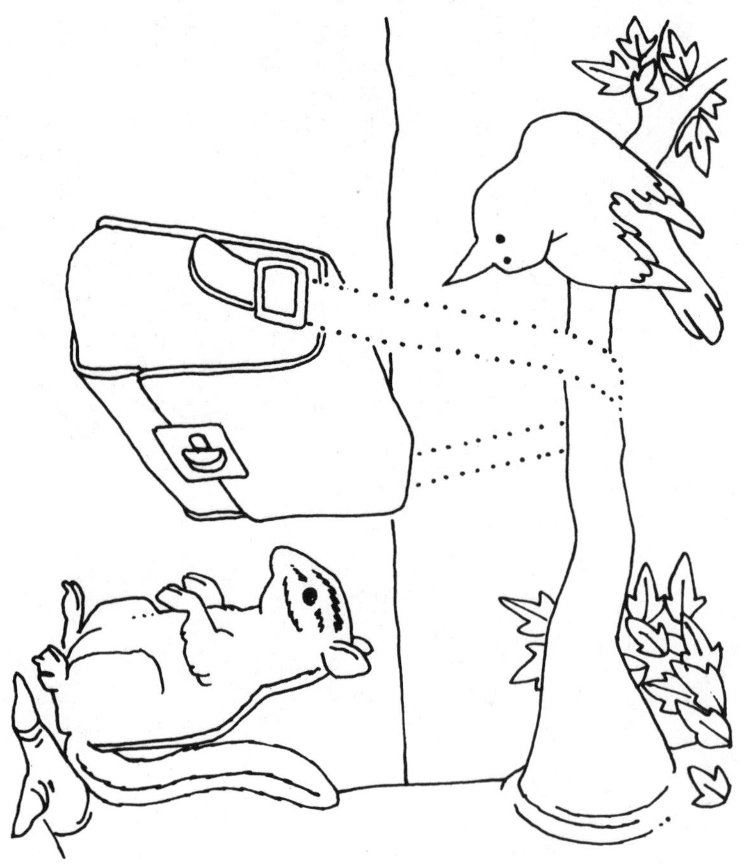

Name ______________________________

R	Red birds	☐
Y	Yellow birds	☐
B	Blue birds	☐
	Other animals	☐

Name ______________________________

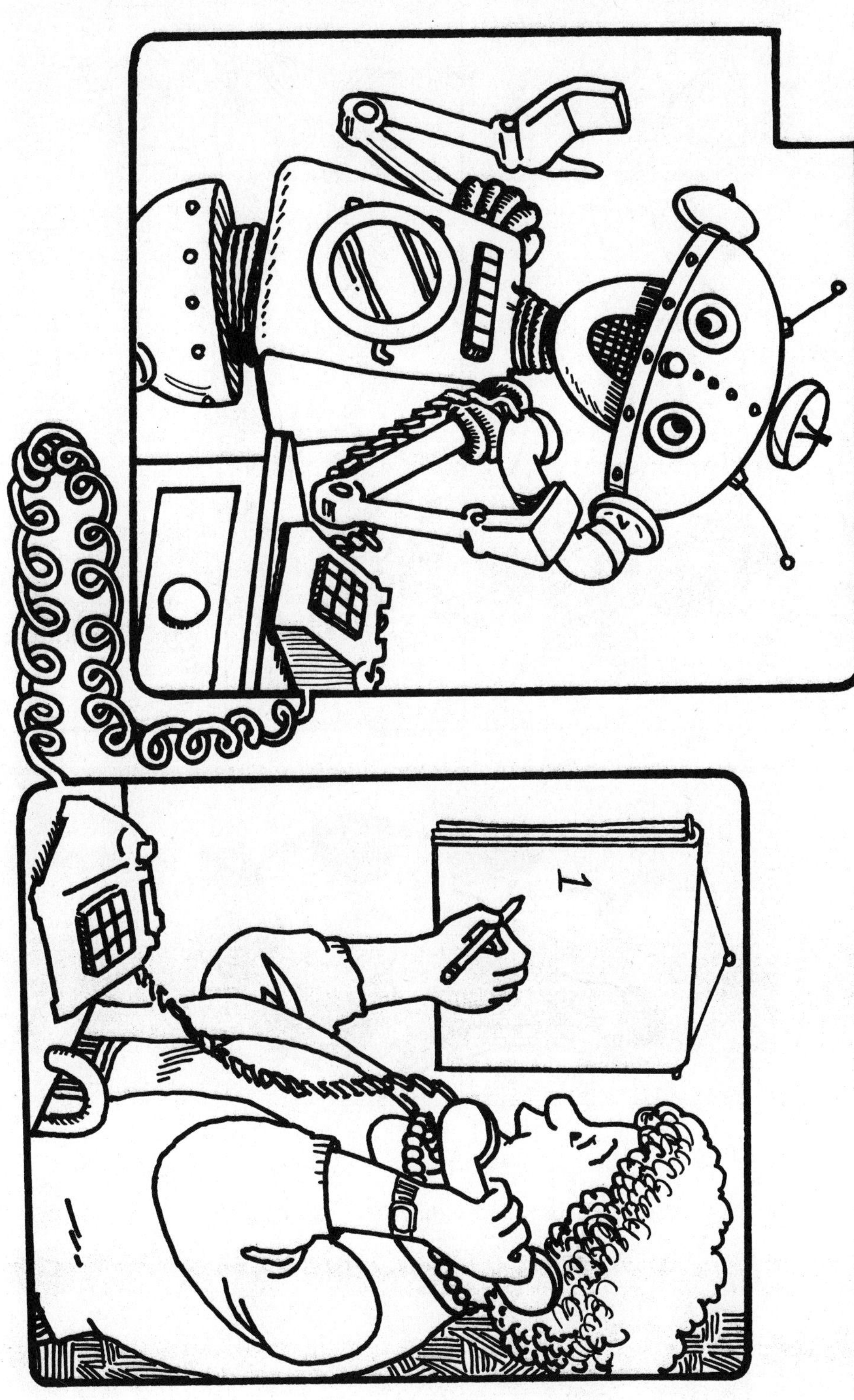

Name ______________________________

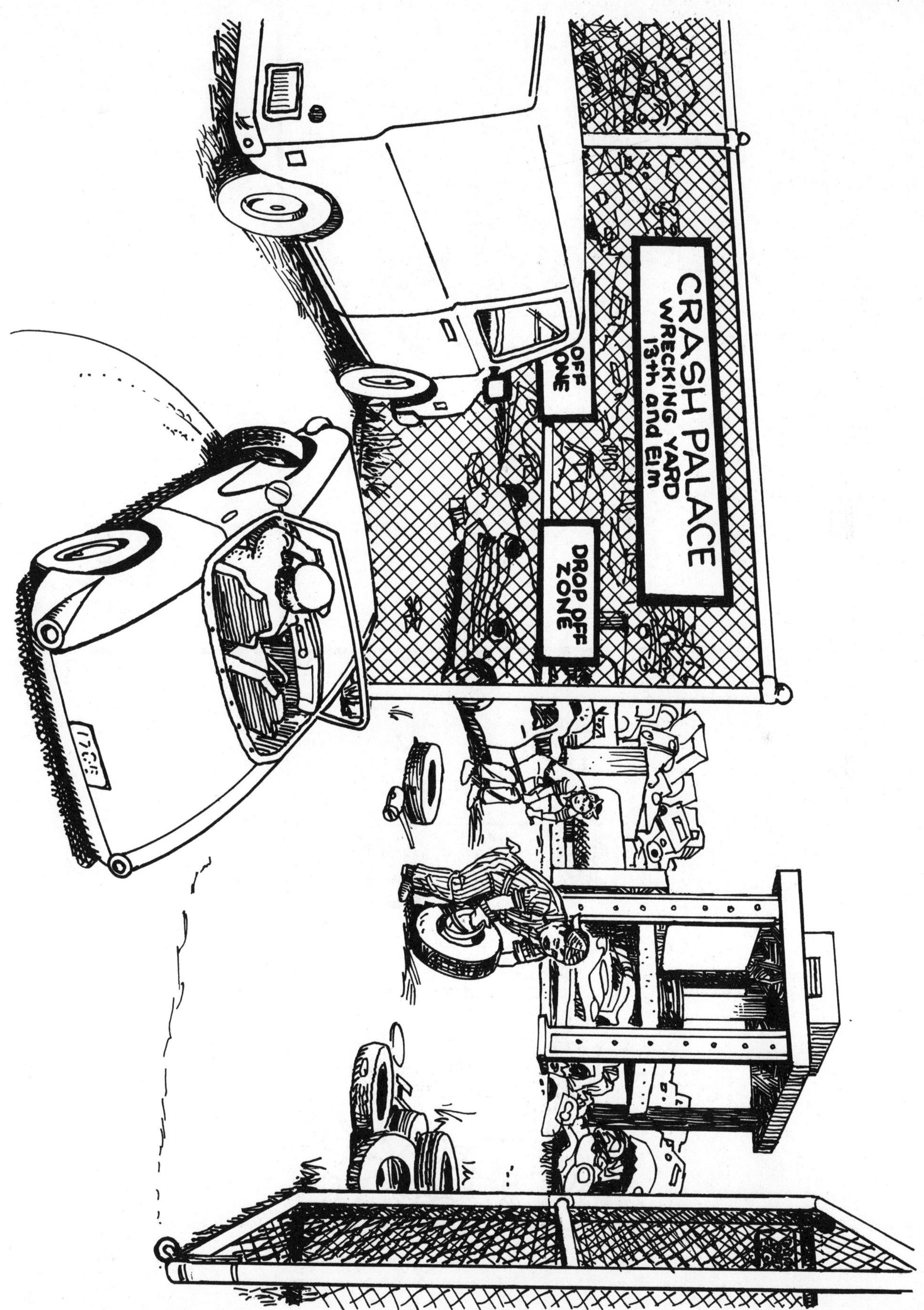
CRASH PALACE
WRECKING YARD
13th and Elm
DROP OFF
ZONE
OFF
ZONE

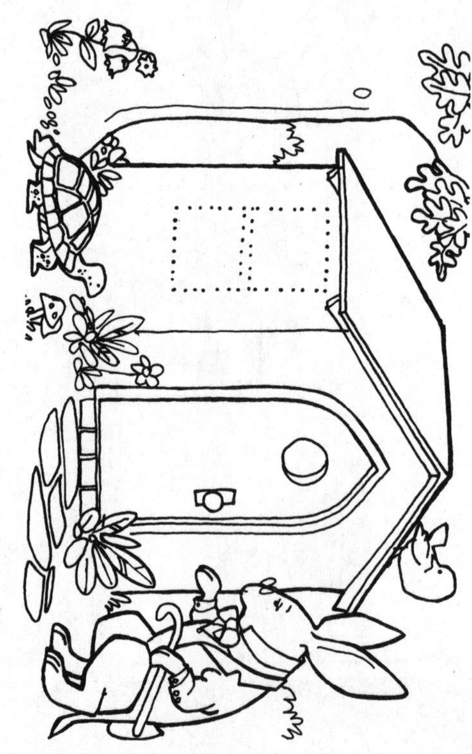

Name ______________________________

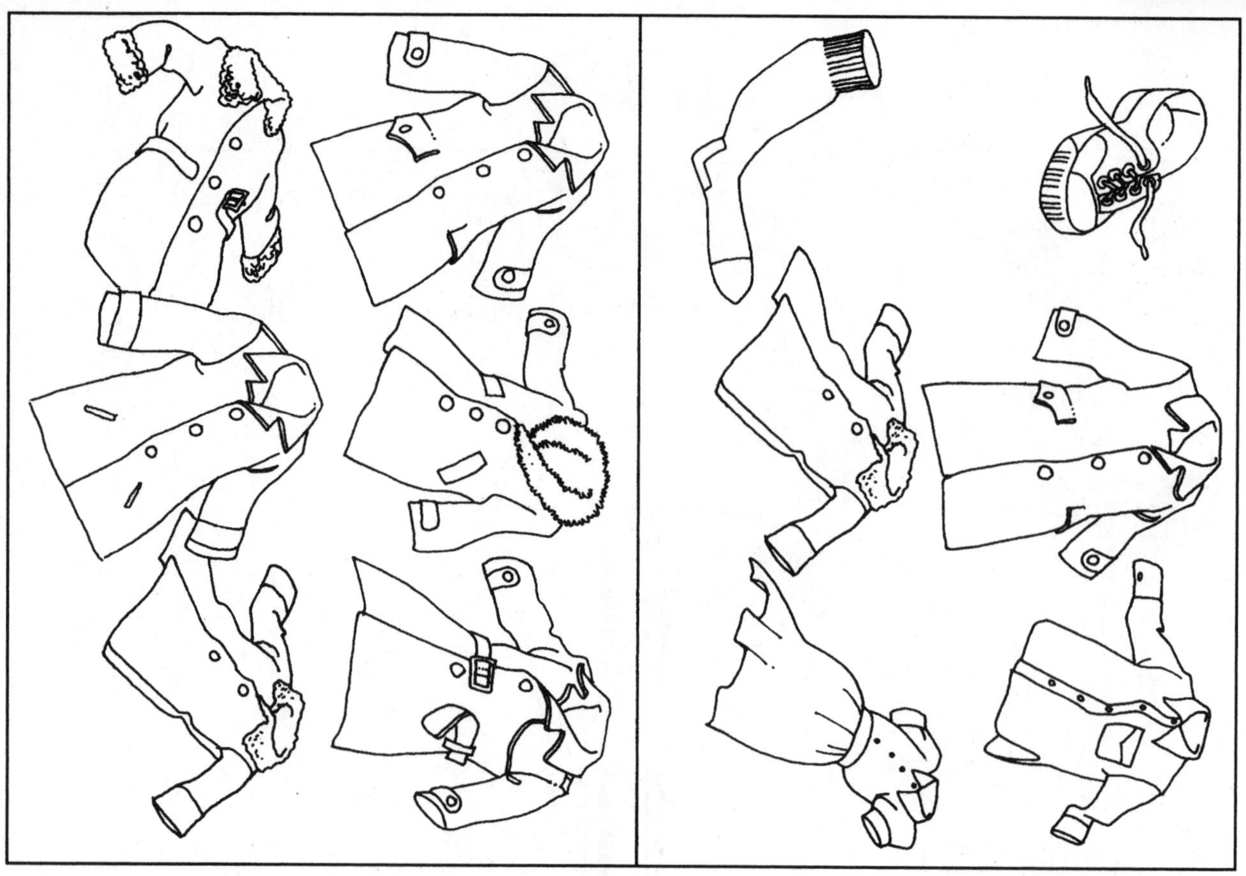

GATE
3

Name ______________________________

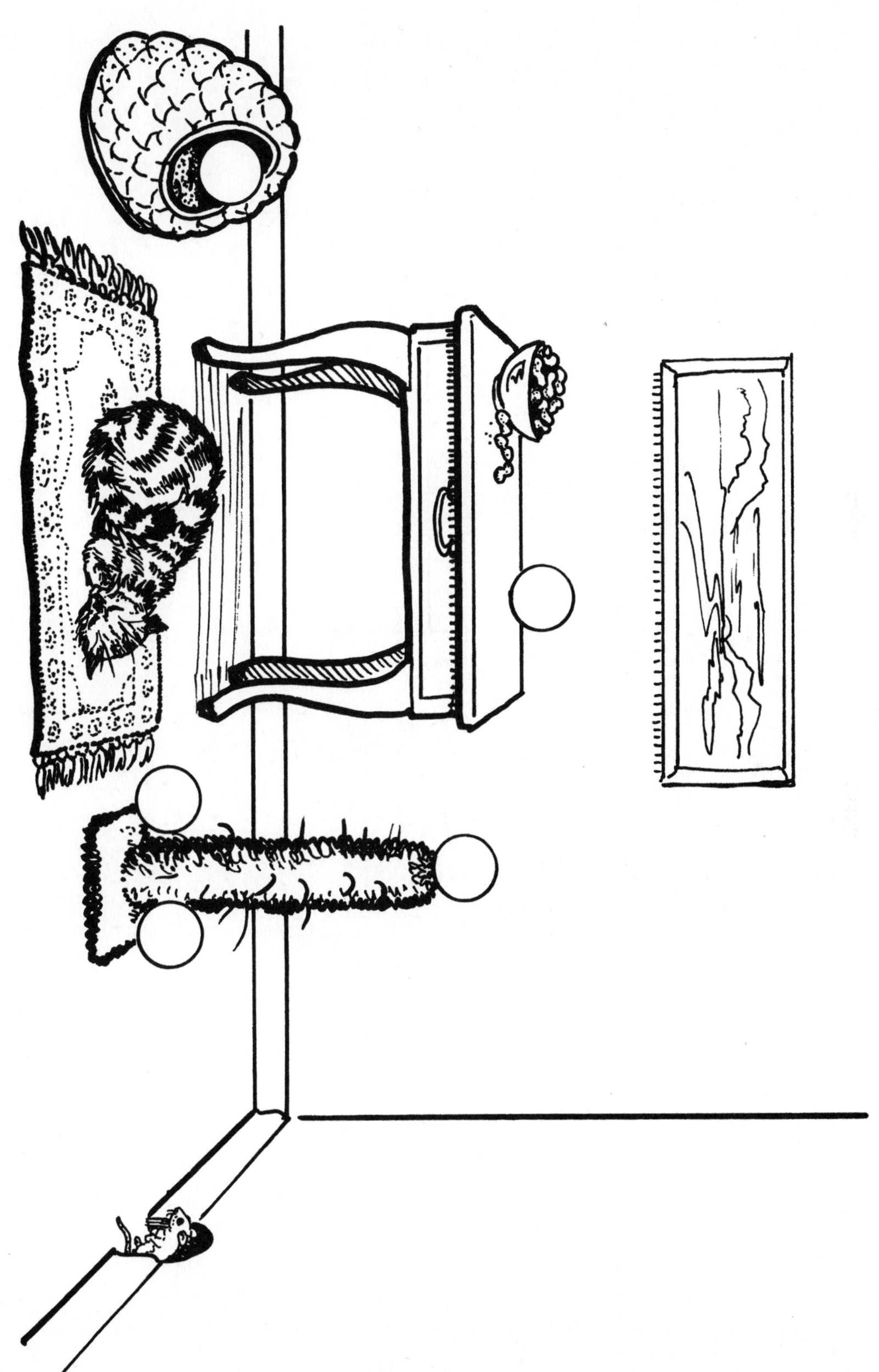

Name ______________________________

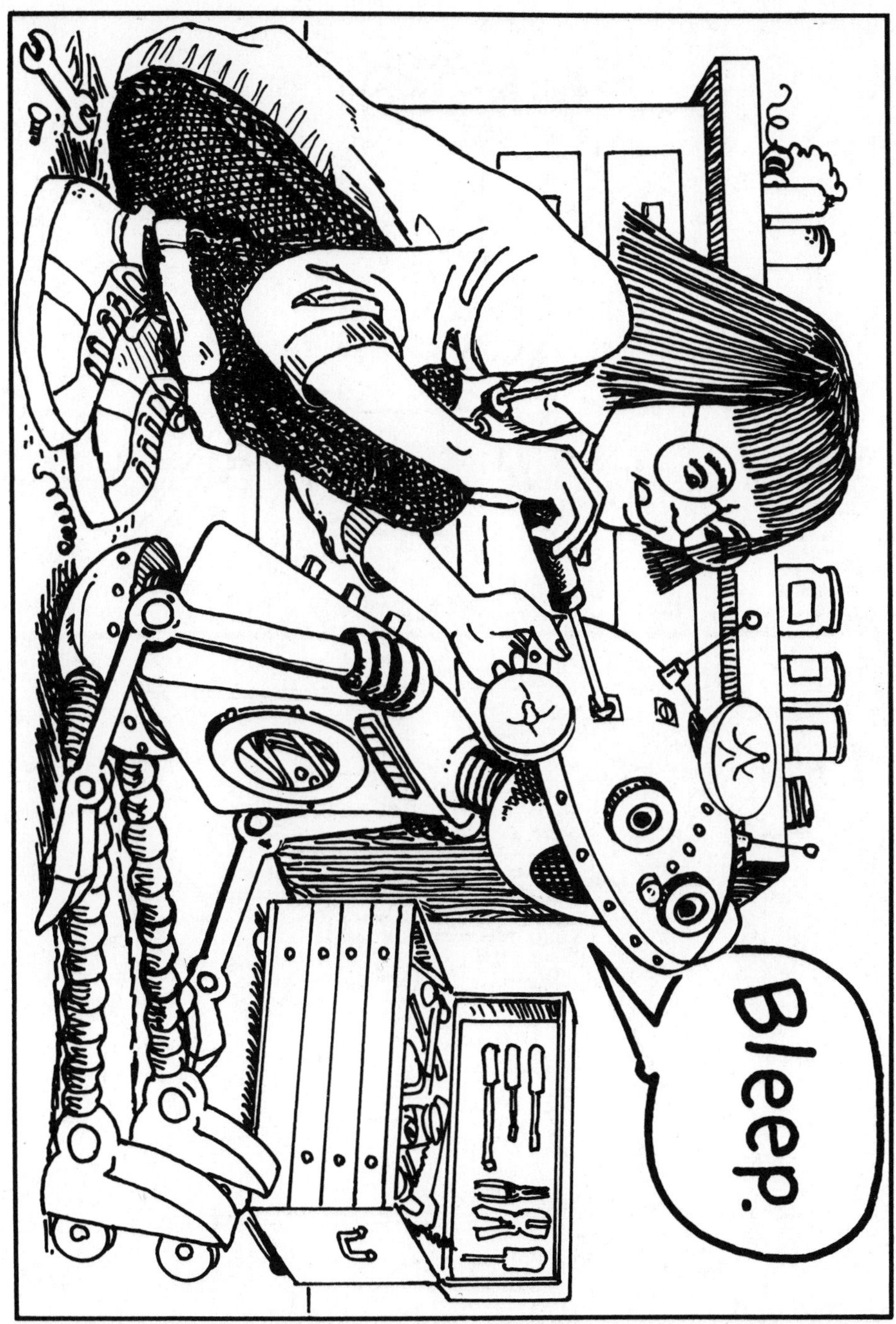

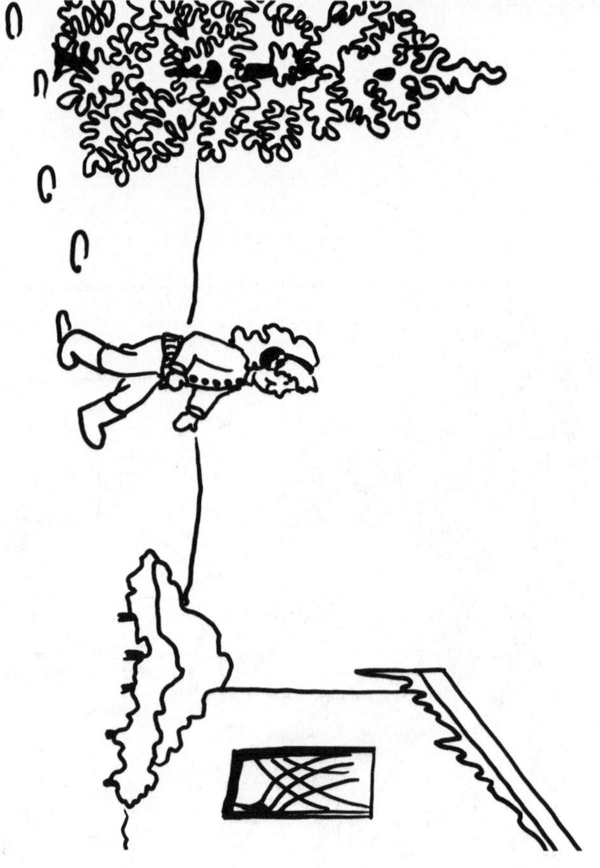

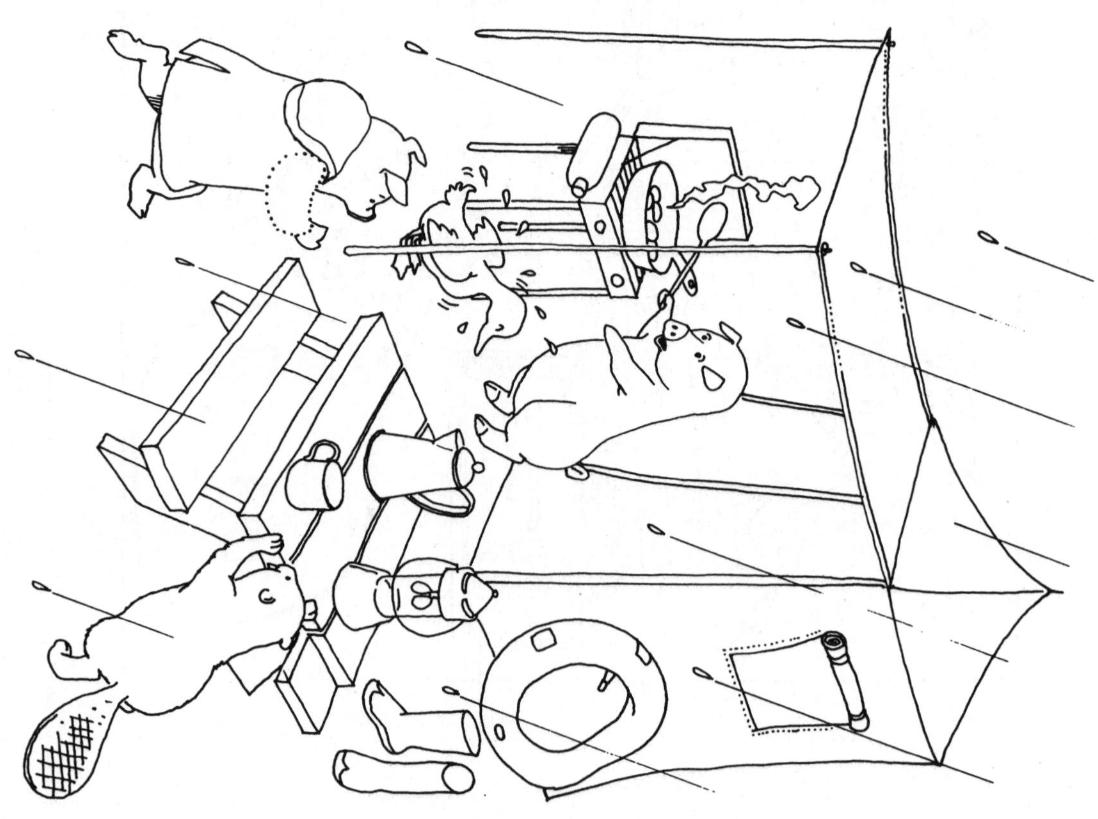

Name ______________________________

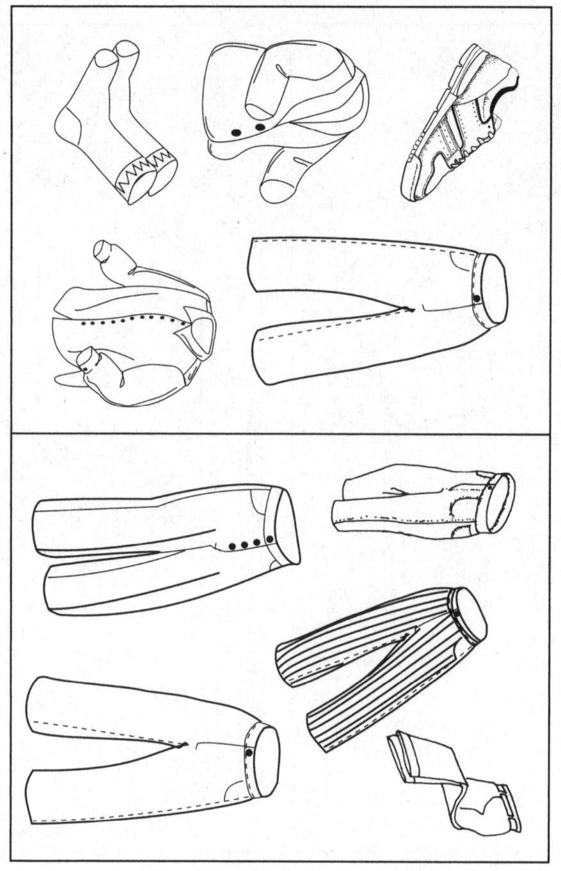

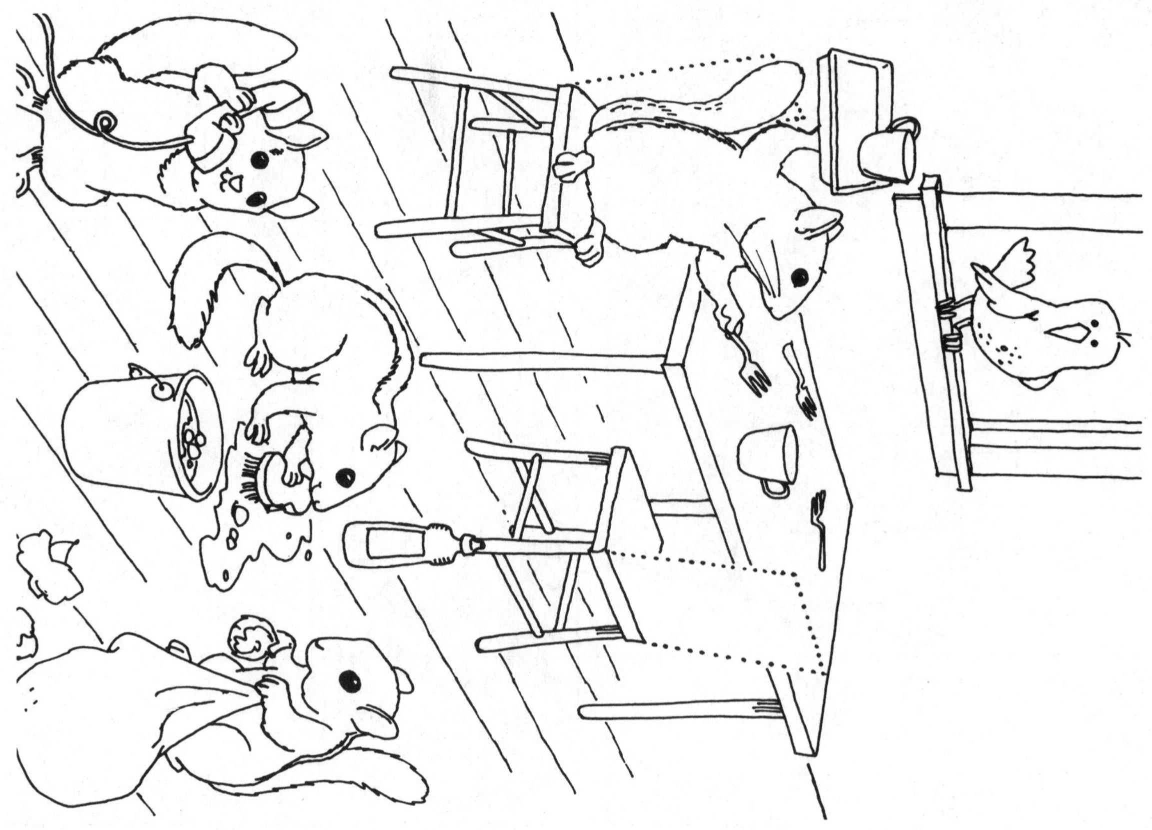

Name ______________________________

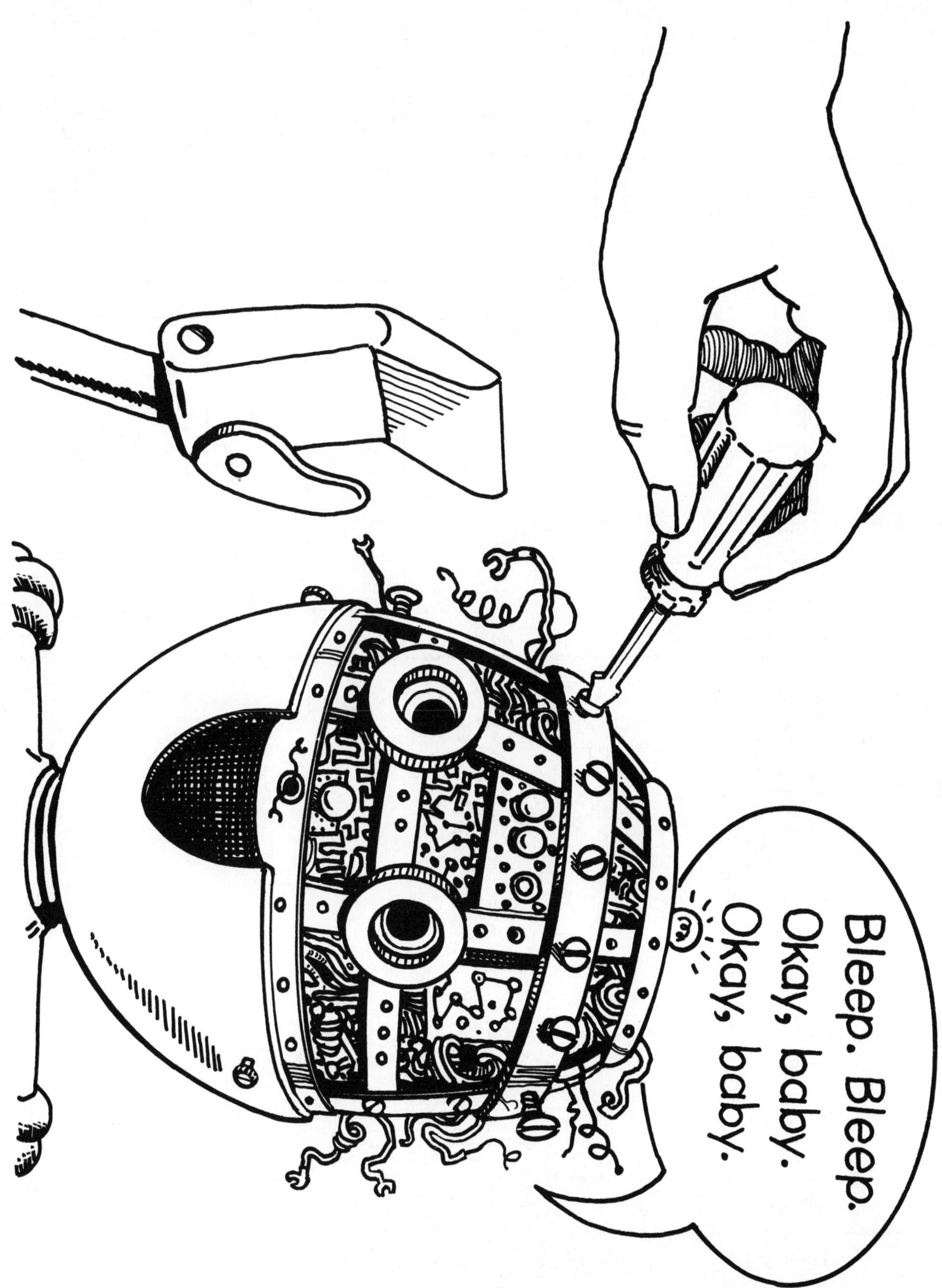

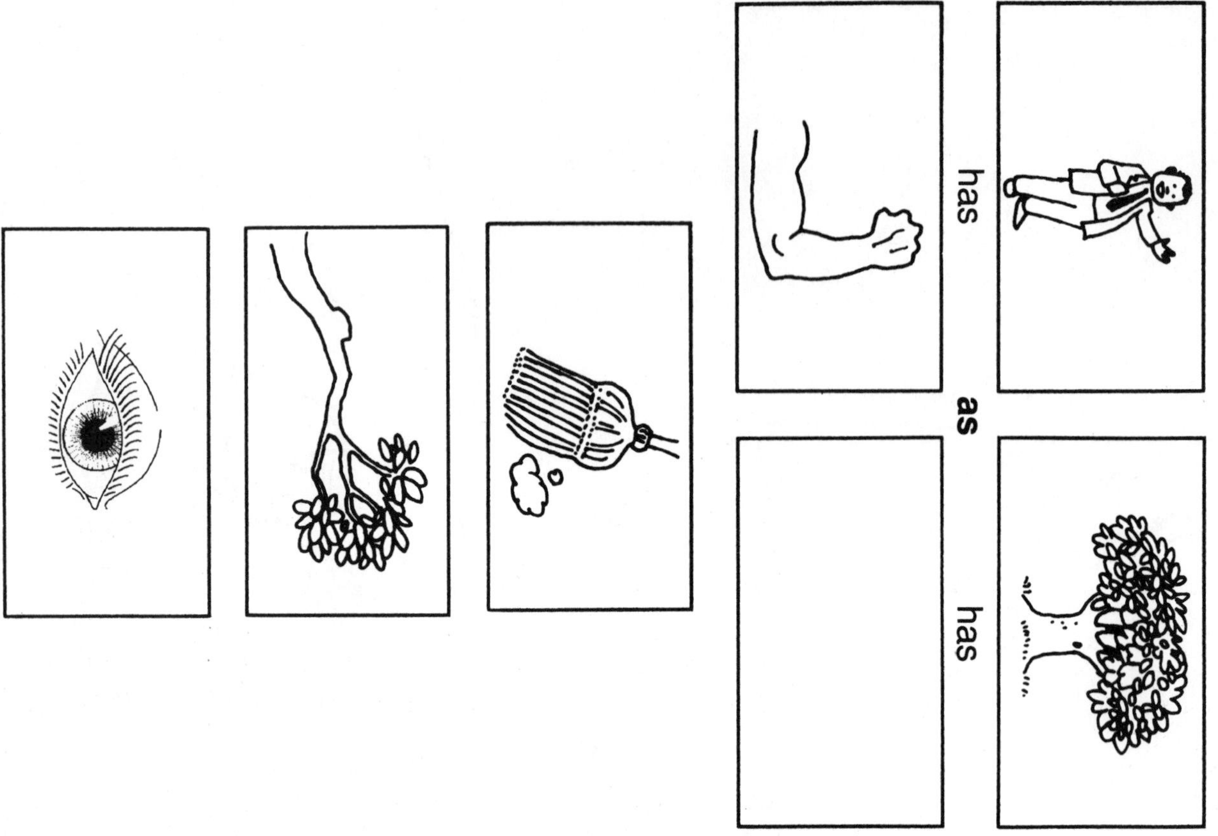
has
as
has

Name ______________________________

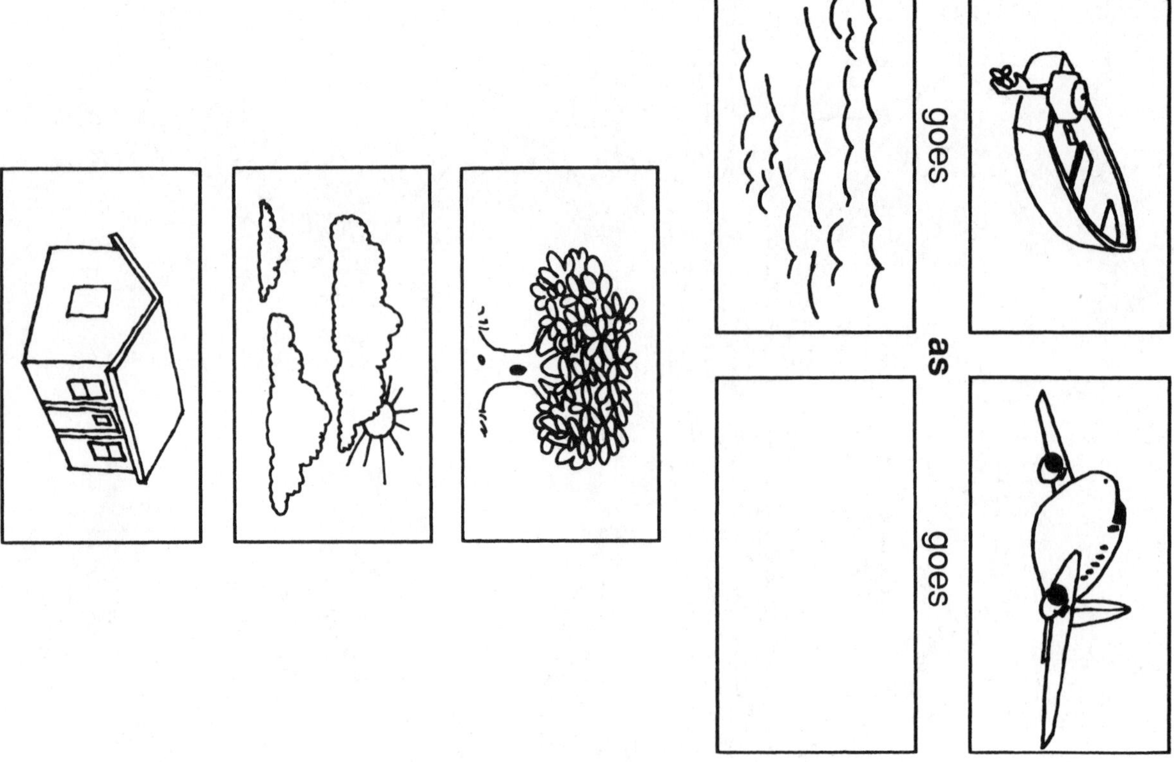
goes
as
goes

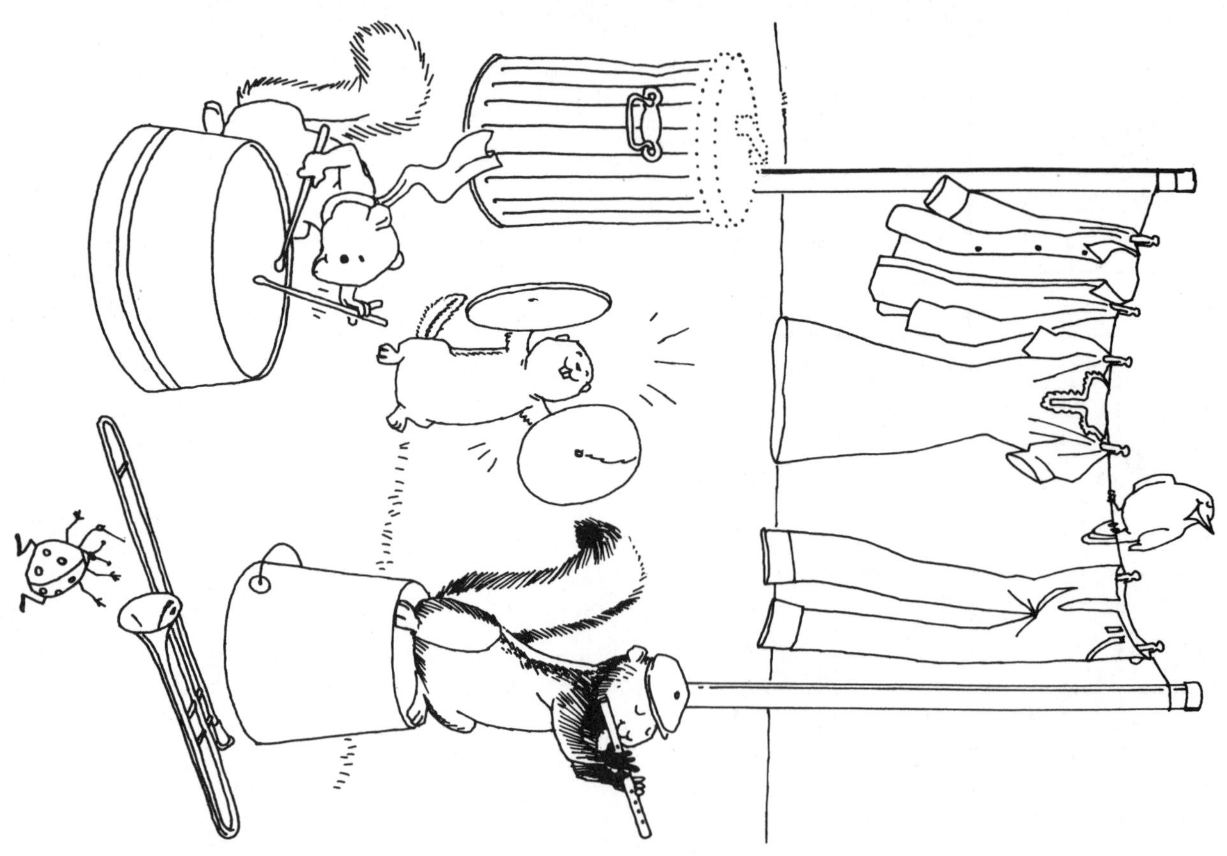

Name ______________________

chased

a bug

a rat

Sweetie

a bird

a skunk

a dog

1.

2.

3.

Name ______________________________

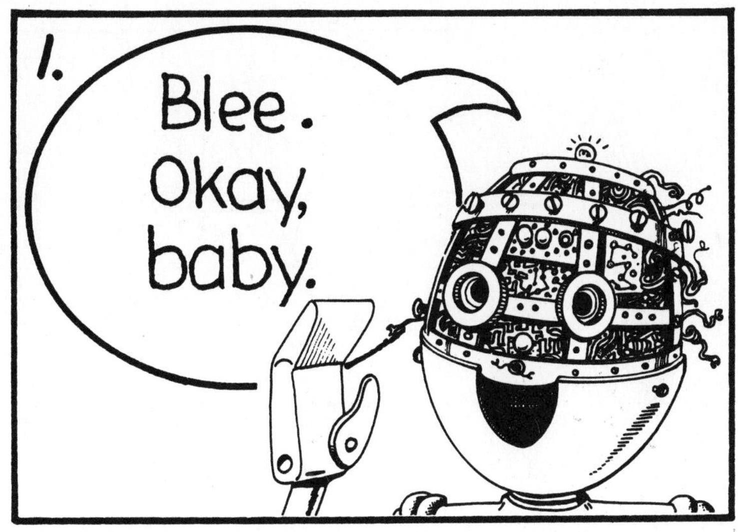
1.
Blee. Okay, baby.

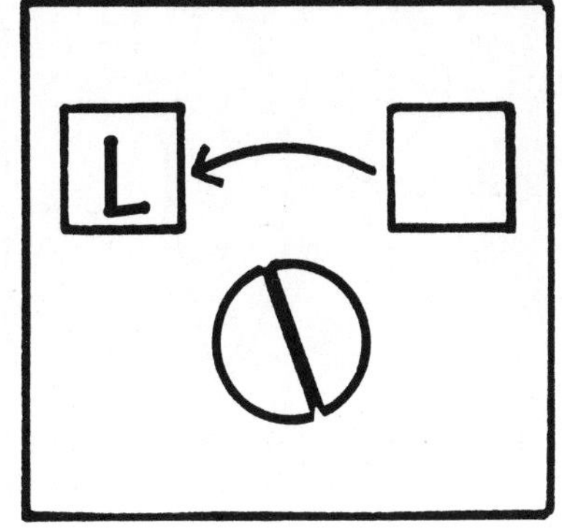
L

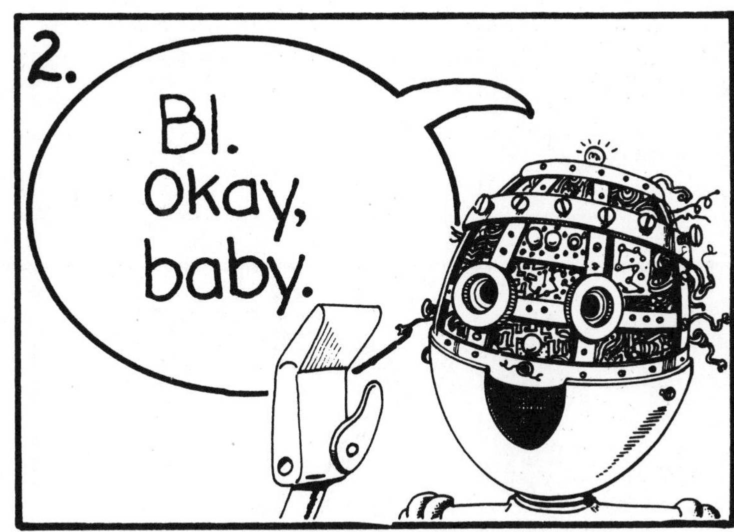
2.
Bl. Okay, baby.

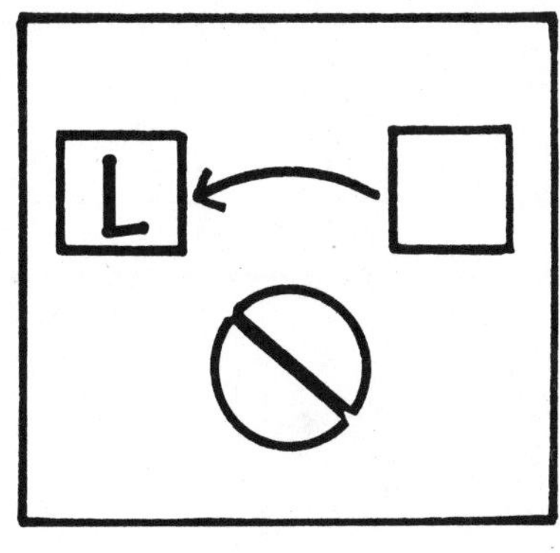
L

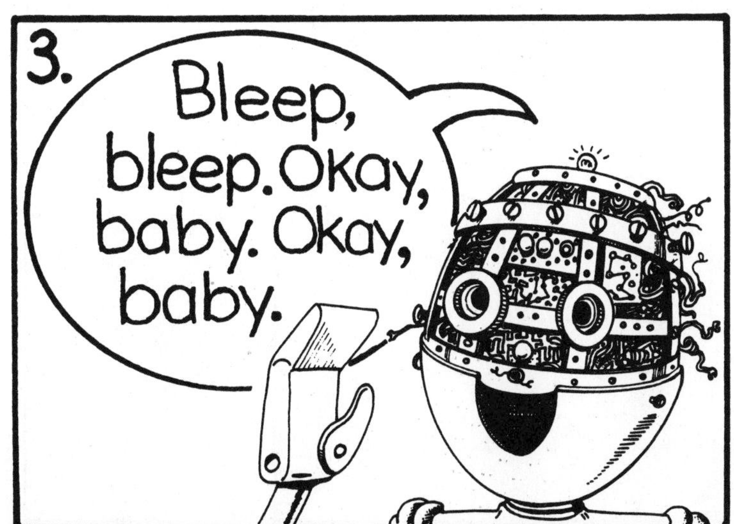
3.
Bleep, bleep. Okay, baby. Okay, baby.

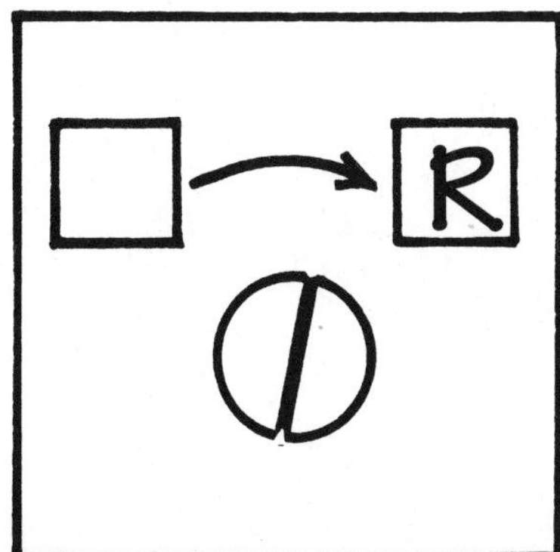
R

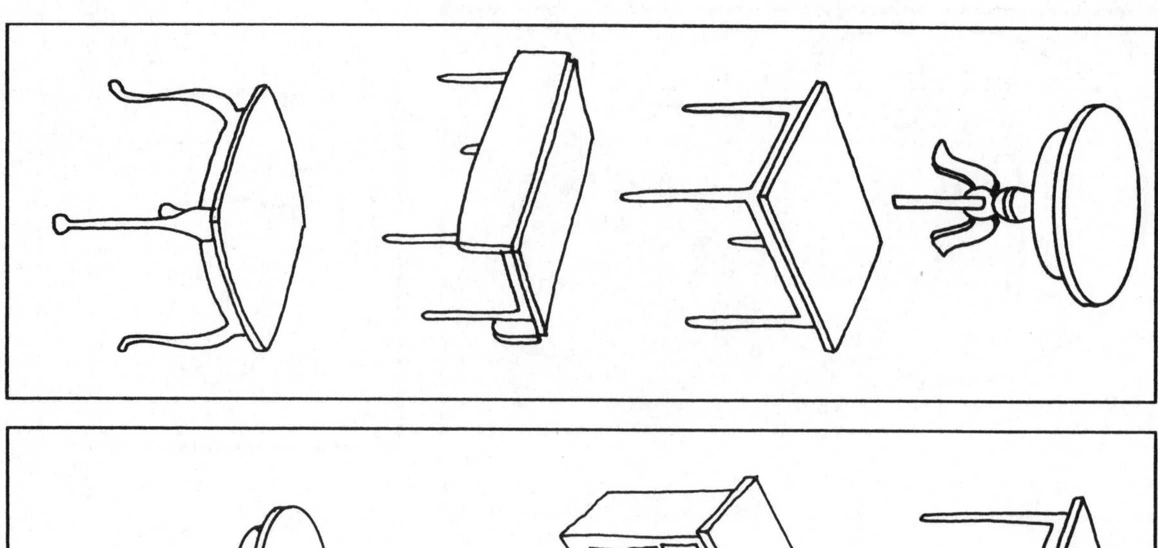

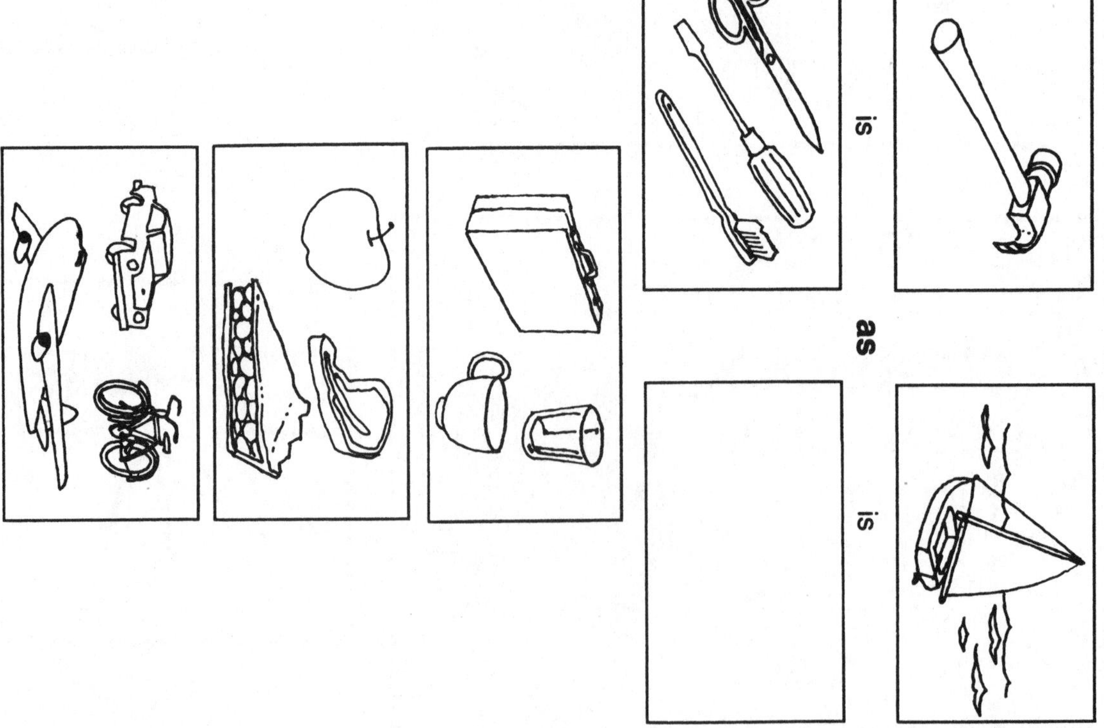
is
as
is

Name ______________________________

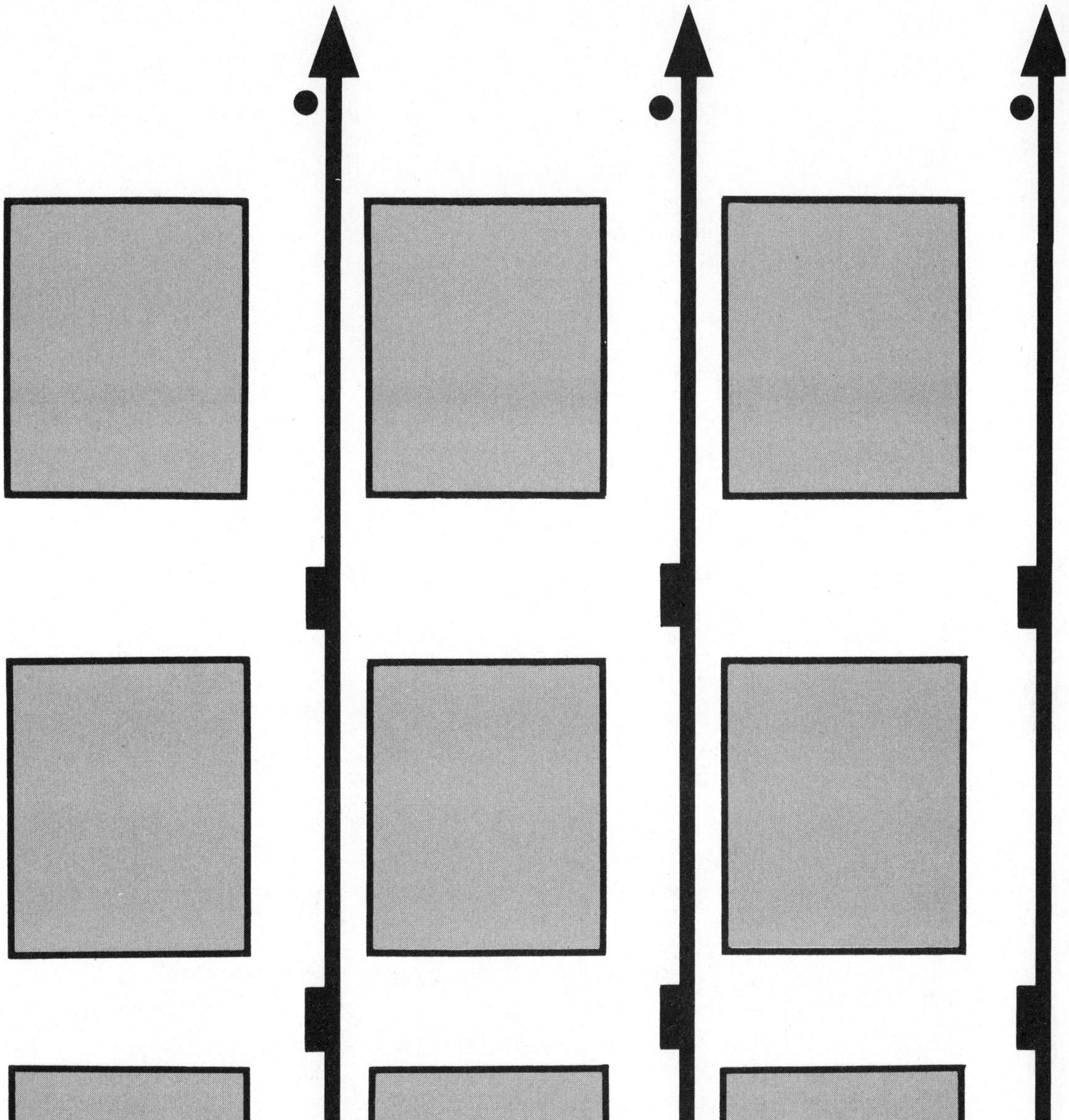

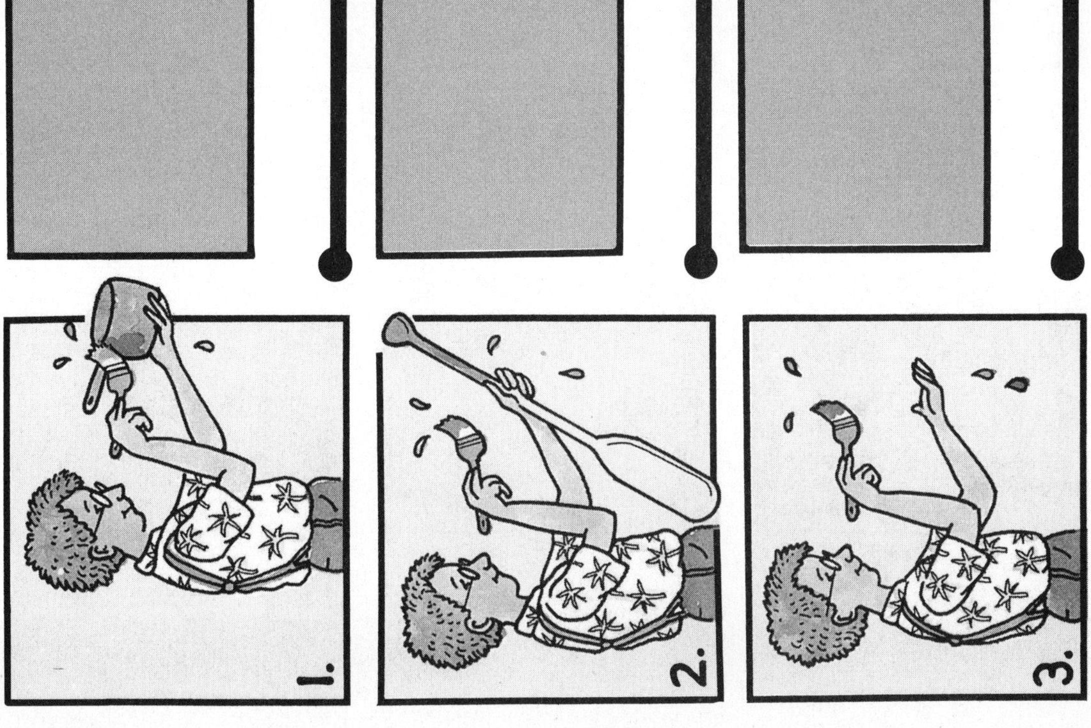

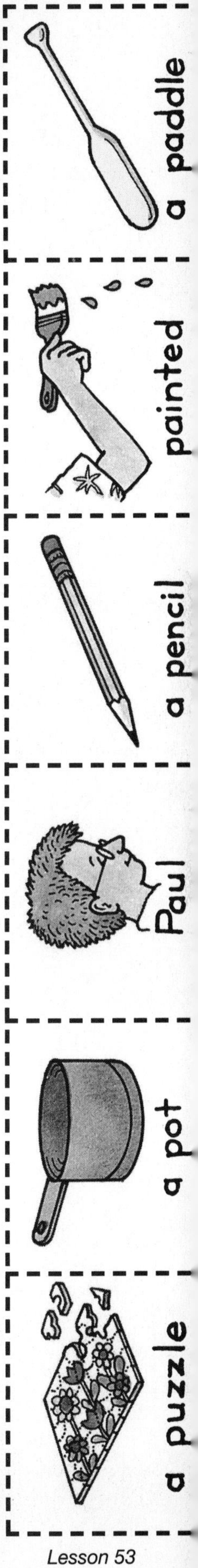

a paddle

painted

a pencil

Paul

a pot

a puzzle

1.

2.

3.

Name ______________________________

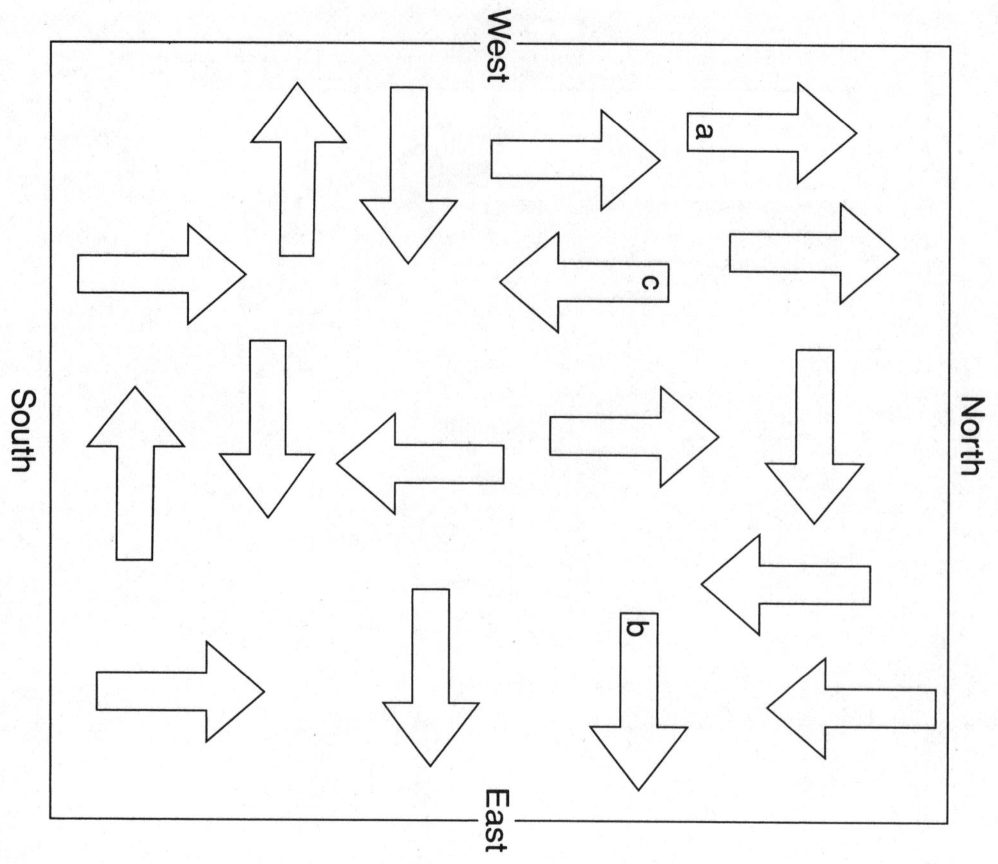
West
South
North
East
a
b
c

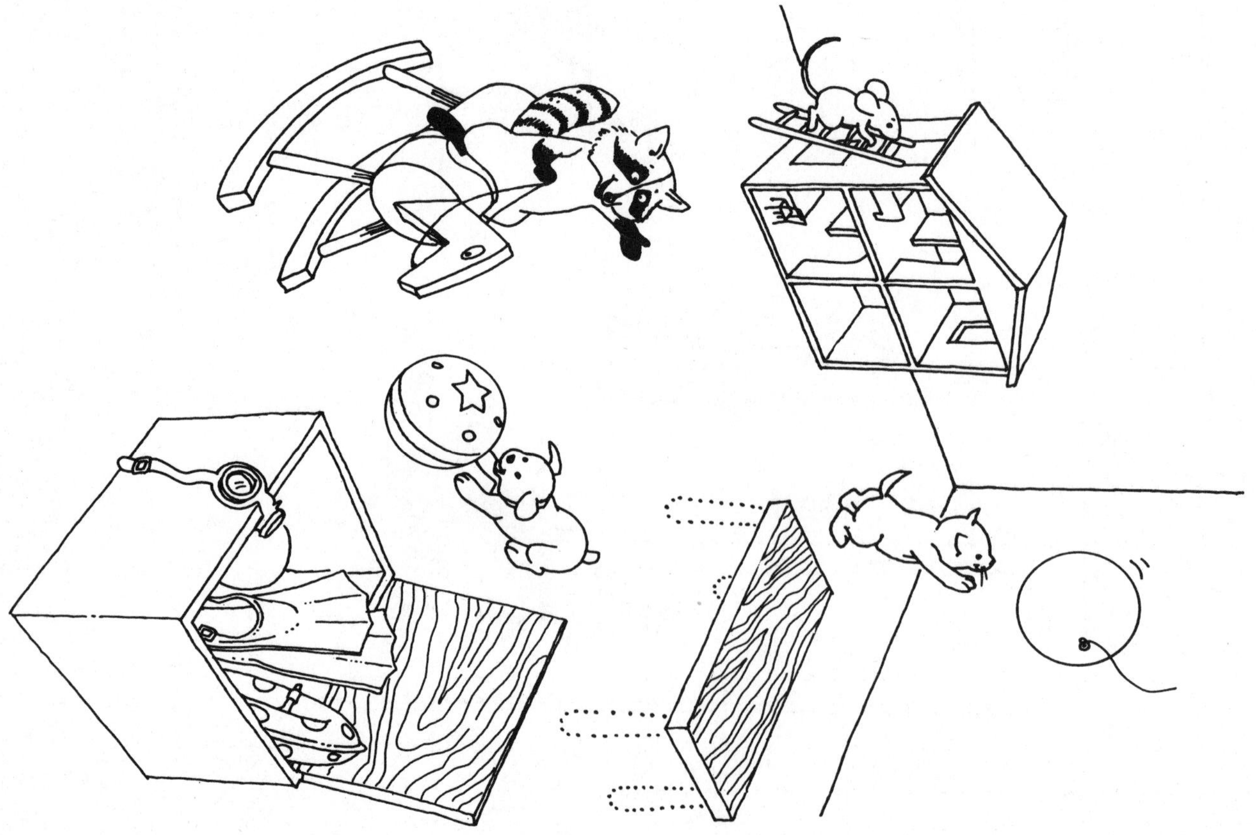

Name ______________________________

Clarabelle

a tree

a ladder

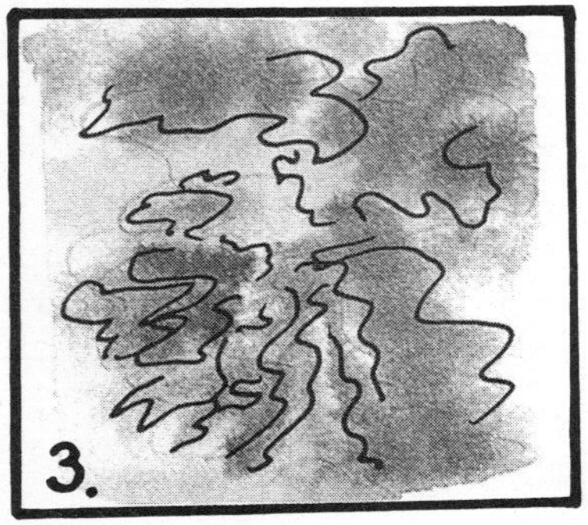

Paul

climbed

Sweetie

Roxie

1.

2.

3.

Name ___________________________

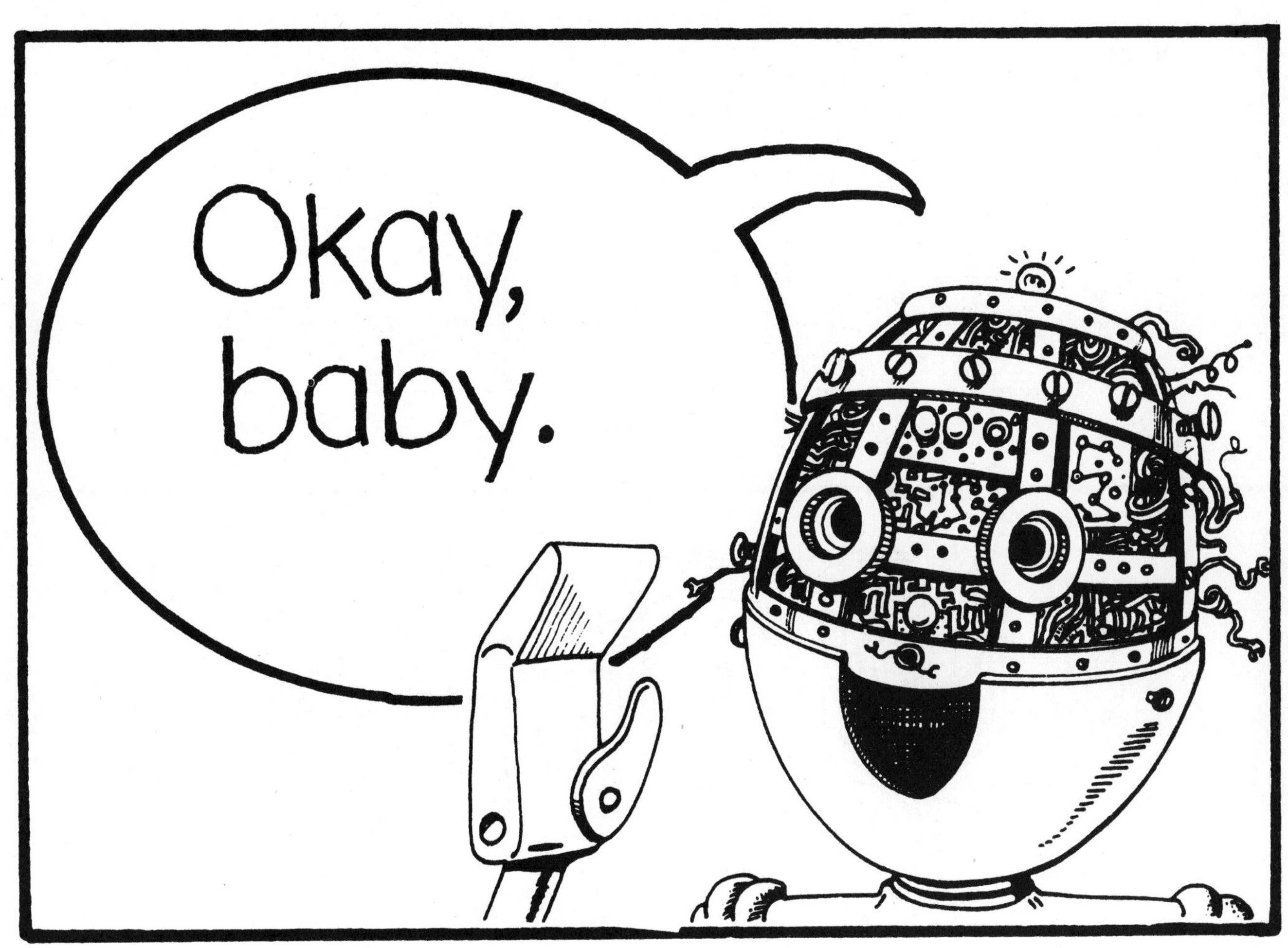

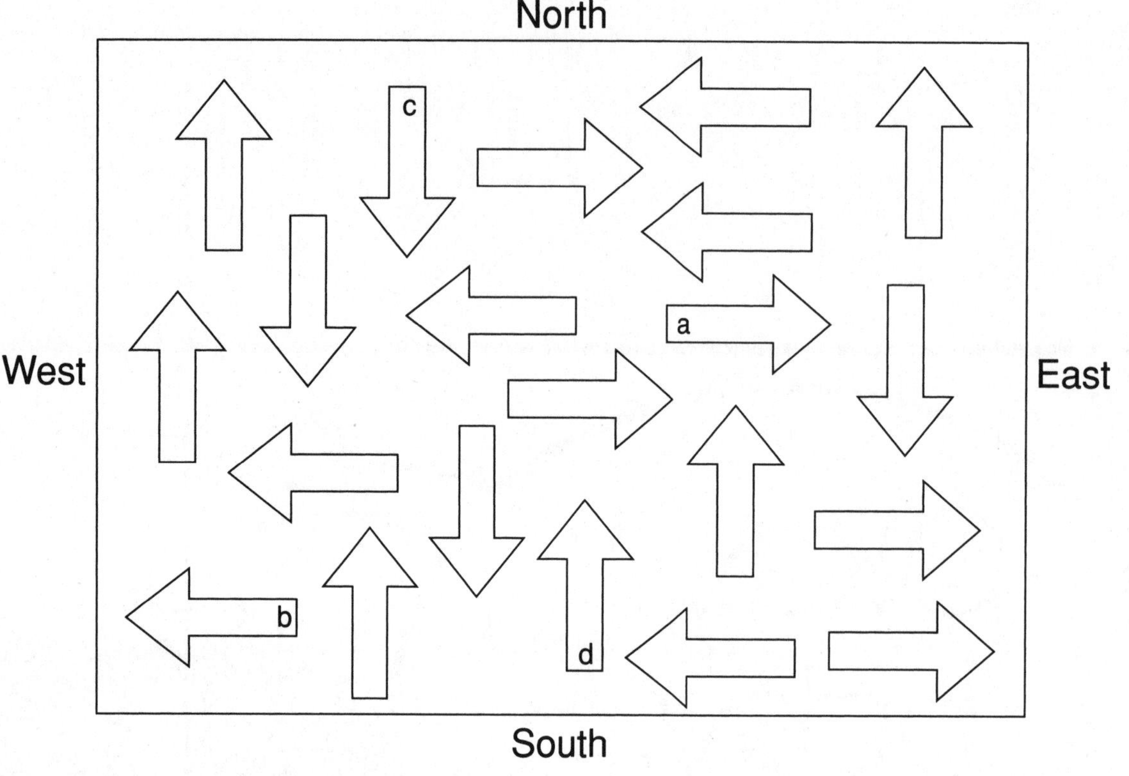
North
West
East
South
a
b
c
d

Name ______________________

1. ______
2. ______
3. ______
4. ______
5. ______
6. ______

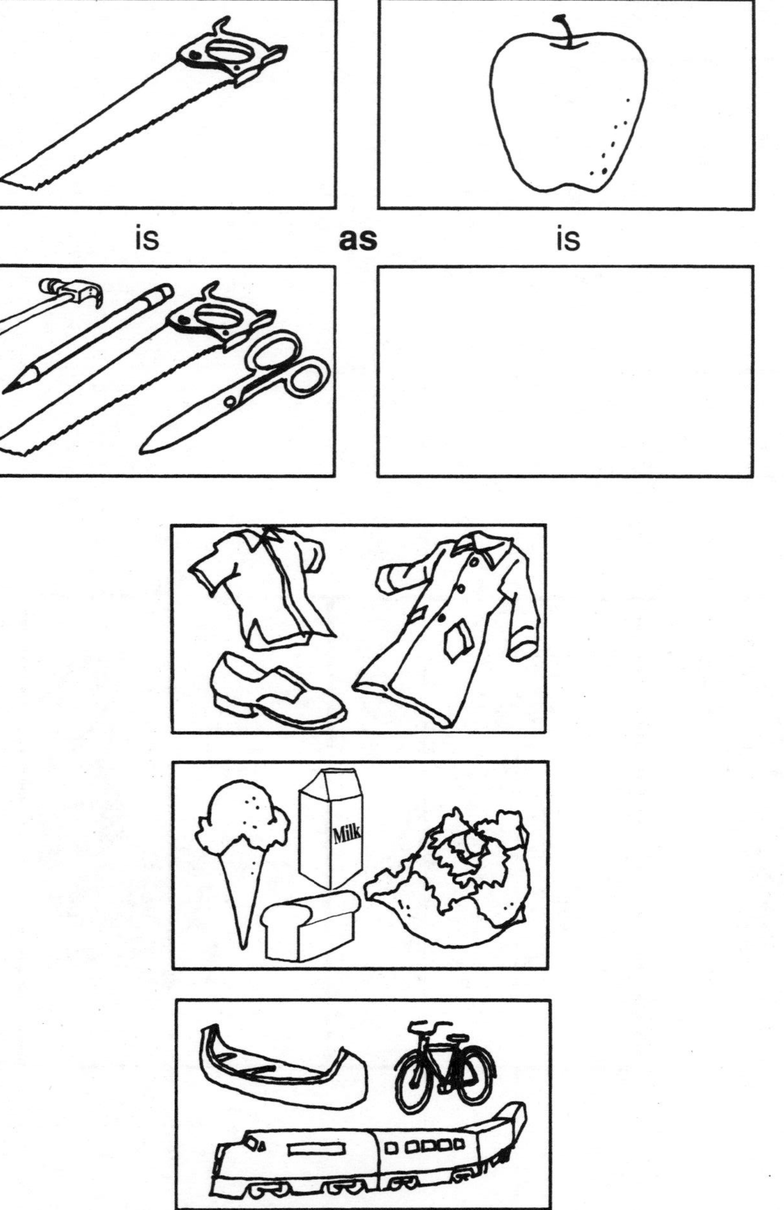
is
as
is
Milk

Name ______________________________

Sunday	Monday	Tuesday	Wednesday

Say the days of the week.

______________,
______________,
______________,
Blurpday.

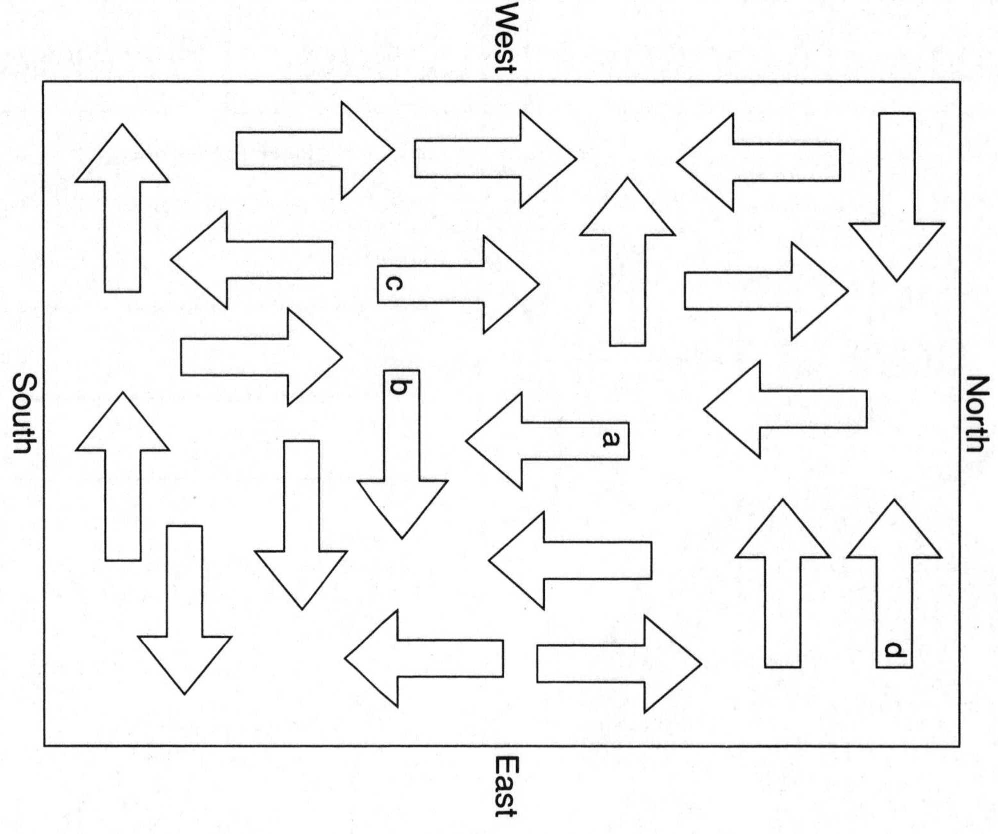

West
North
South
East
a
b
c
d

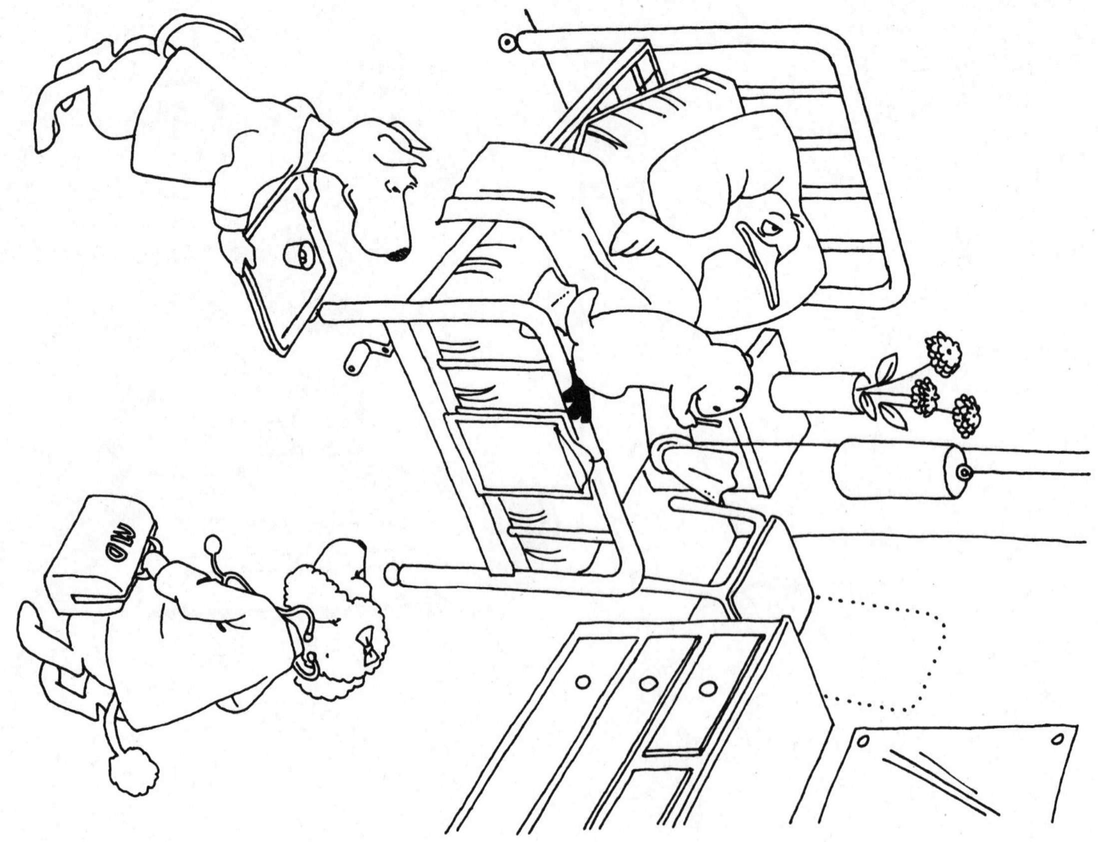

MD

Name ______________________________

Wednesday	Thursday	Friday	Saturday

Name ____________________

Why did you say

__________,

Bleep?

Sunday

____

Monday

____

Tuesday

____

Wednesday

____

Thursday

____

Blurpday

____

Saturday

____

Name ____________________________

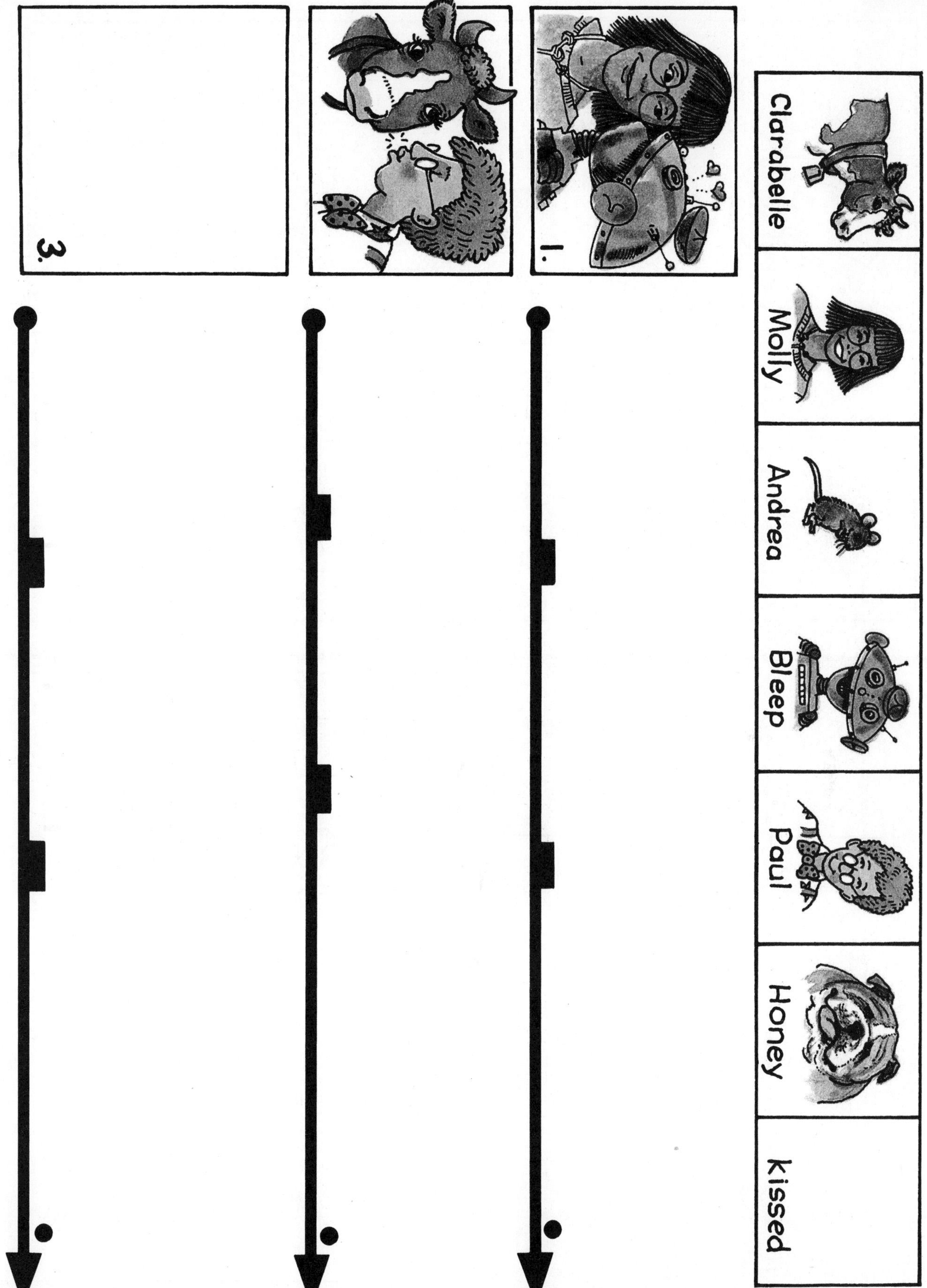

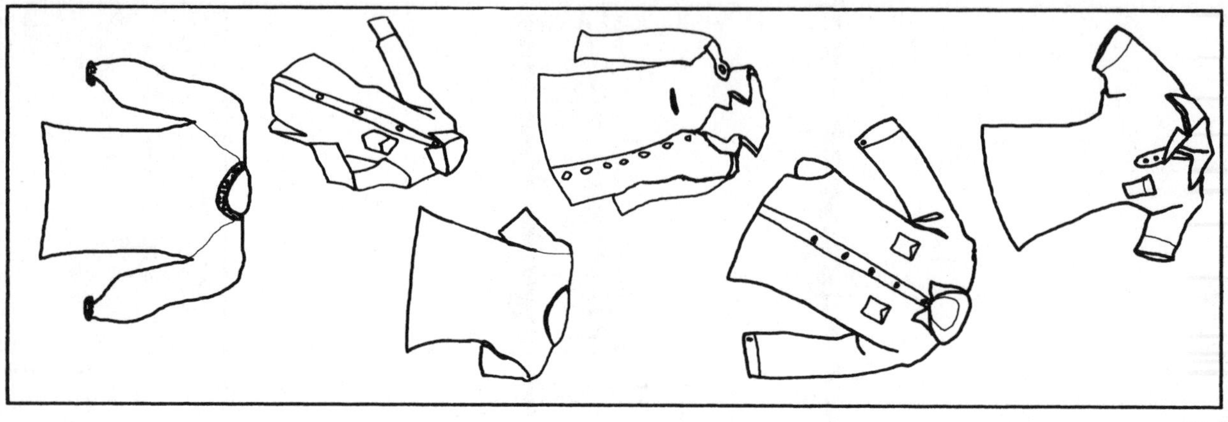

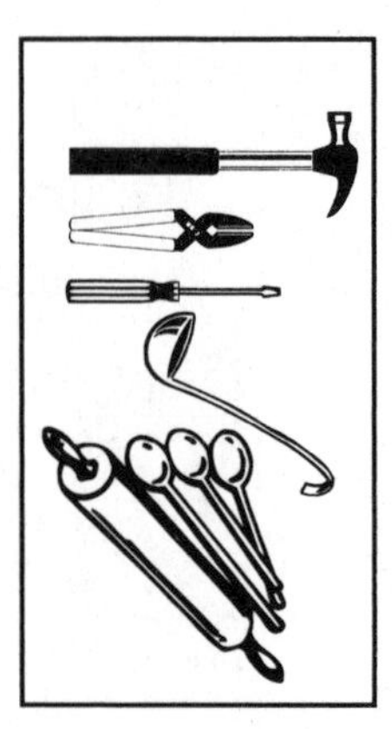

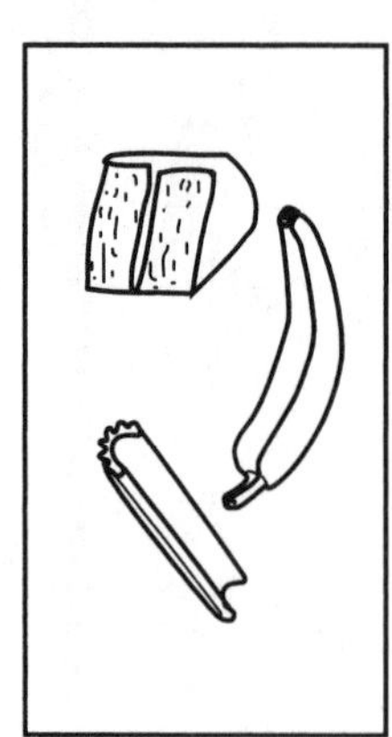

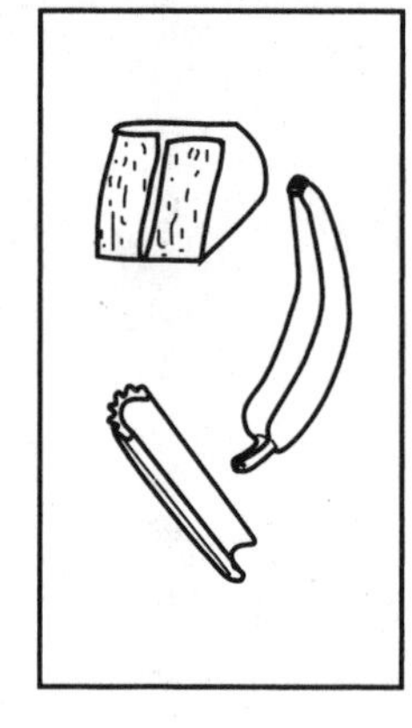

is

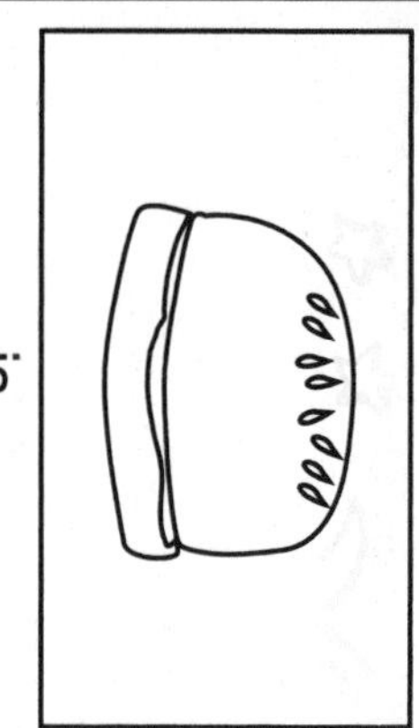

as

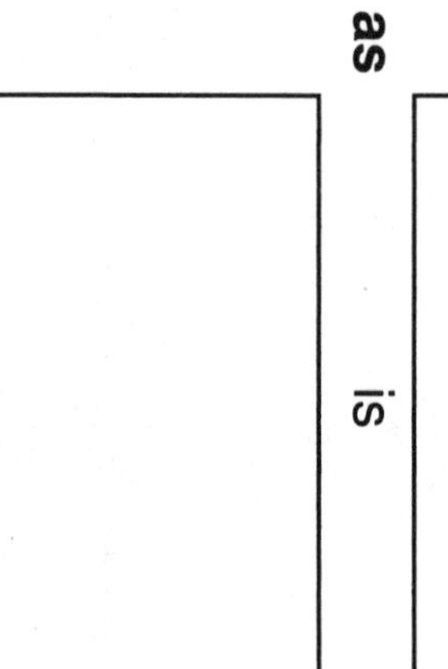

is

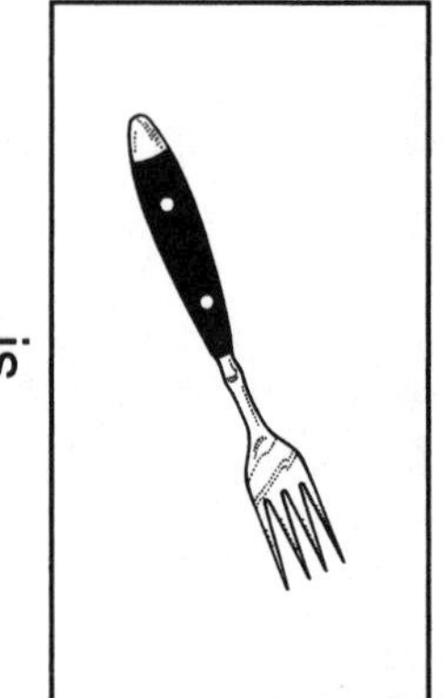

Name ________________________________

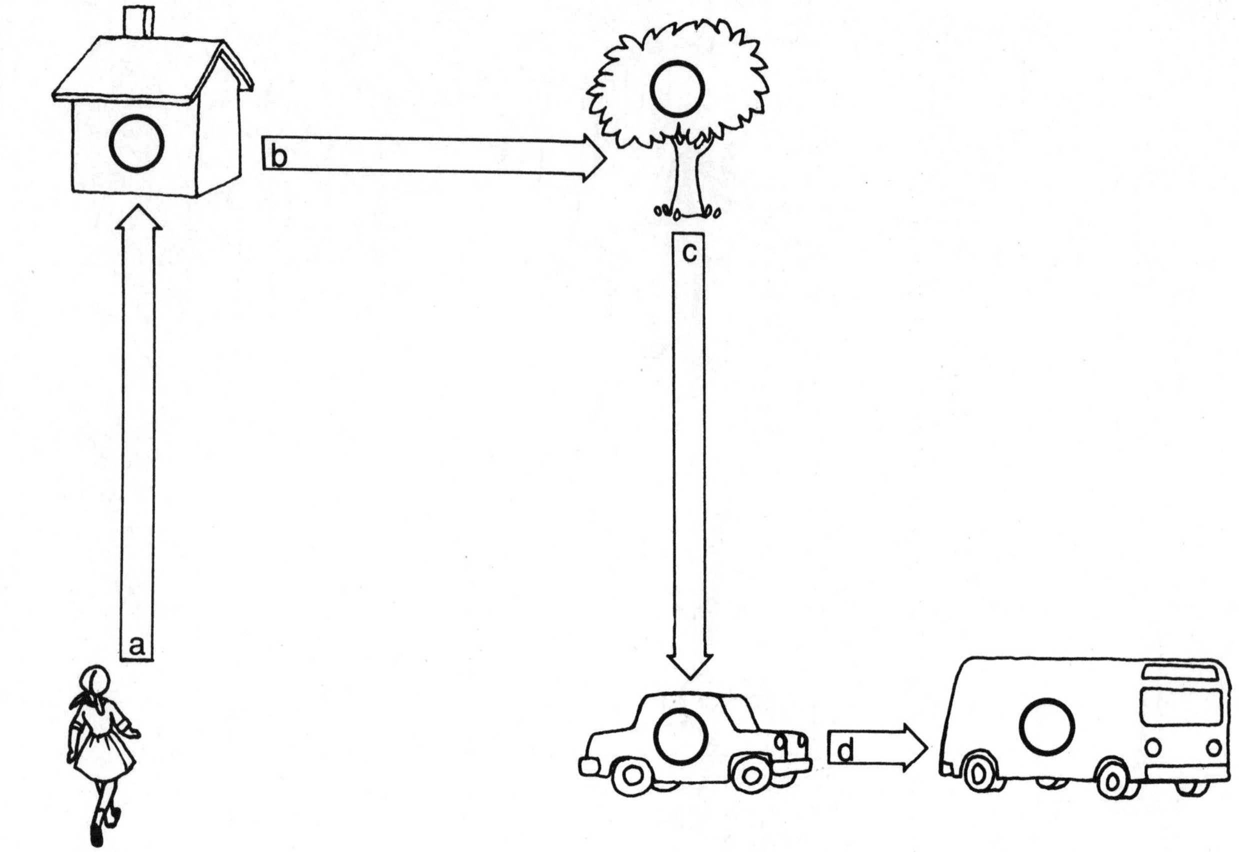

b

c

a

d

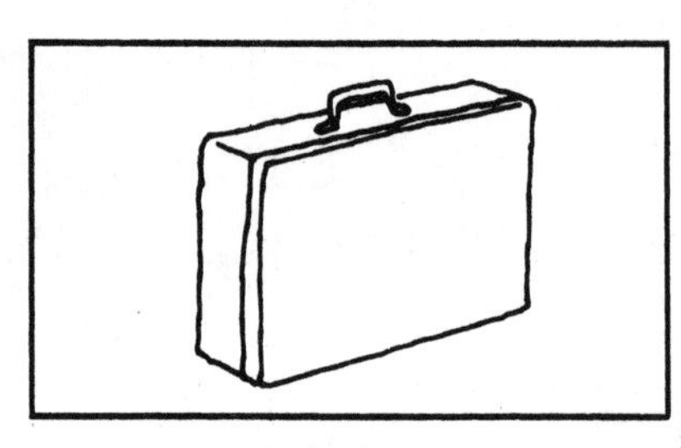

is as is

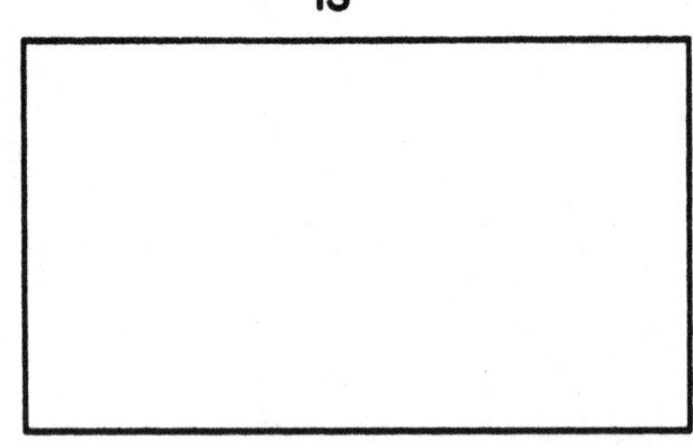

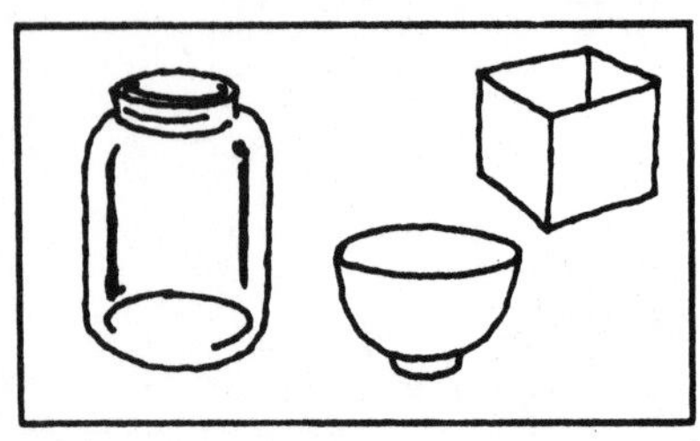

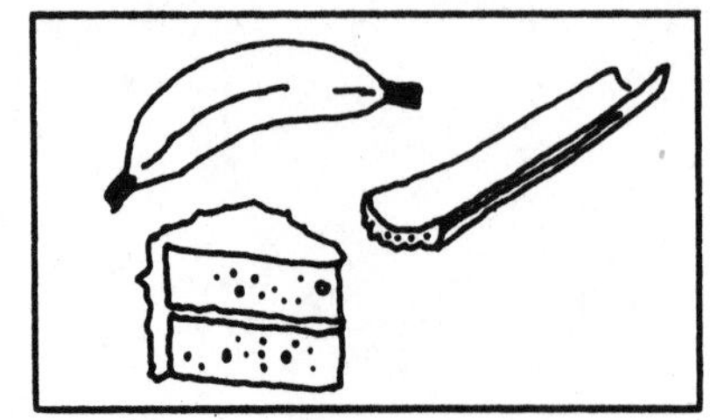

Name ______________________________

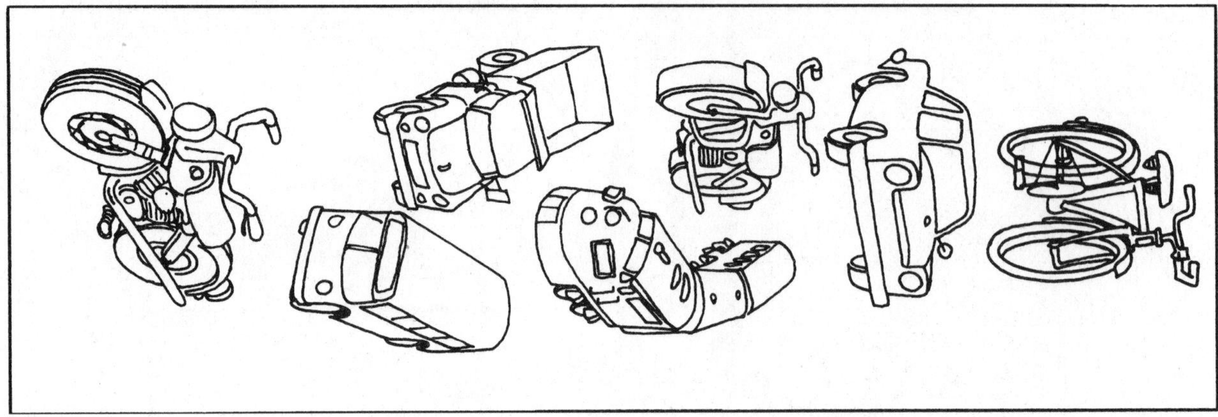

Name ____________________

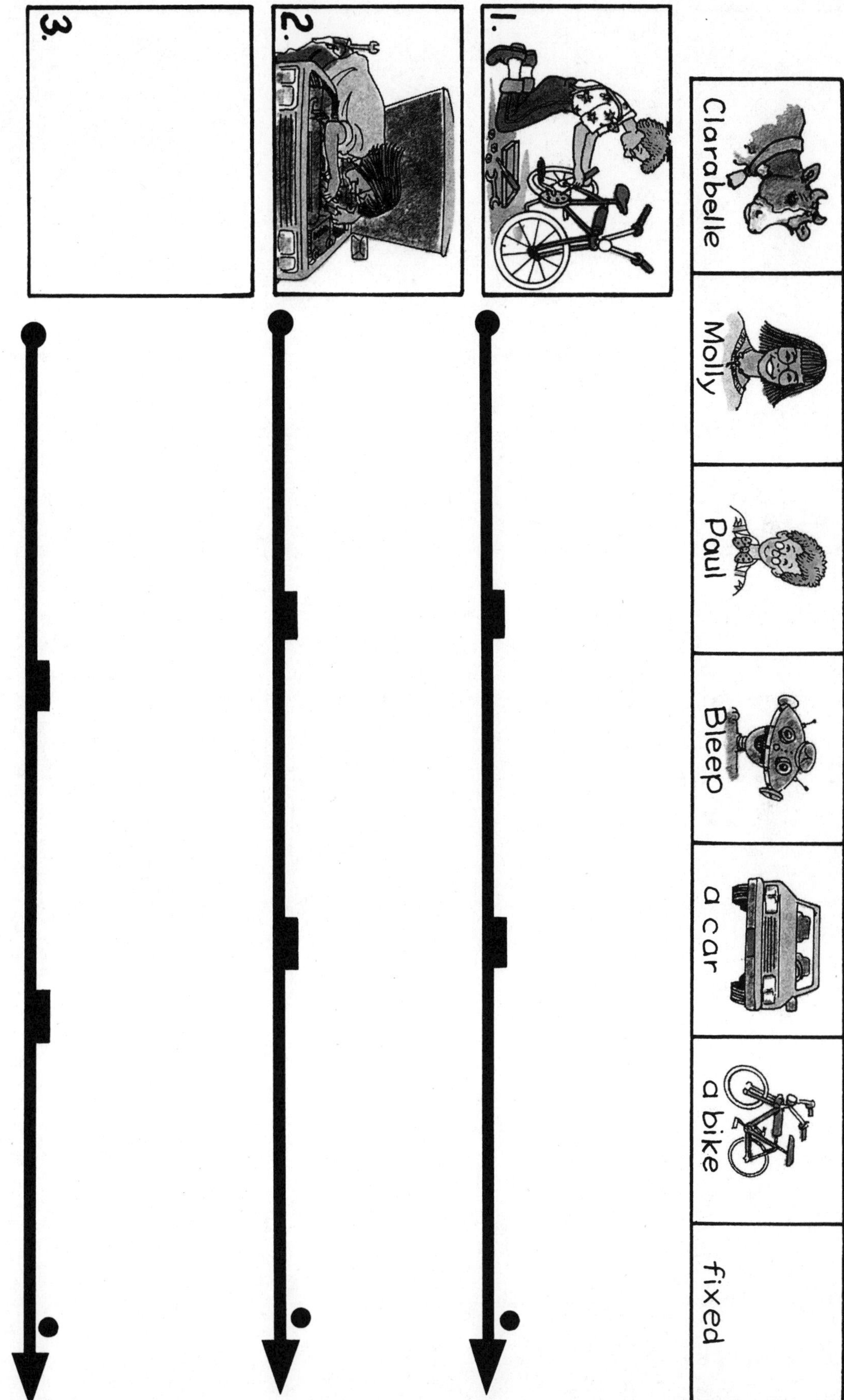

January
February
March
April
May
June
January,
February,
Blurp.

Name ____________________________

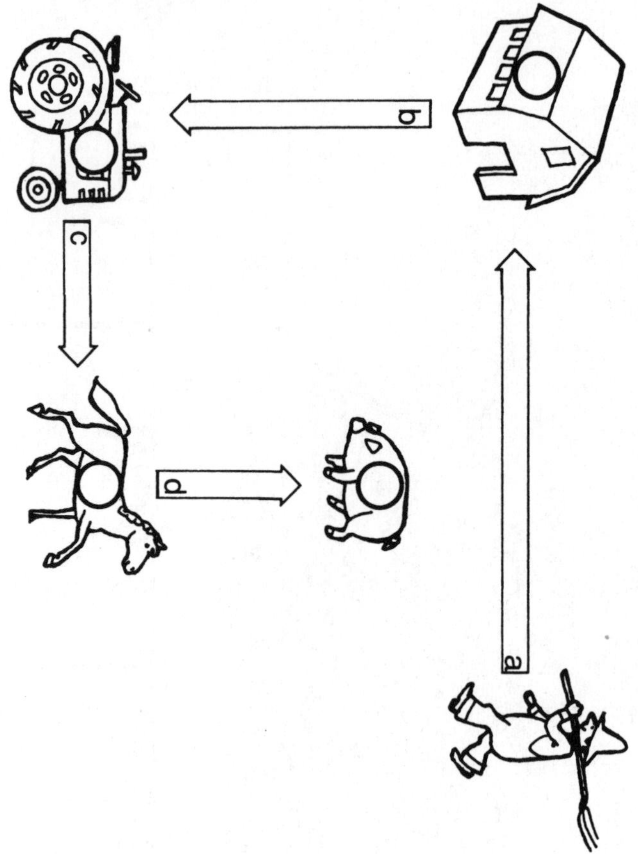
a
b
c
d

Name ______________________________

September			
March	June	February	May
November	January	April	July
October	August	December	

Name ______________________________

Name ________________________________

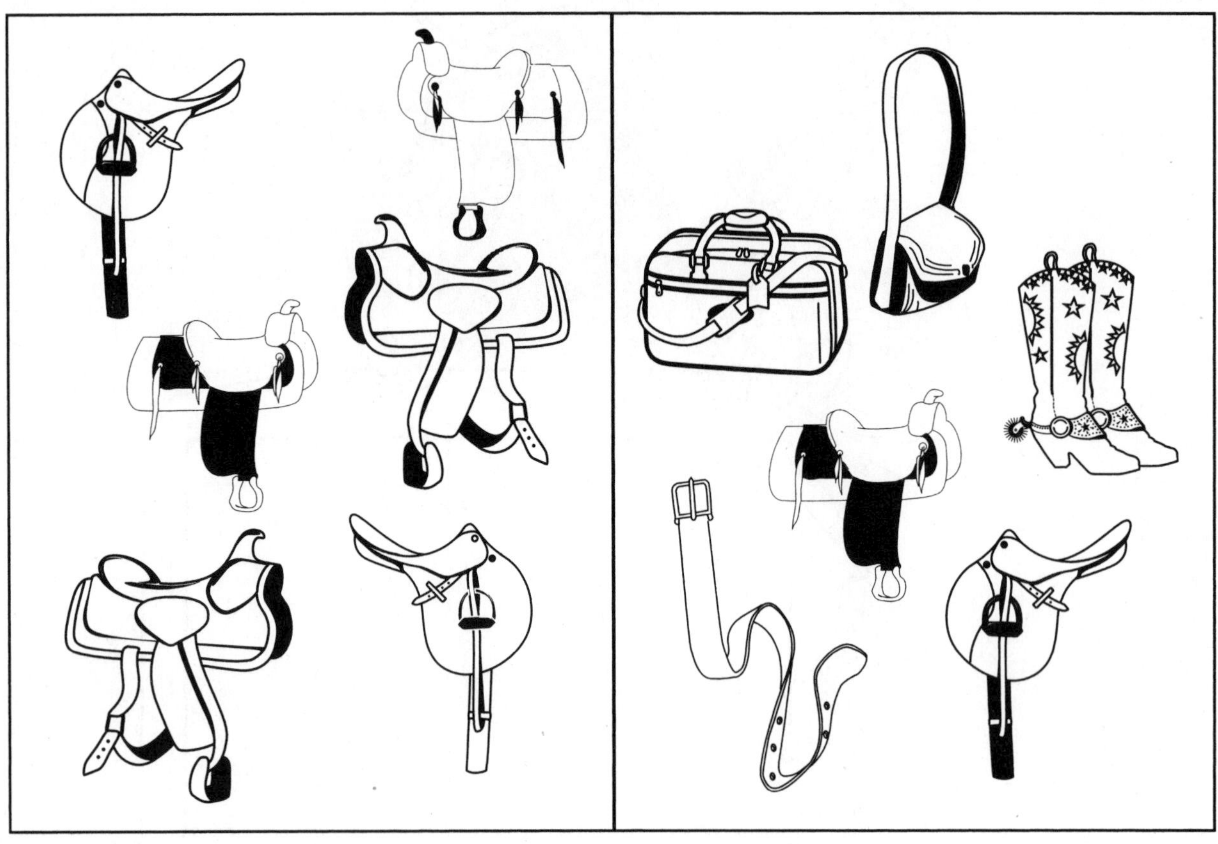

is

as

is

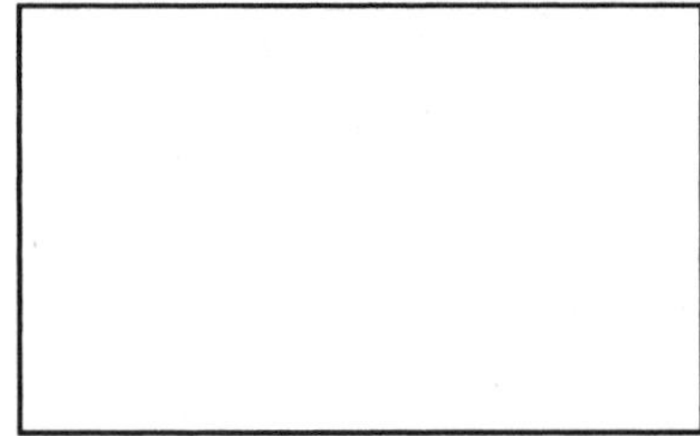

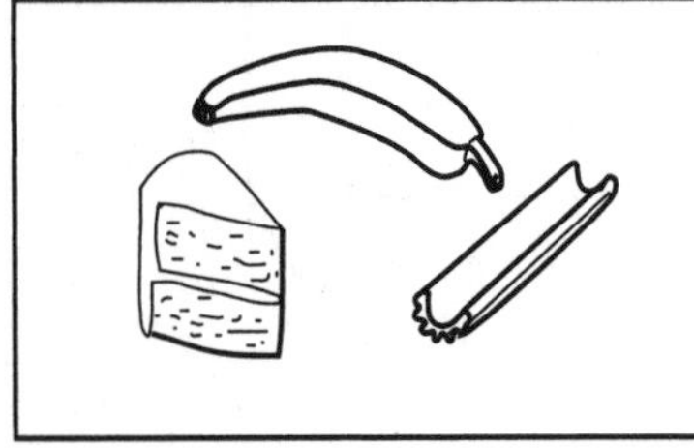

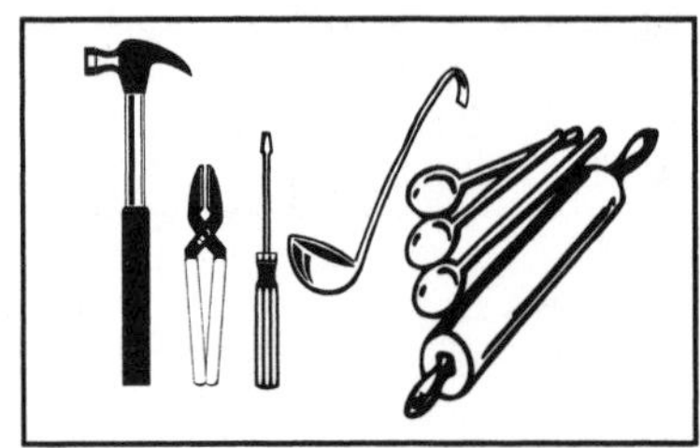

Name ___________________________

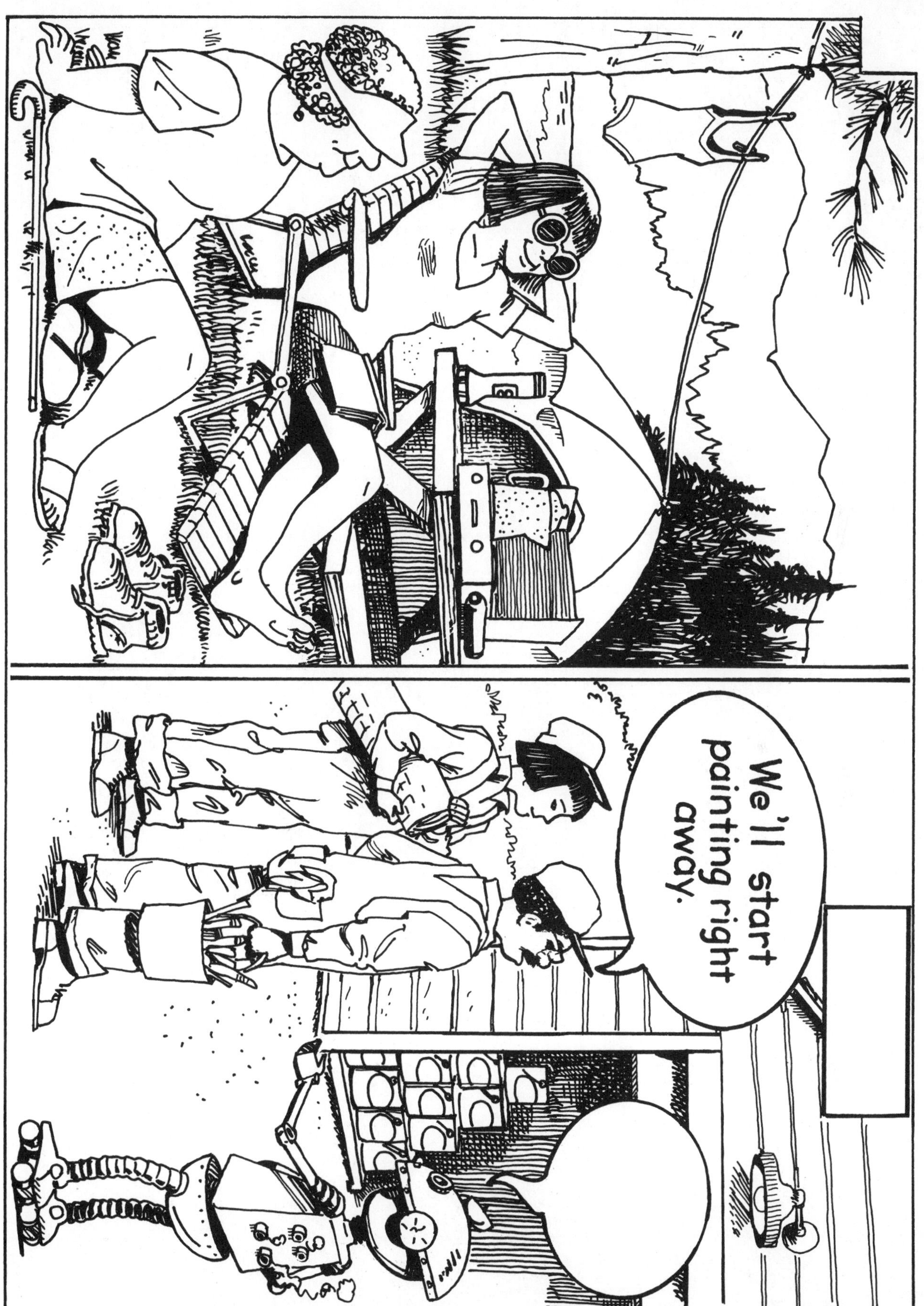

Name ______________________________

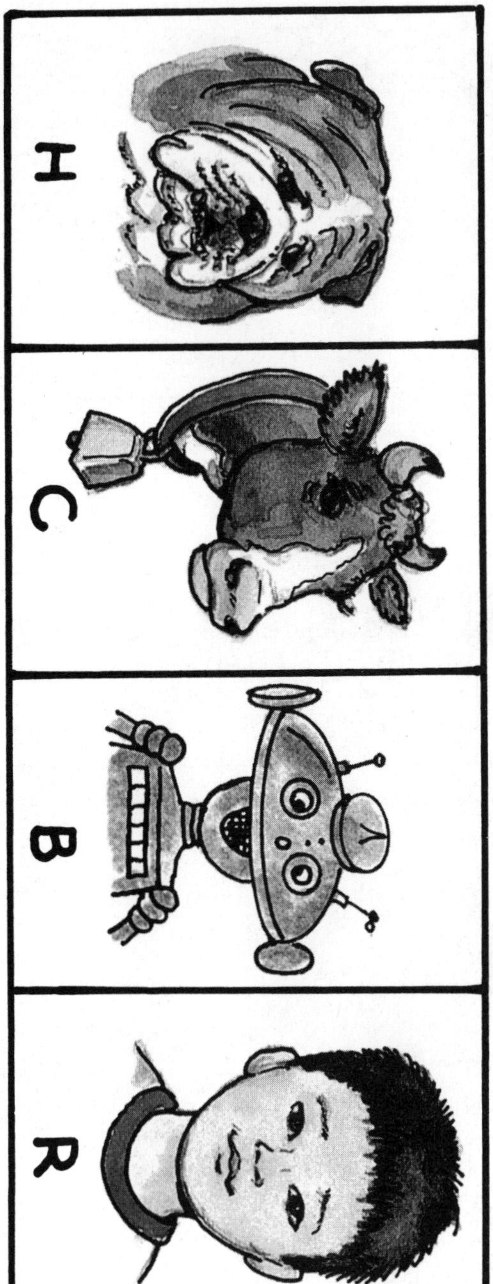

H

C

B

R

S

1. ______________

2. ______________

3. ______________

4. ______________

5. ______________

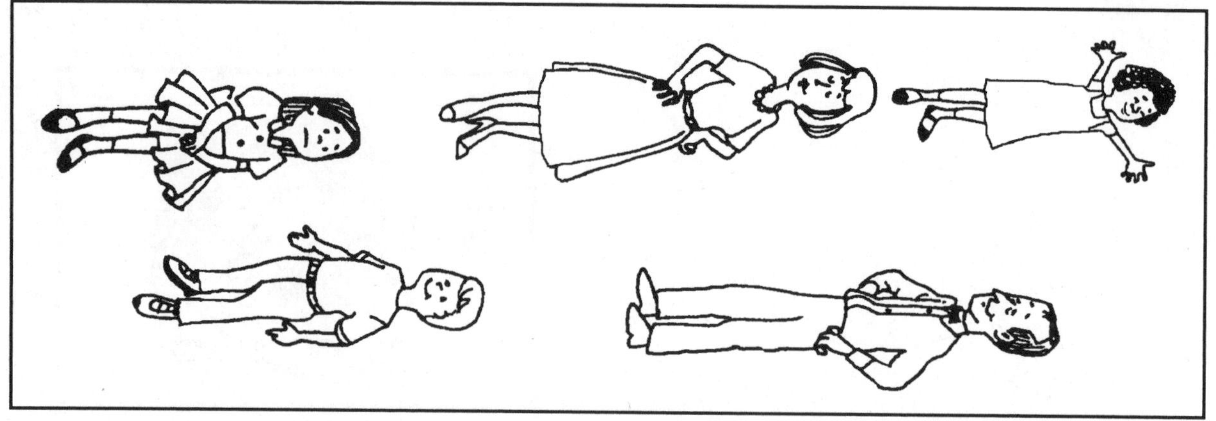

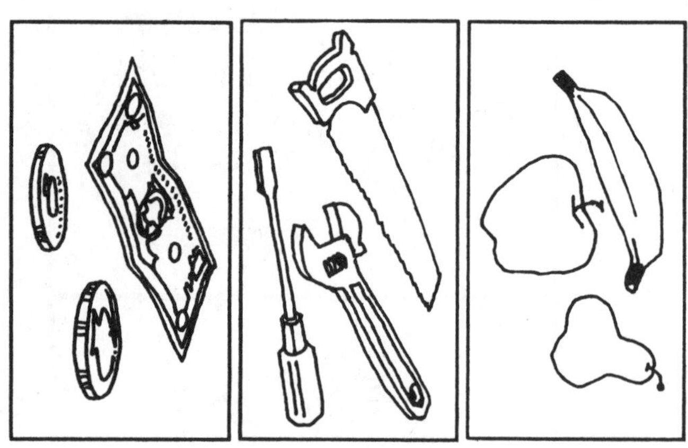

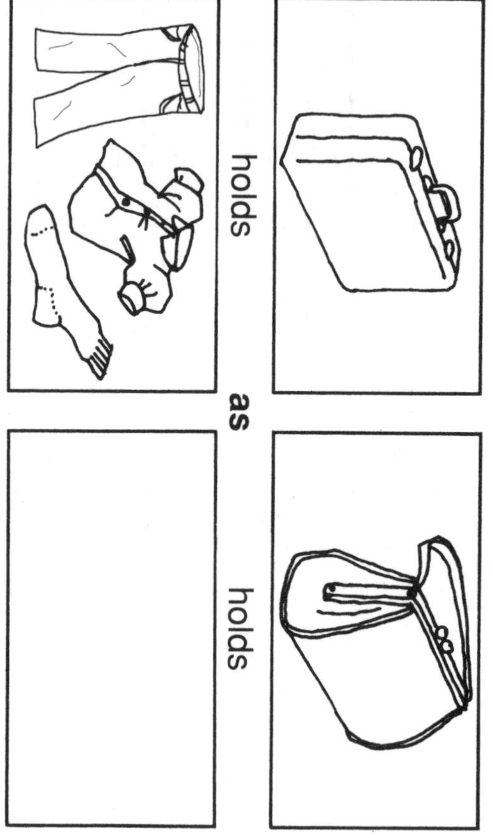
holds
as
holds

Name ______________________________

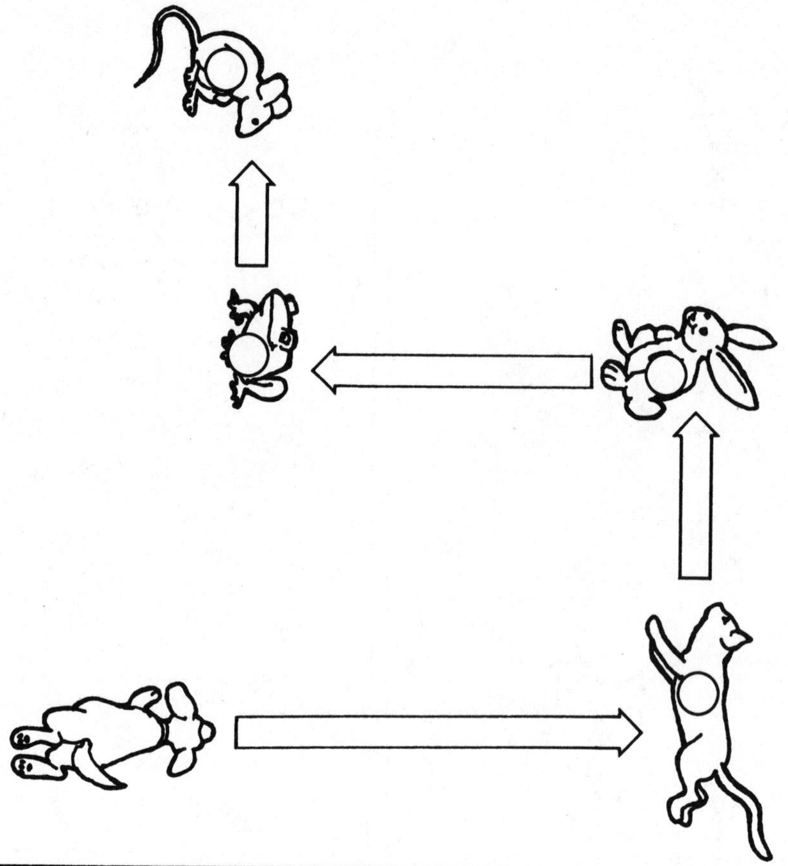

Name ______________________________

1. ____________________
2. ____________________
3. ____________________
4. ____________________
5. ____________________

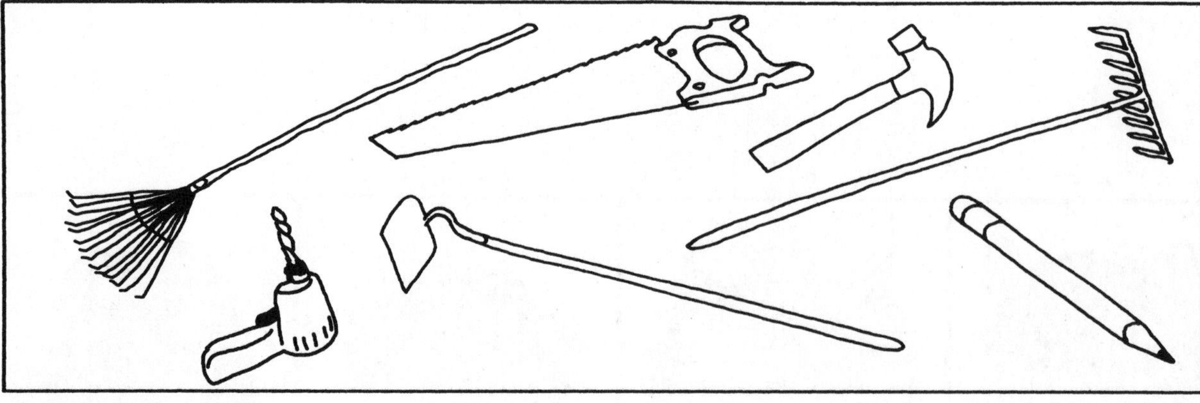

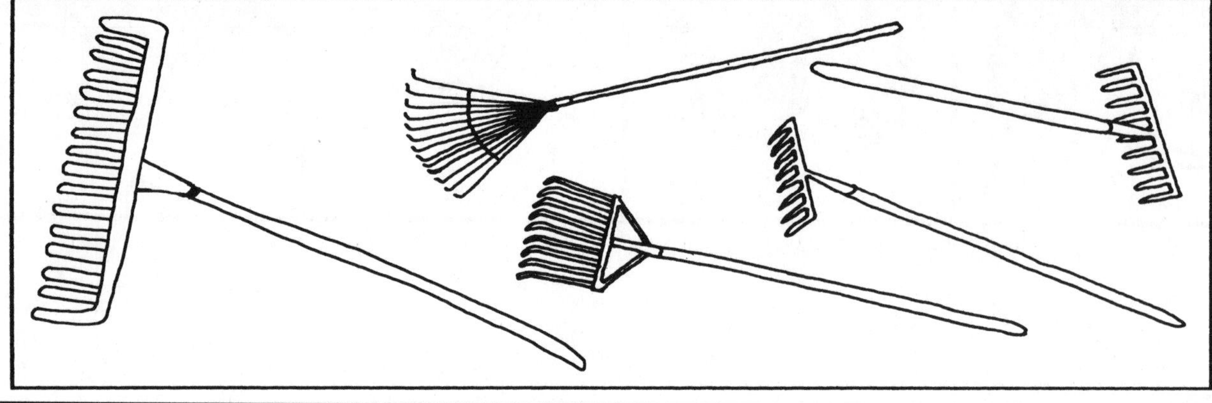

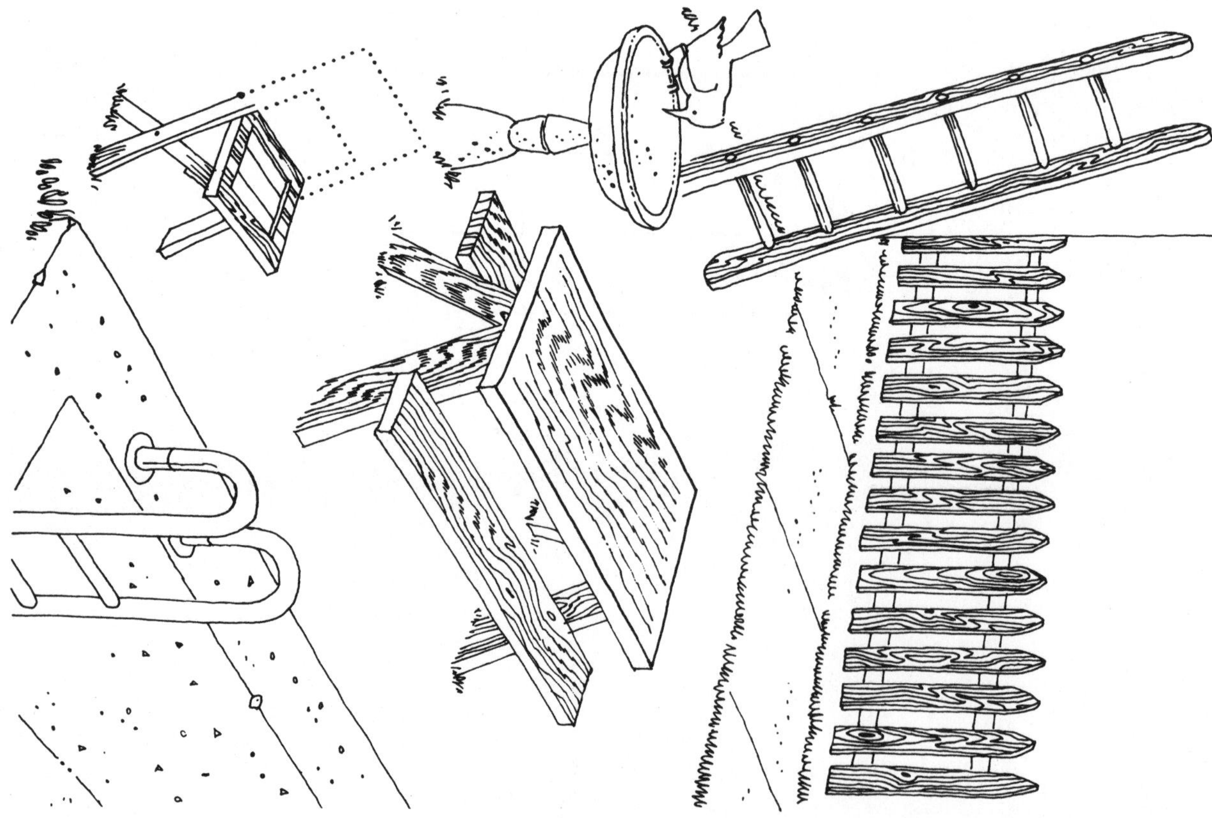

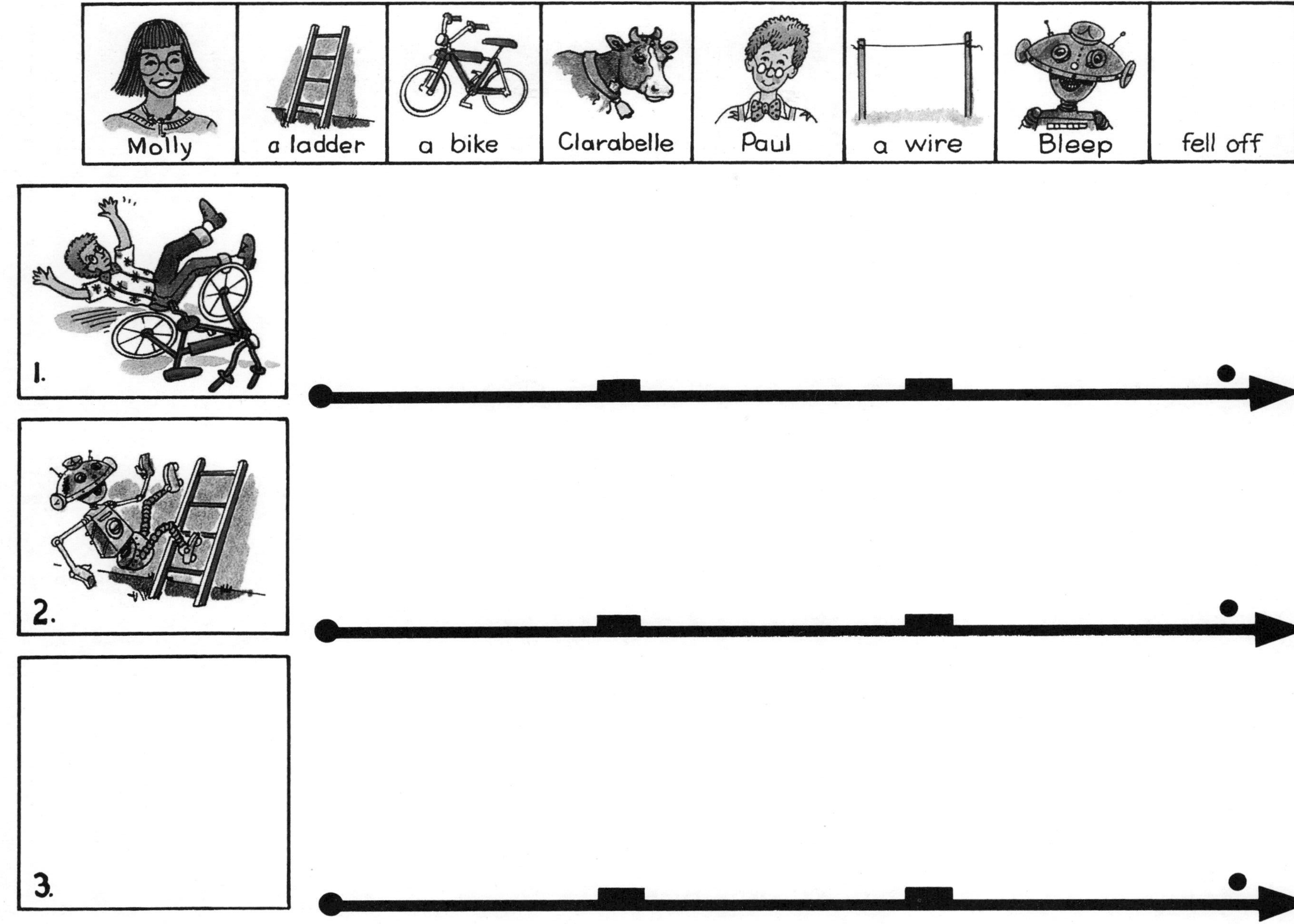

Molly
a ladder
a bike
Clarabelle
Paul
a wire
Bleep
fell off
1.
2.
3.

Name ____________________

Name ________________________________

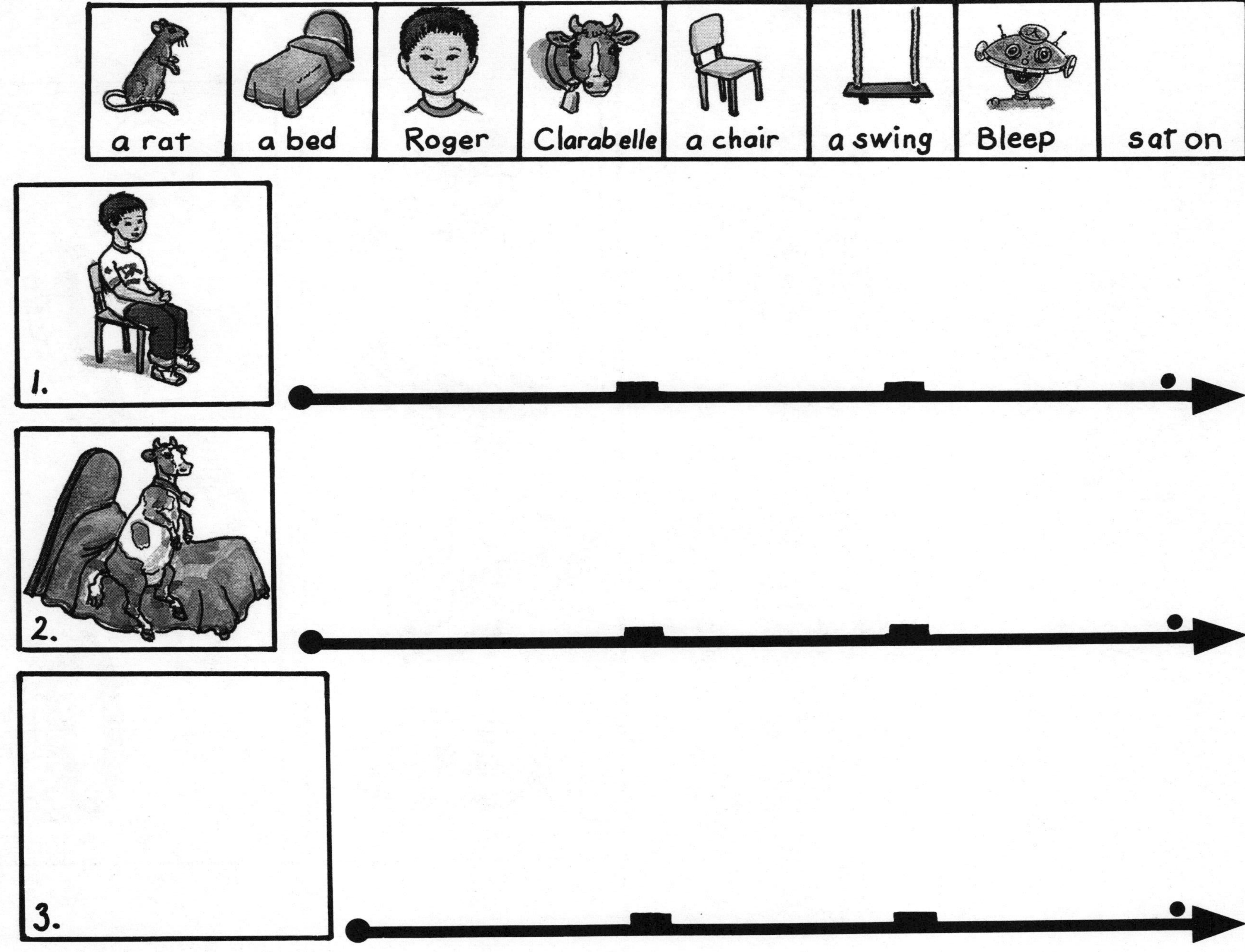

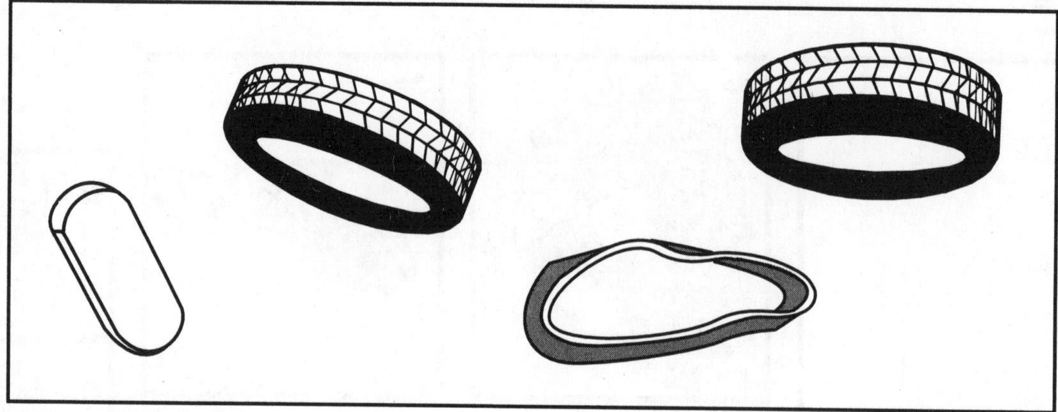

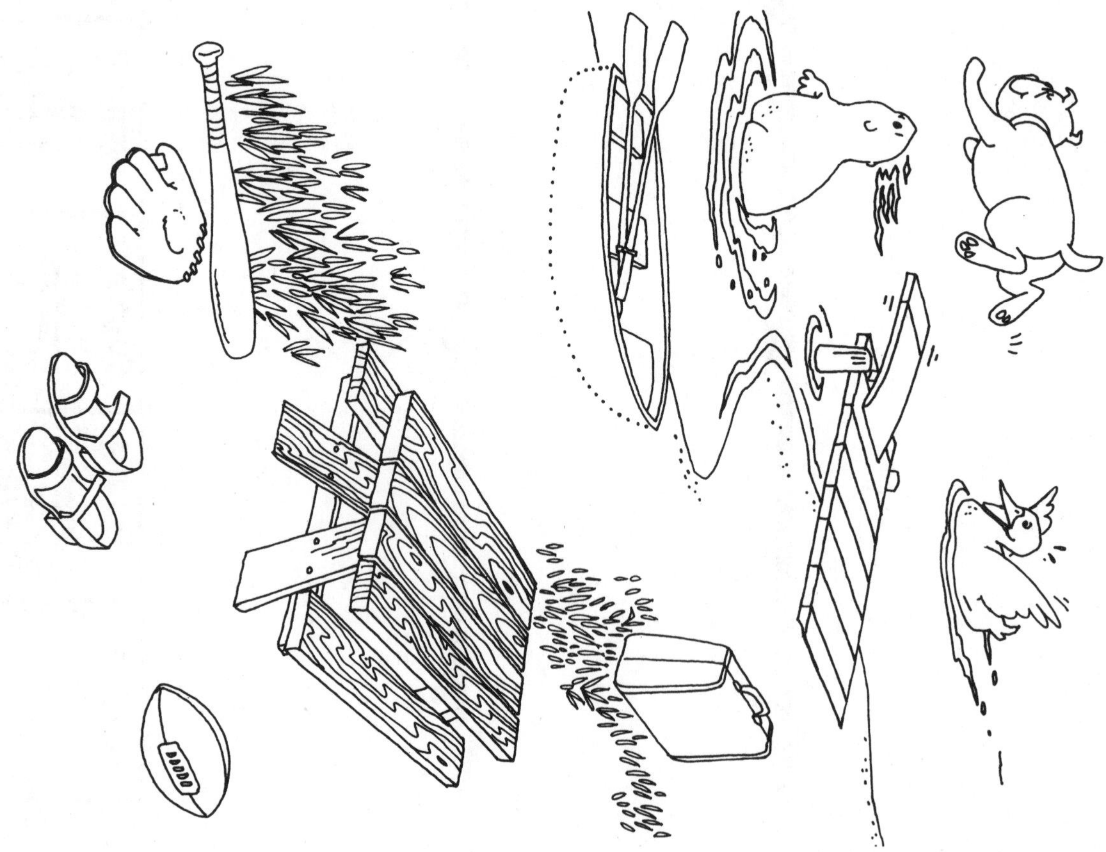

Name ______________________

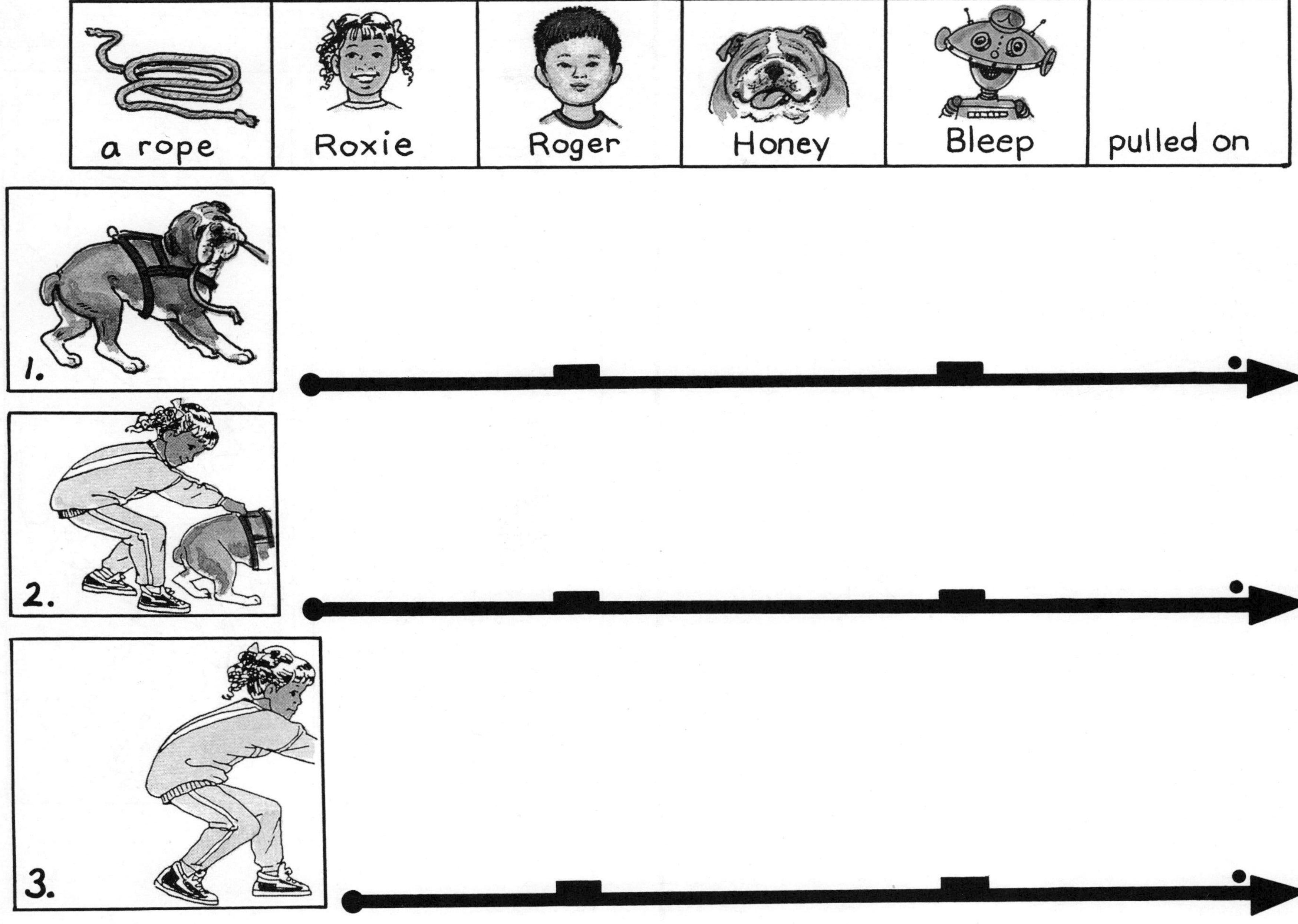

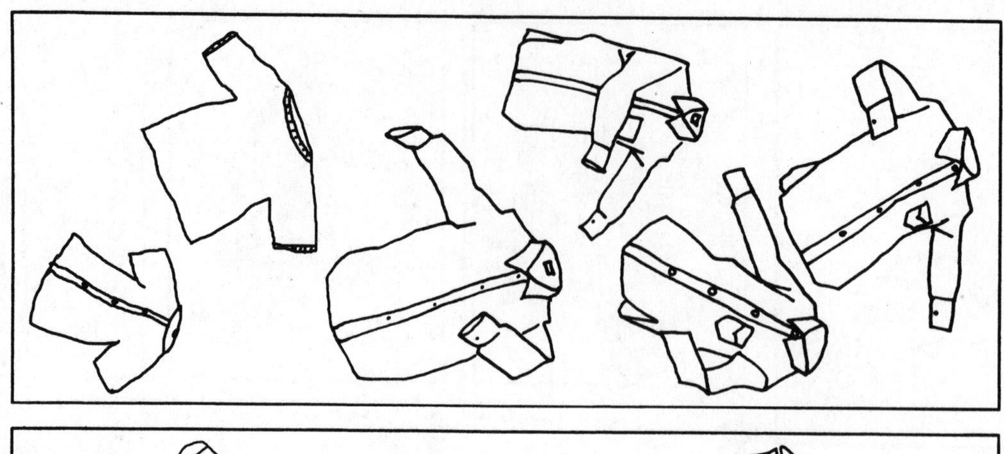

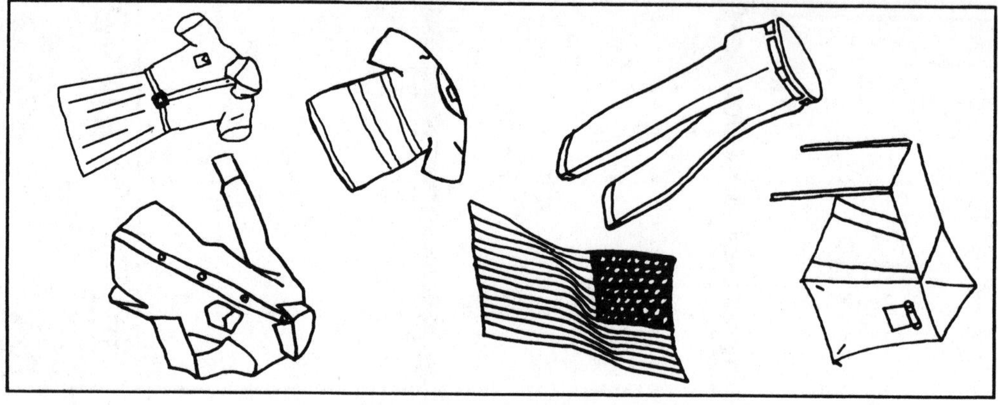

Name ______________________

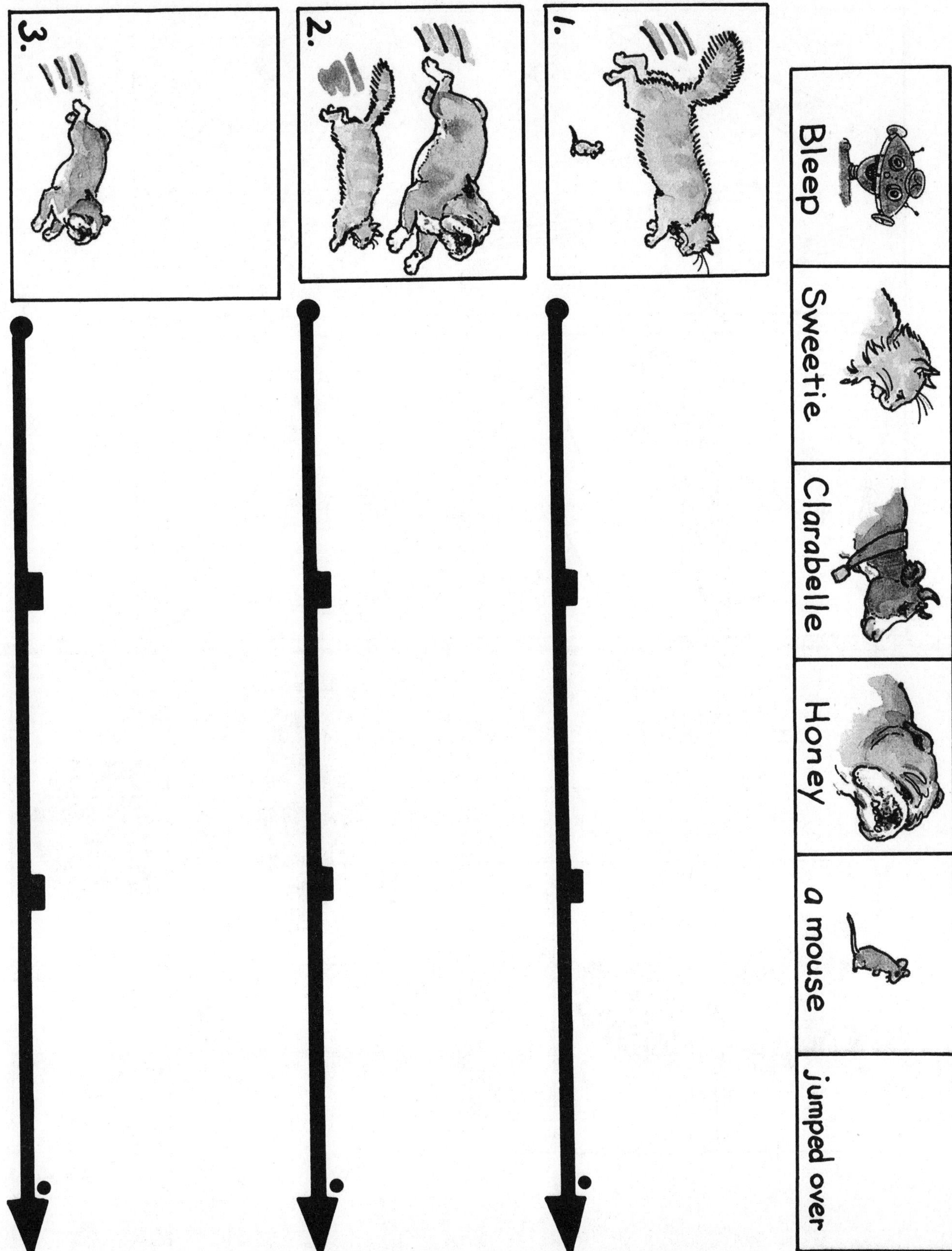

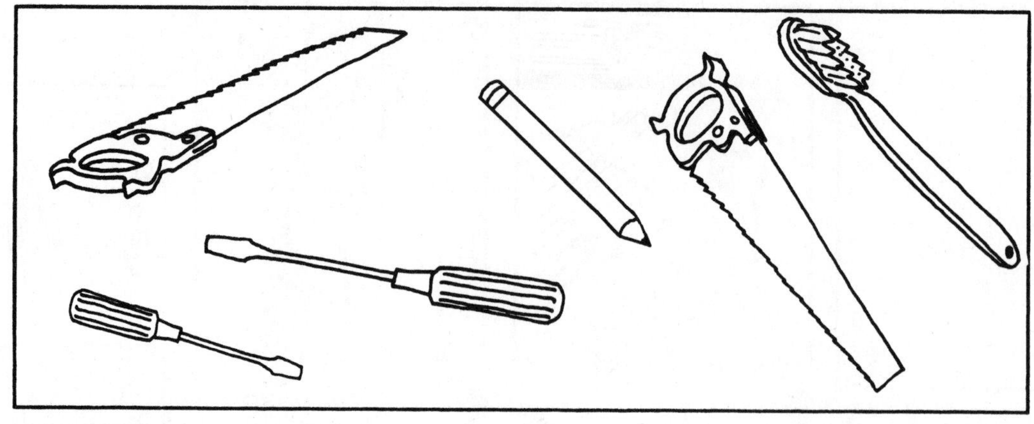

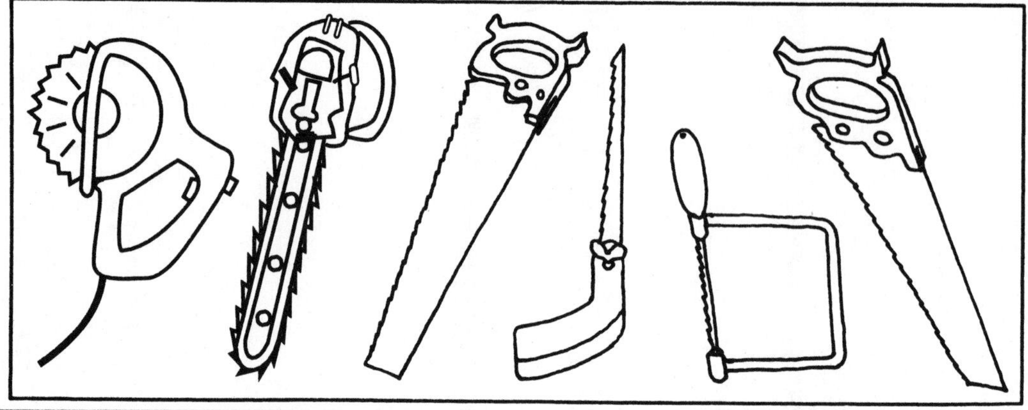

holds

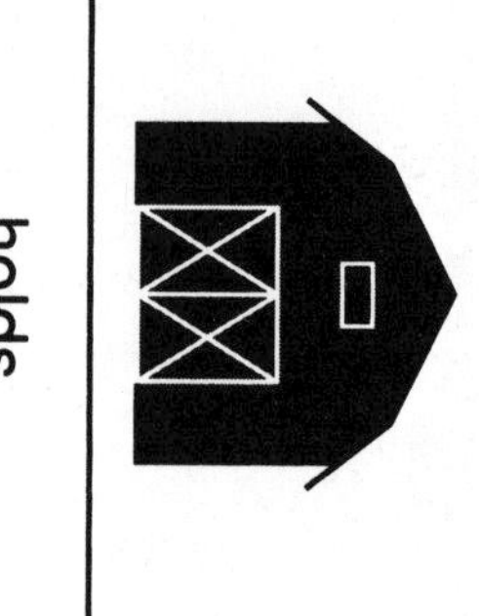

as

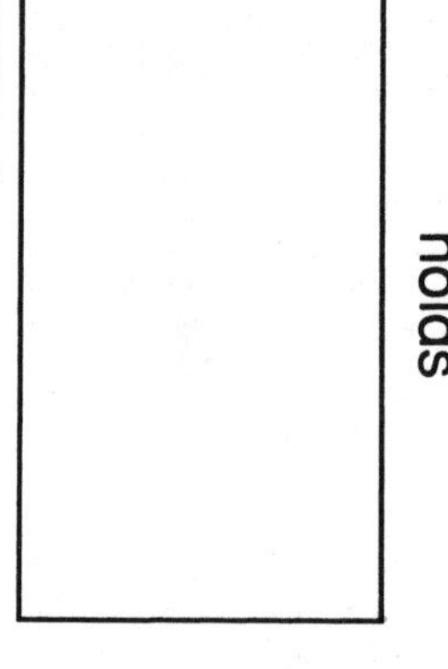

holds

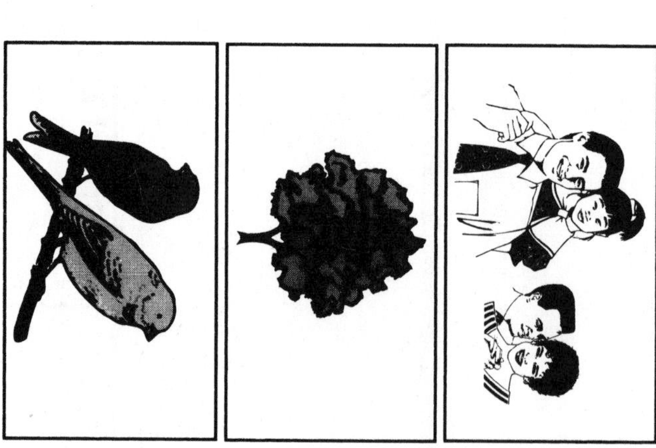

Name ______________________

Name ______________________

 rocks	 Sweetie	 Honey	 skunks	 hats	carried	 paint

1. Roxie

2. Paul

3. Clarabelle

Name ____________________

Name ______________________

cone the fox

The

____

____

____

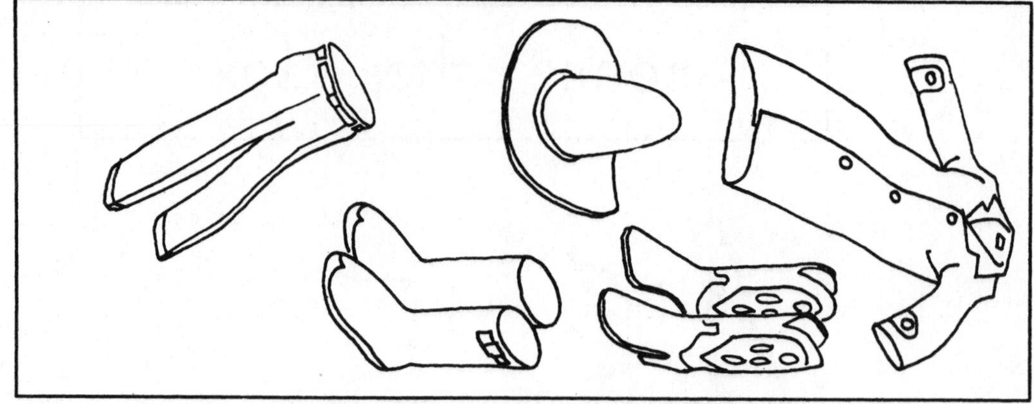

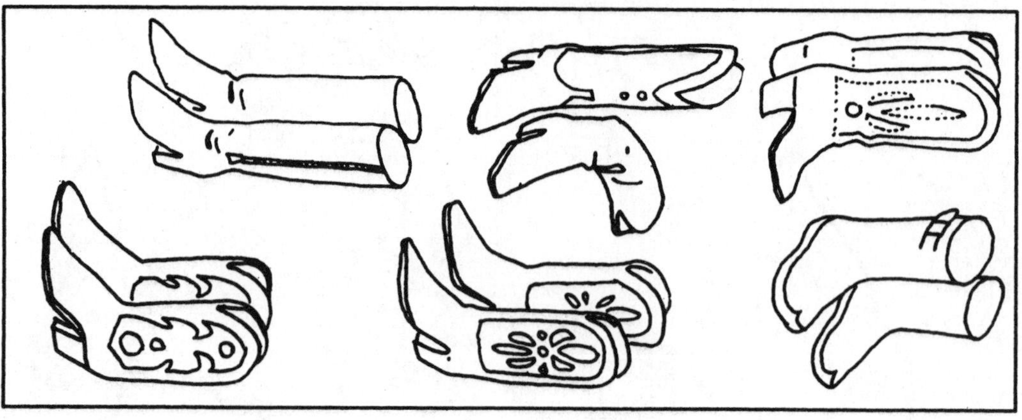

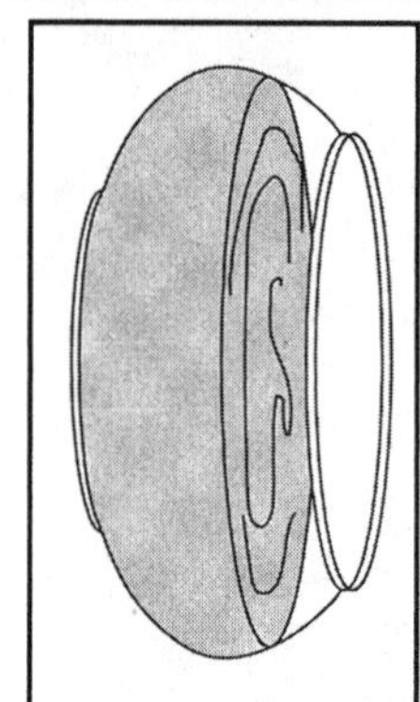

holds

as

holds

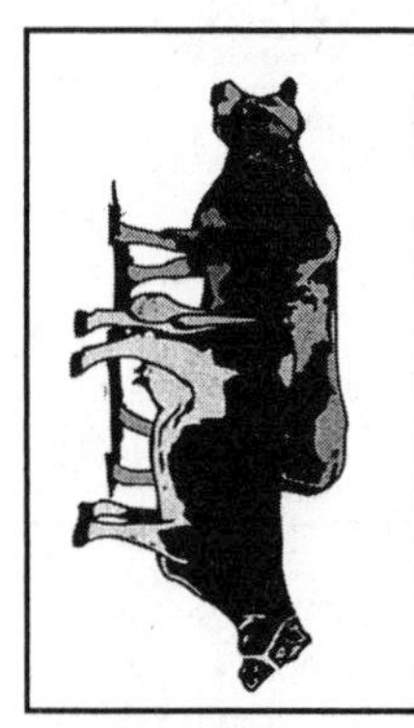

Name ____________________

cake fox

____

____

____

____

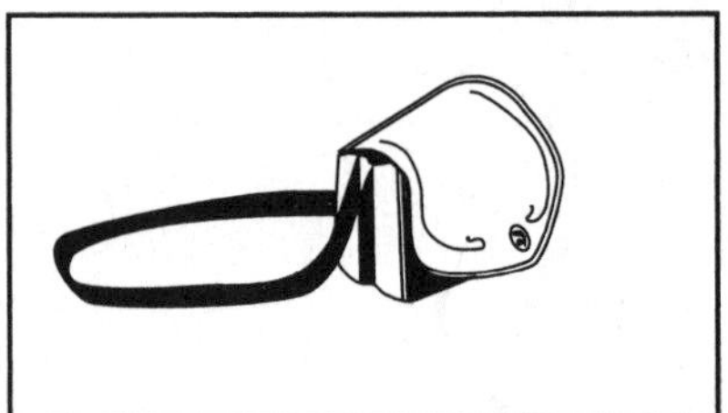

holds

as

holds

Name ________________________________

A.

Name ______________________________

fish bird under coat

____

____

____

____

TRY
HARD
WHAT

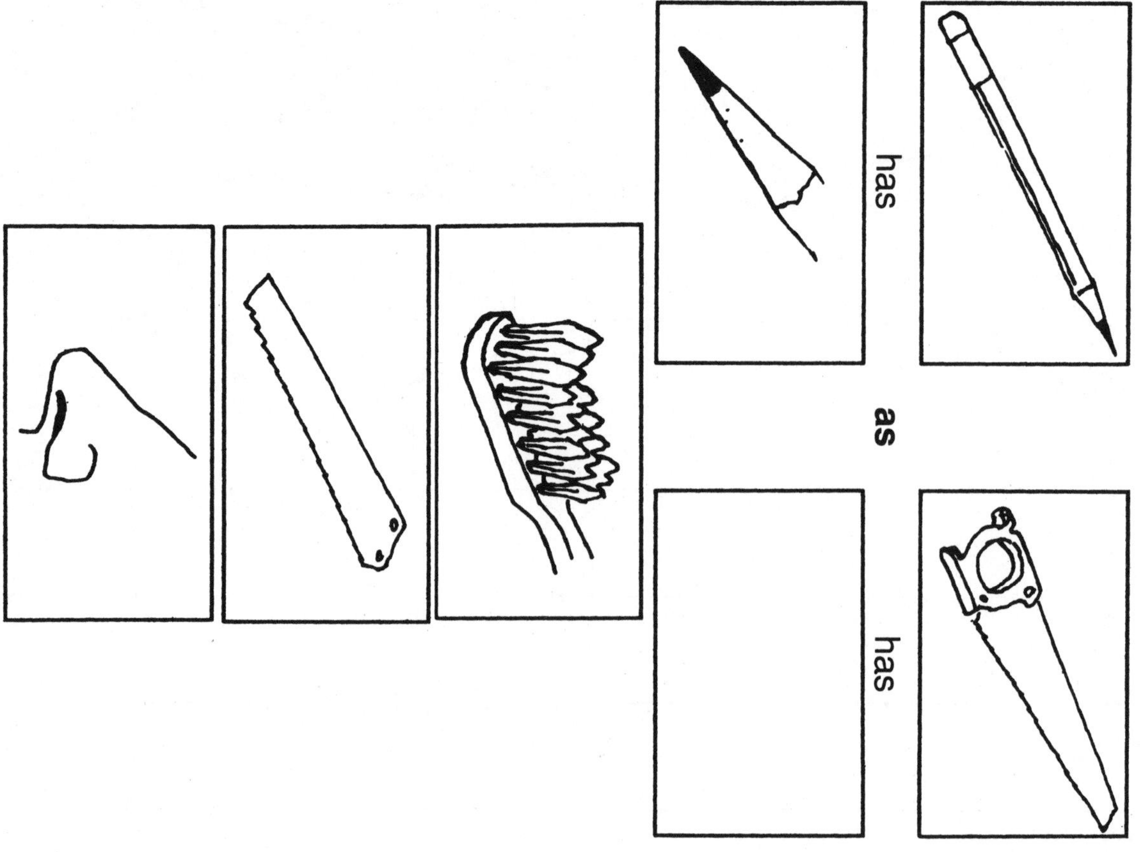
has
as
has

Name ______________________________

hat

____

____

____

____

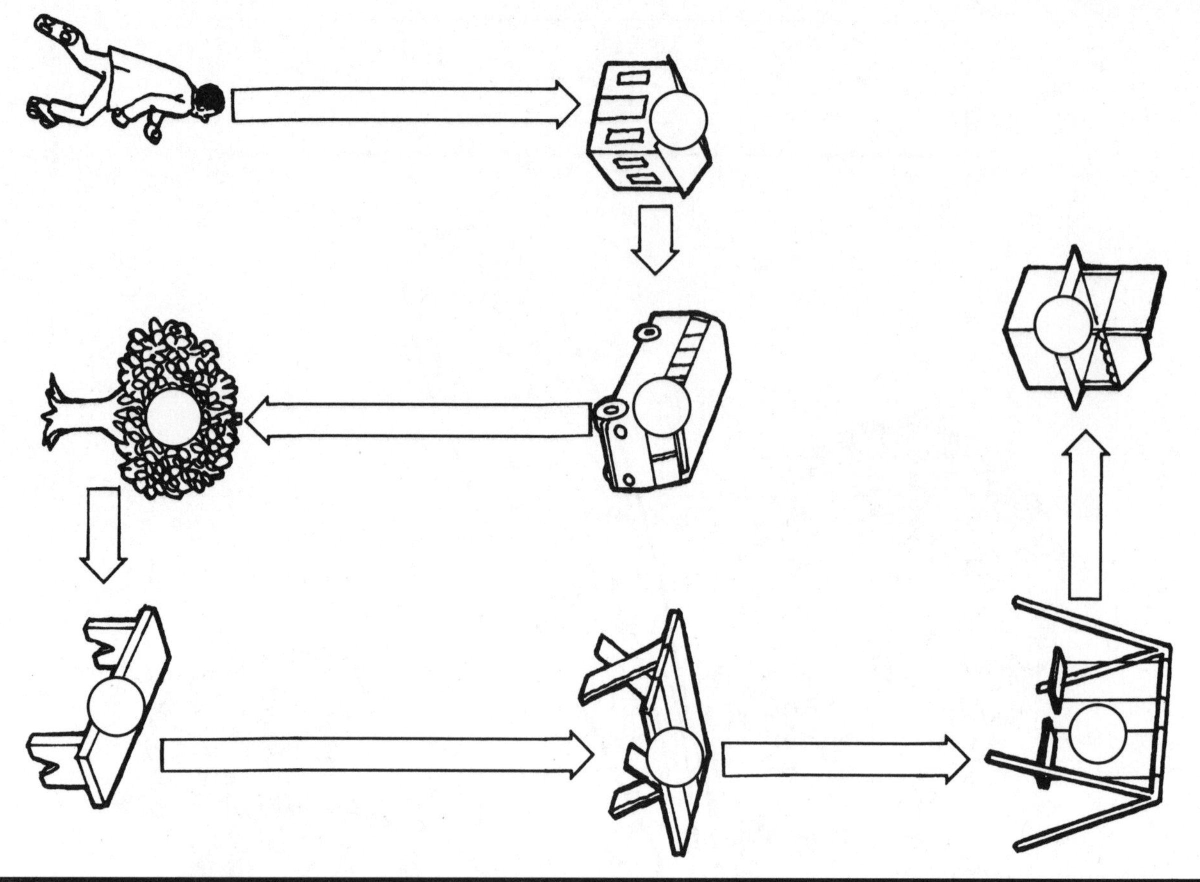

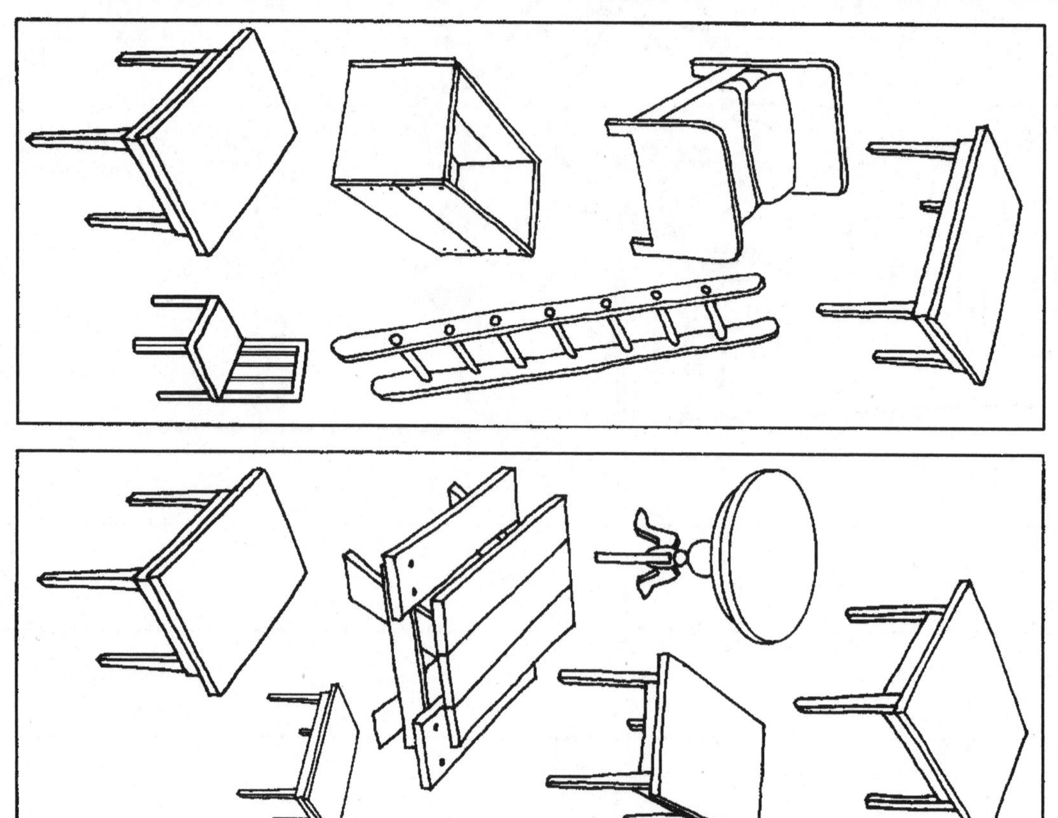

Name ____________________

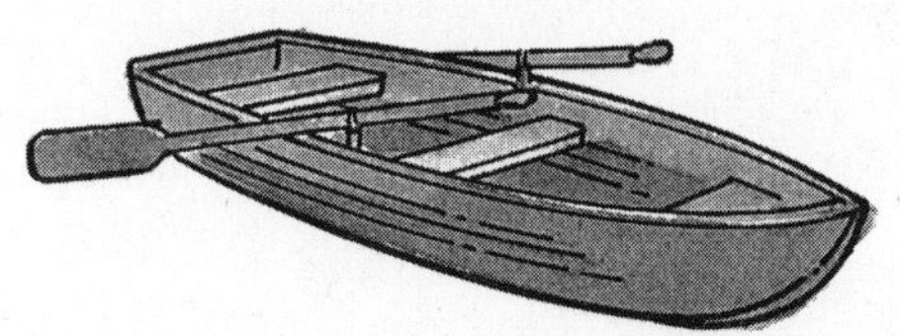

1
2
3
4
5

Name ________________________________

car toad bug

____

____

____

____

Name ______________________________

his	her	socks	shoes	feet

____

____

____

____

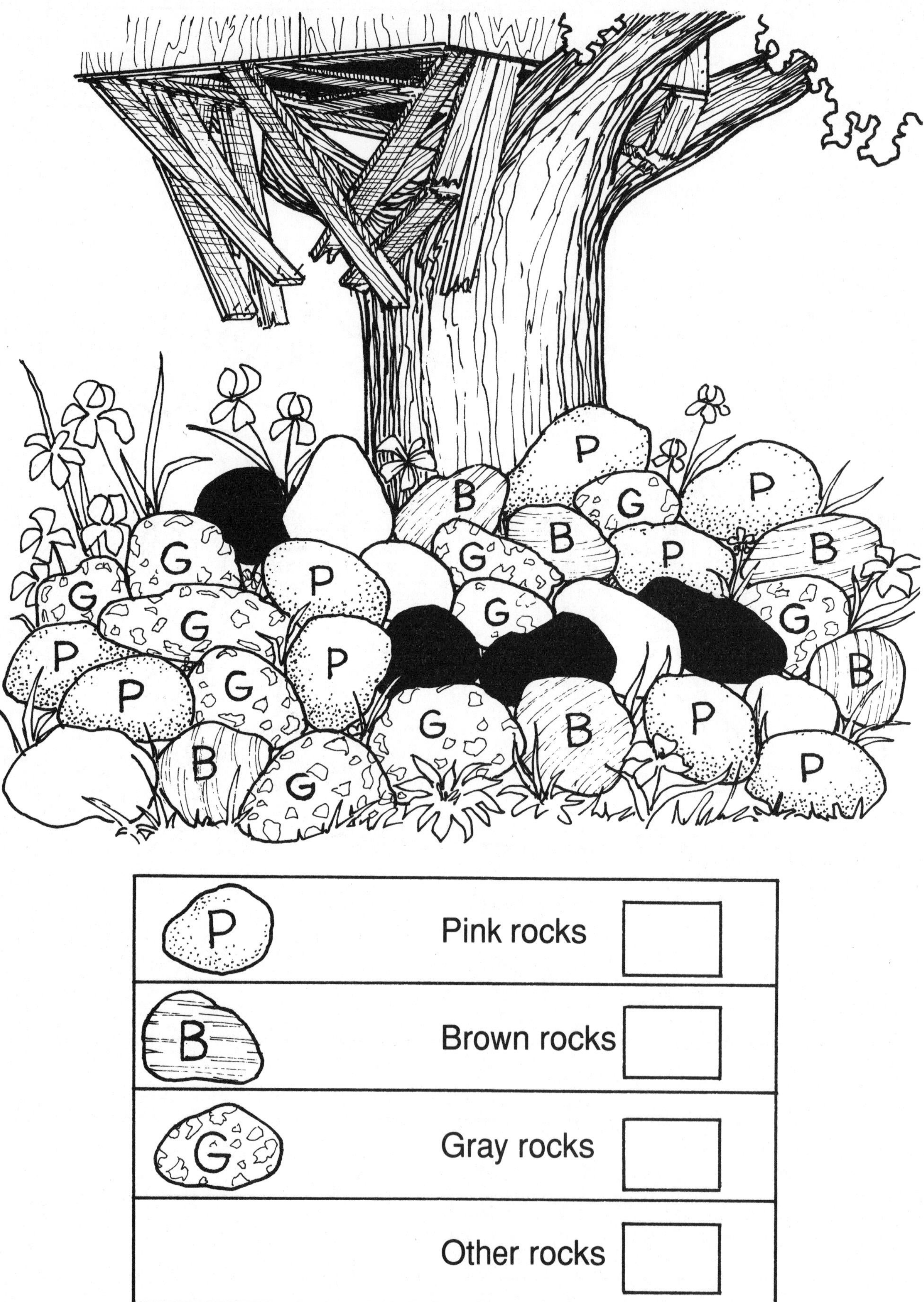
P
Pink rocks
B
Brown rocks
G
Gray rocks
Other rocks

Name ______________________________

bird man

____

____

____

____

Name ______________________________

mole	under	coat

____

____

____

____

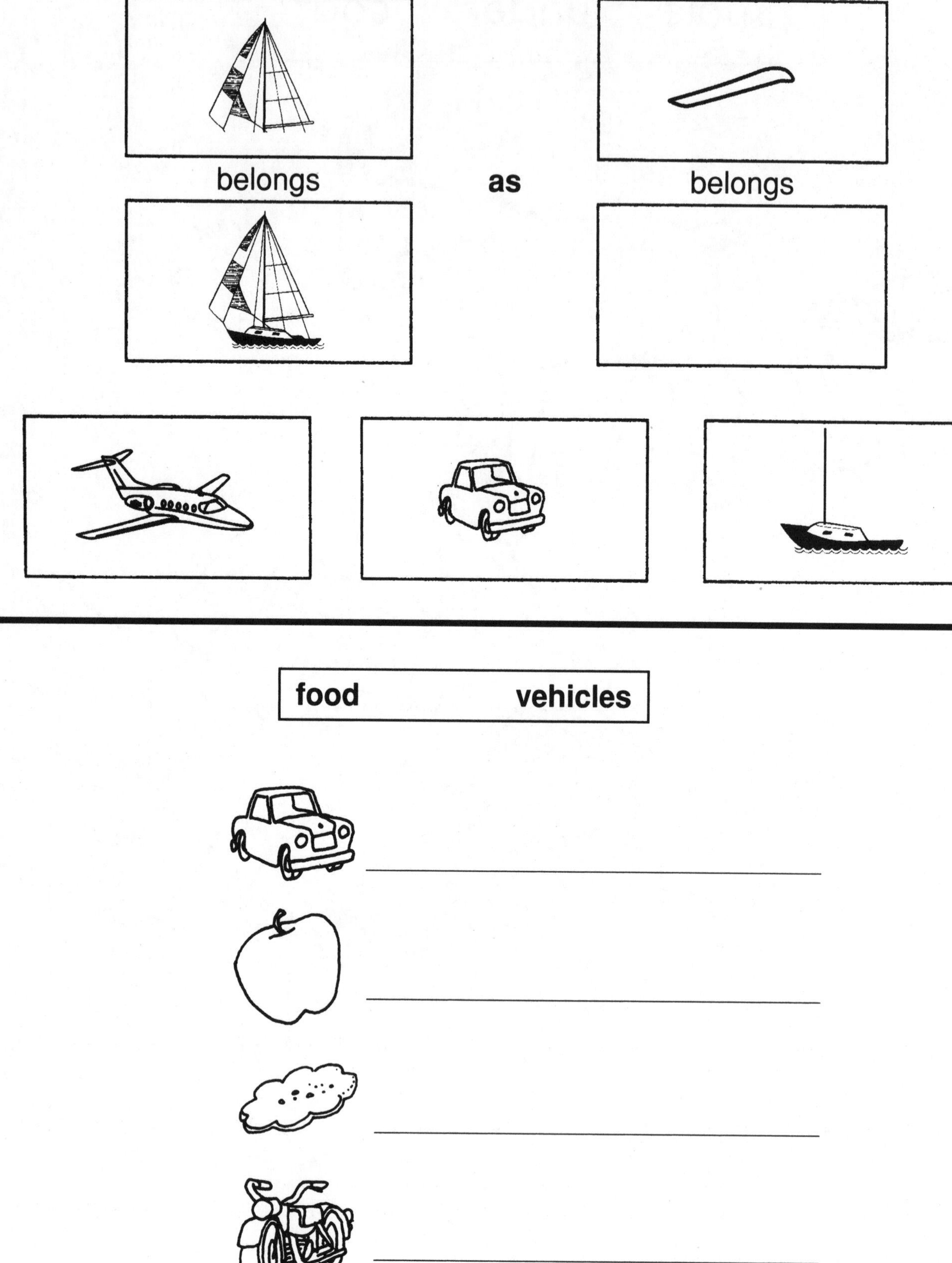
belongs
as
belongs
food
vehicles

Name ______________________________

ant cake

____

____

____

____

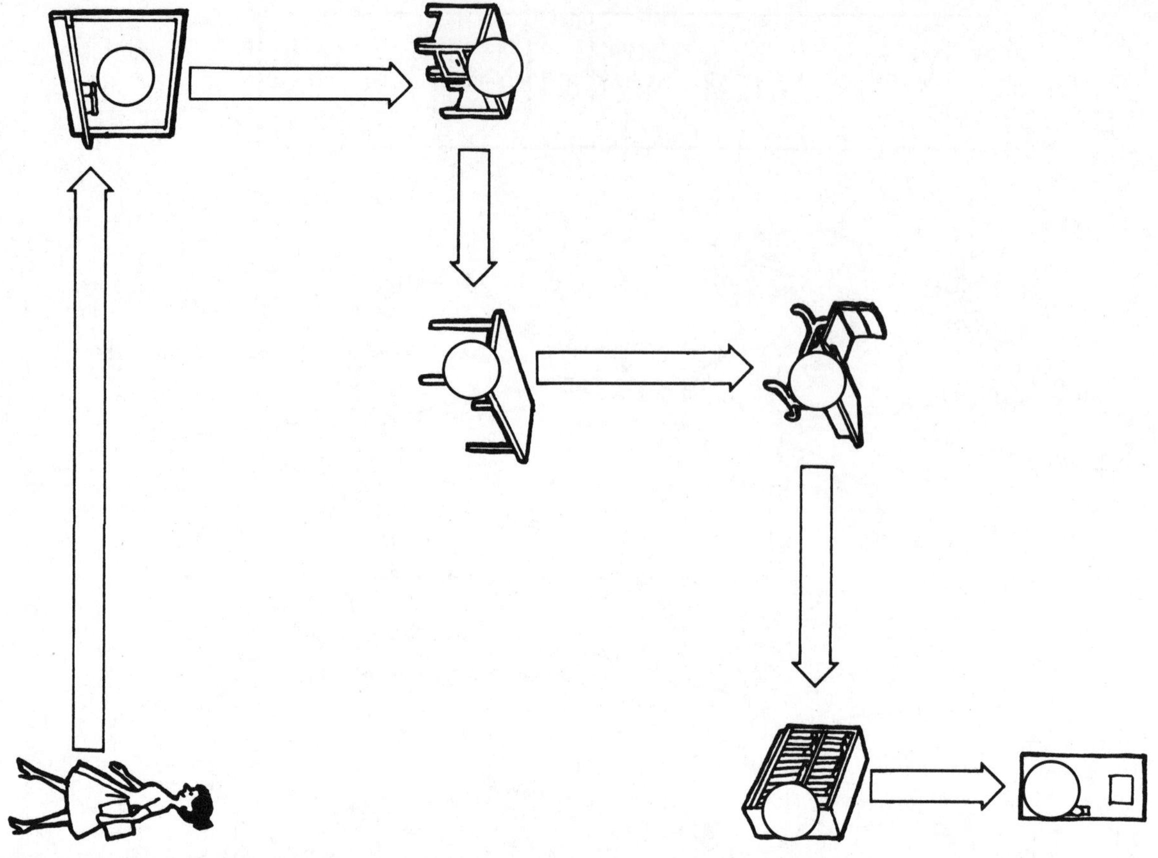

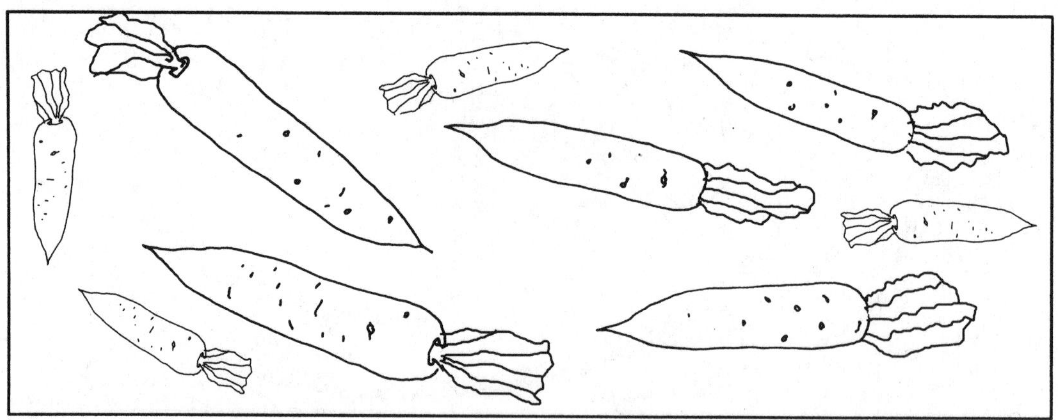

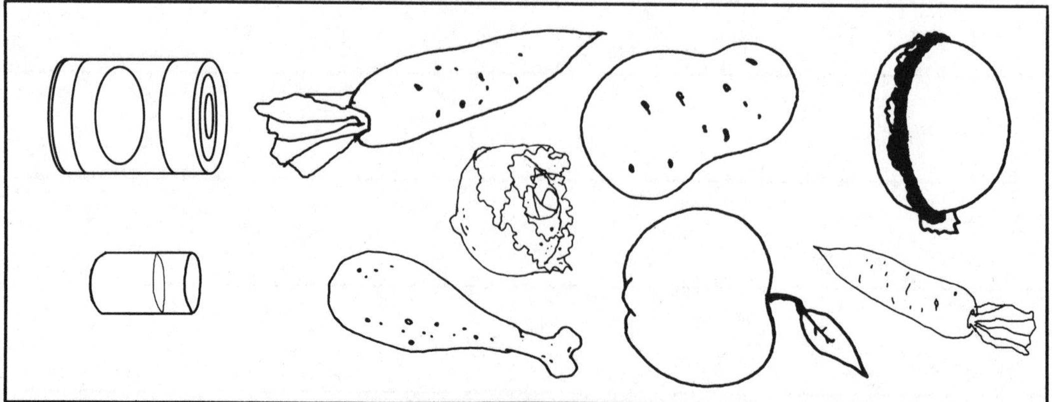

Name ______________________

clock will sing

____

____

____

____

1.
2.
3.
4.

Name ______________________________

baby plane cry

____

____

____

____

1.

2.

3.

4.

Name ______________________________

mail

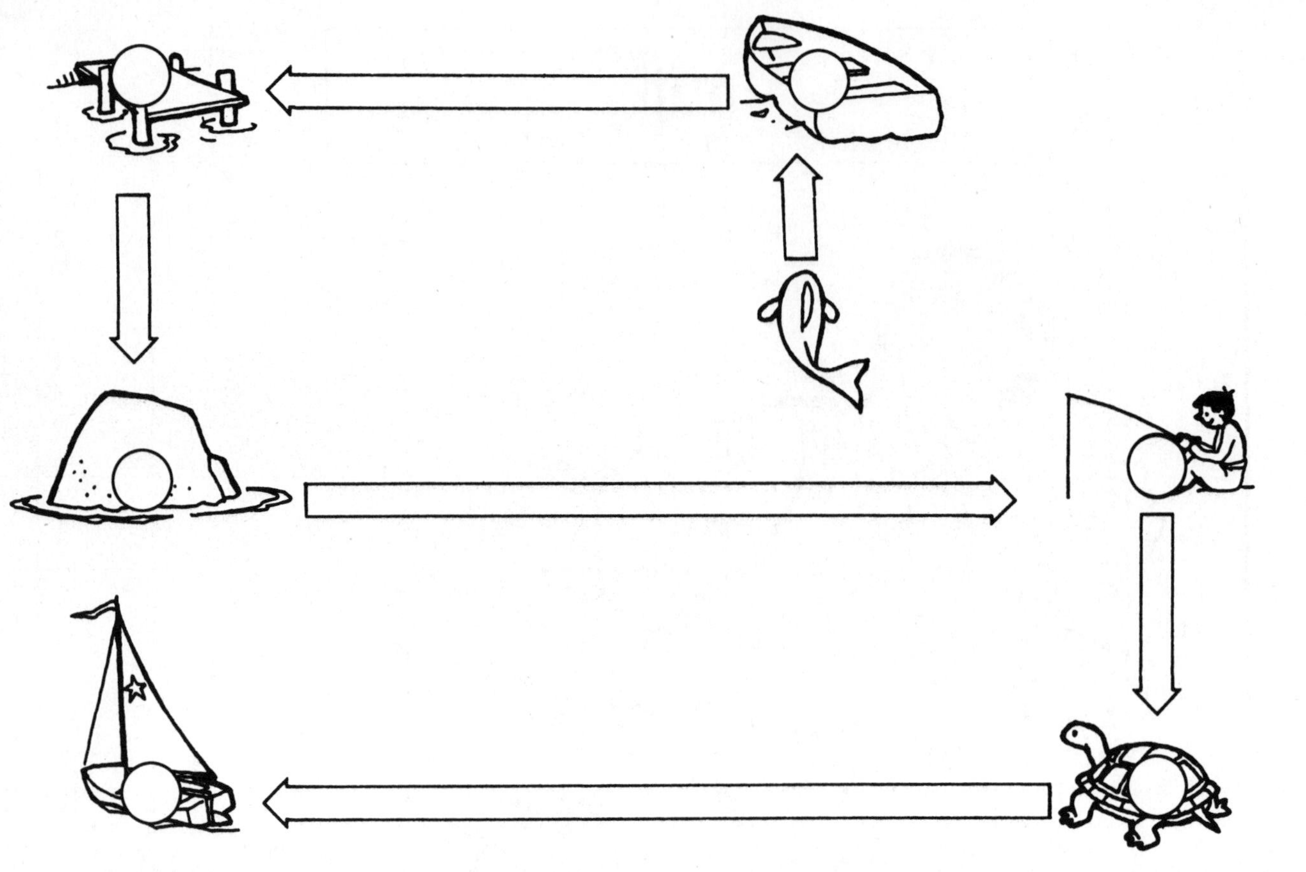

containers	furniture

____

____

____

____

____

Name ____________________

woman rock

Name ____________________________

buildings plants

Name ______________________________

short	boat	sail

____

____

____

____

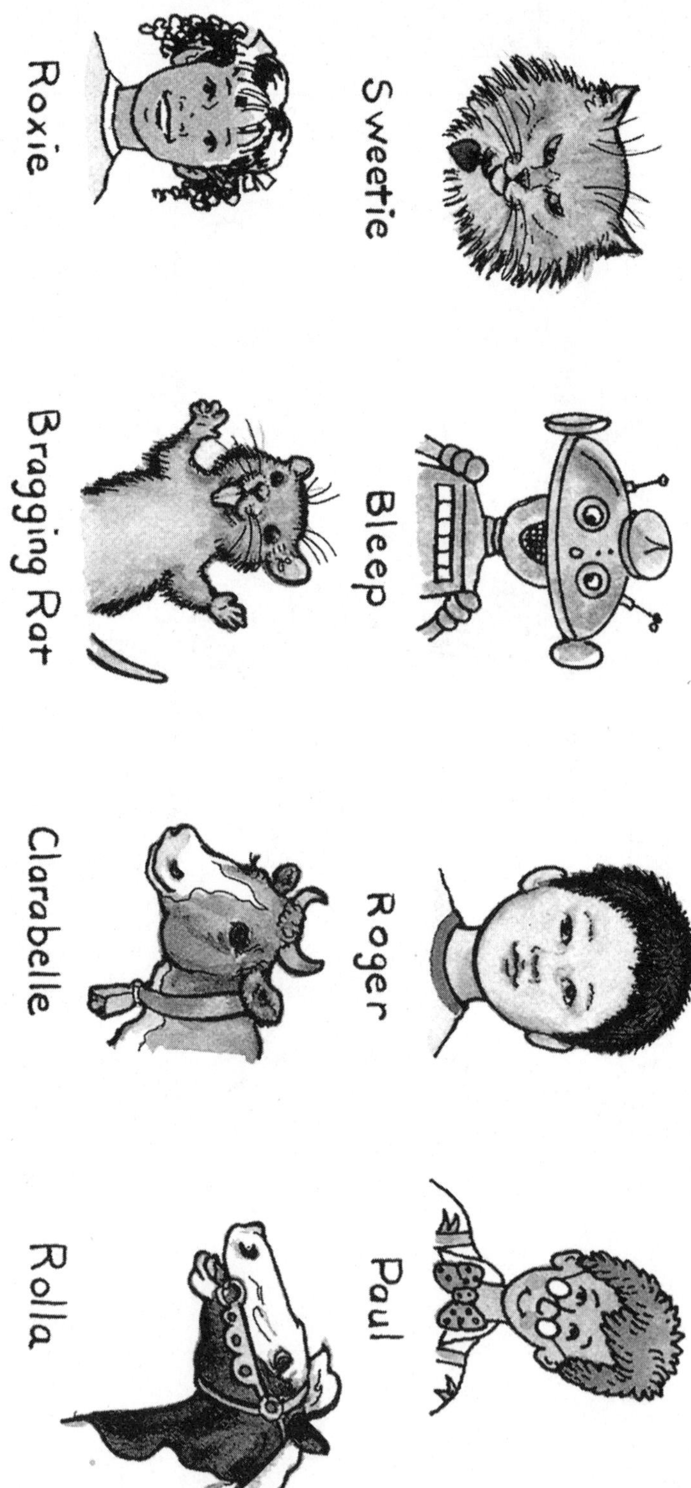
Sweetie
Bleep
Roger
Paul
Roxie
Bragging Rat
Clarabelle
Rolla

Name ________________________________

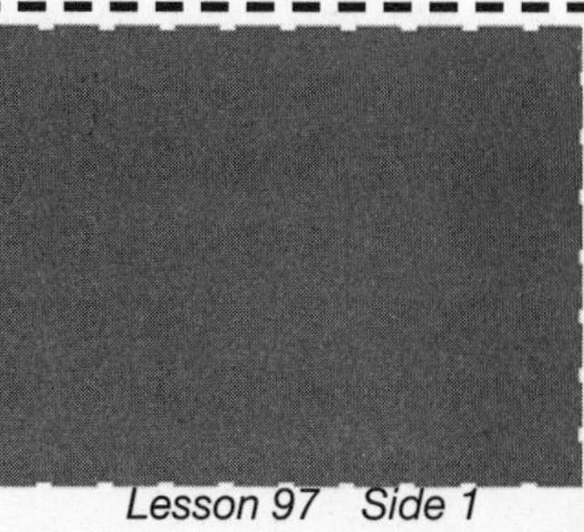

Name ____________________

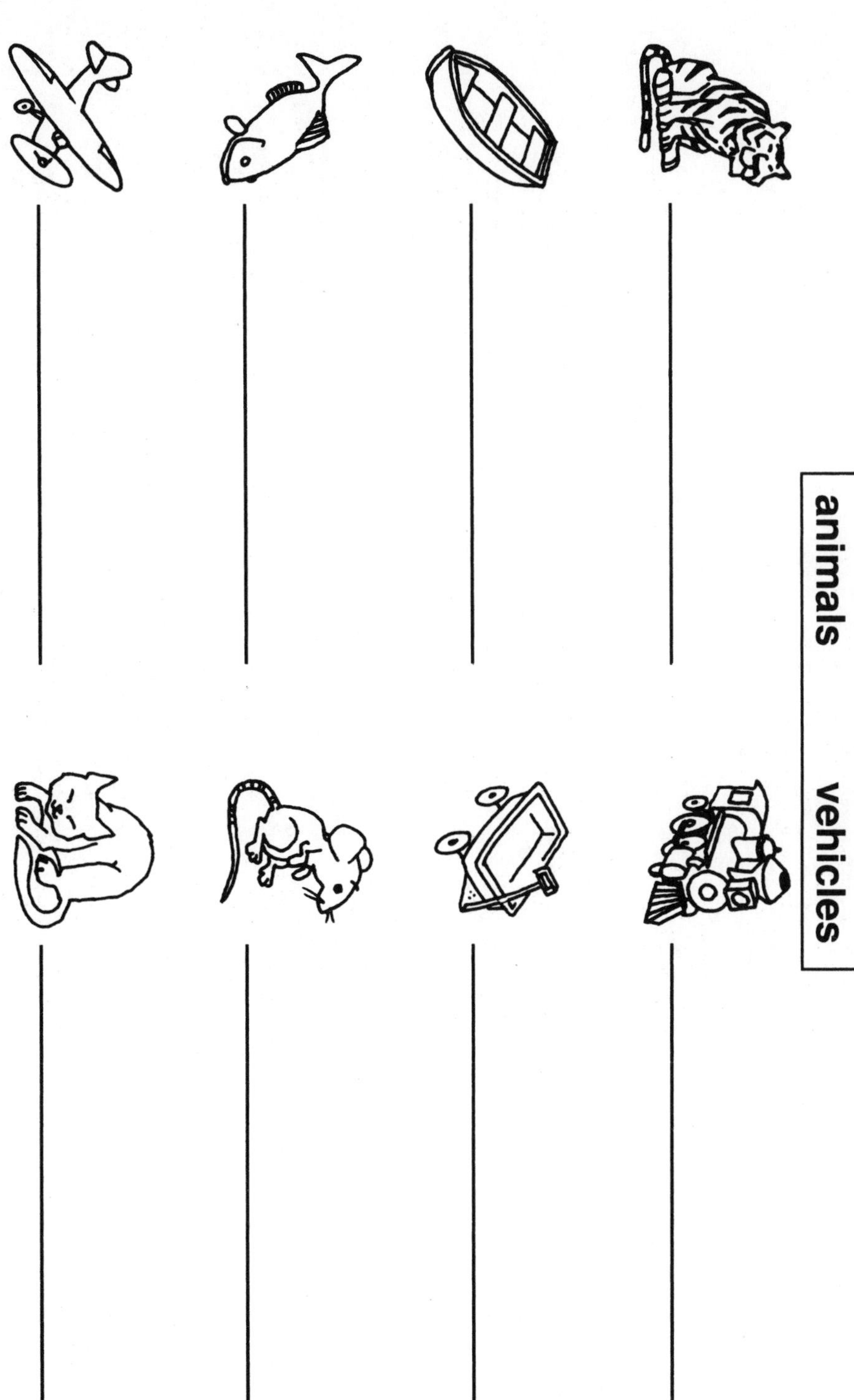

Name ______________________________

girl	boy	sock

____

____

____

____

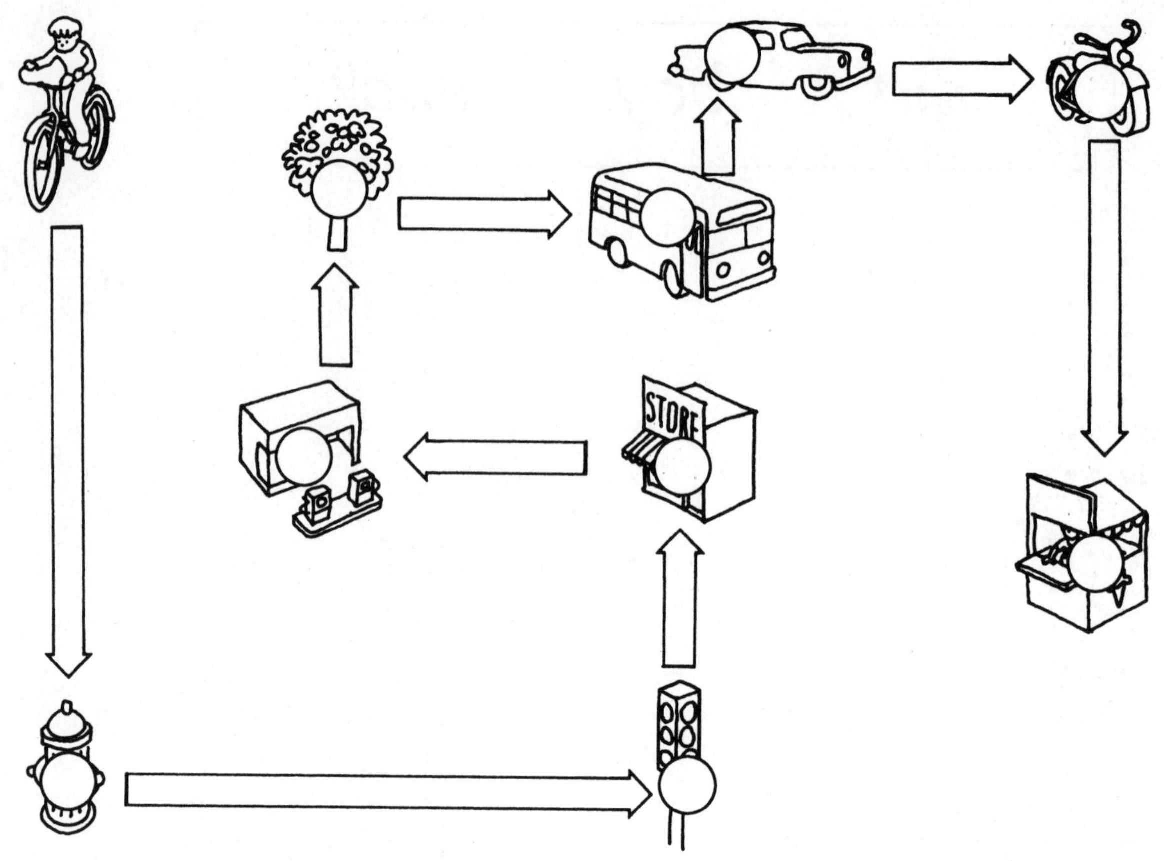
STORE

has
as
has

Name ______________________________

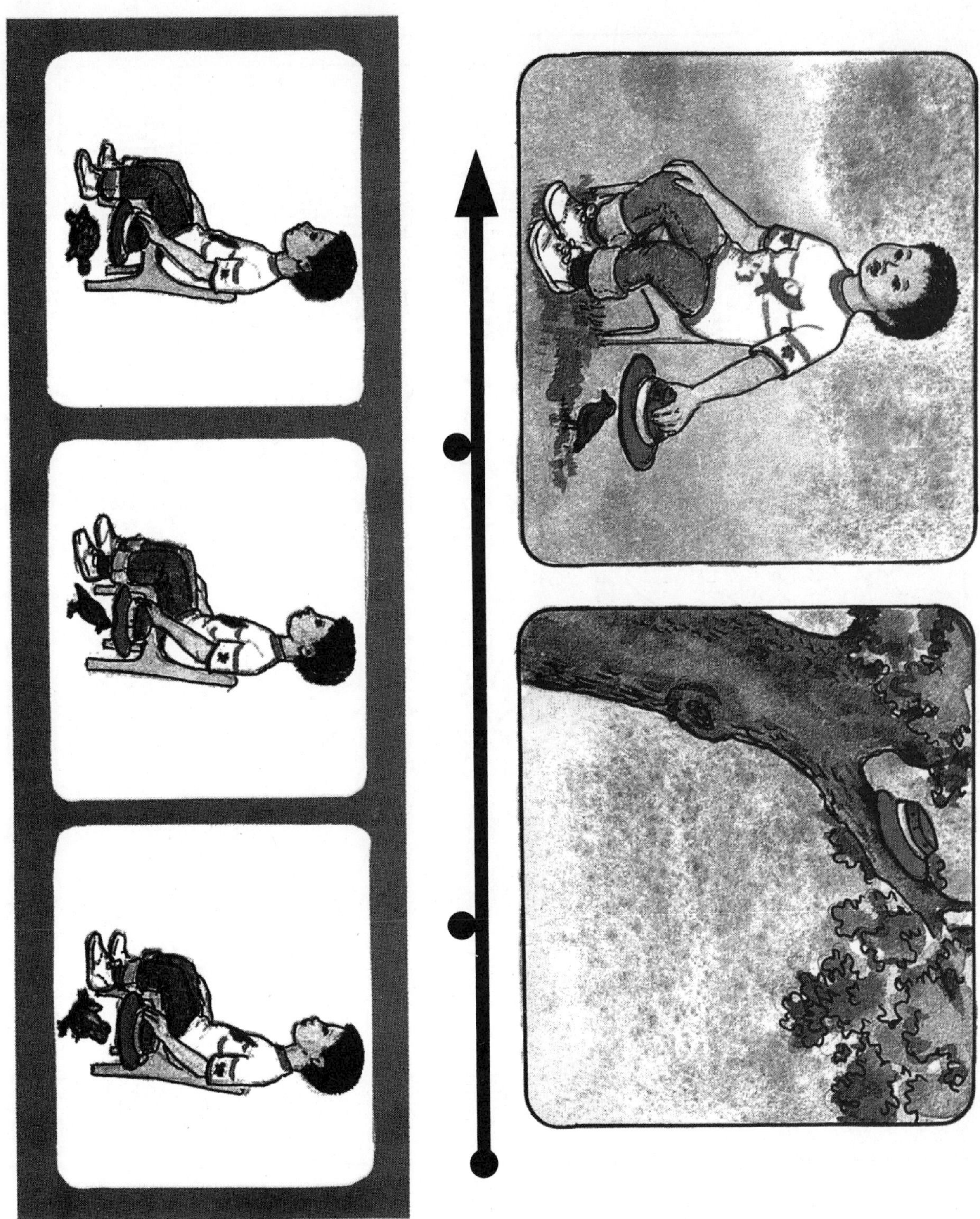

swim

Name ______________________________

girl	drink	eat	boy

Name ______________________________

stick

____

____

____

____

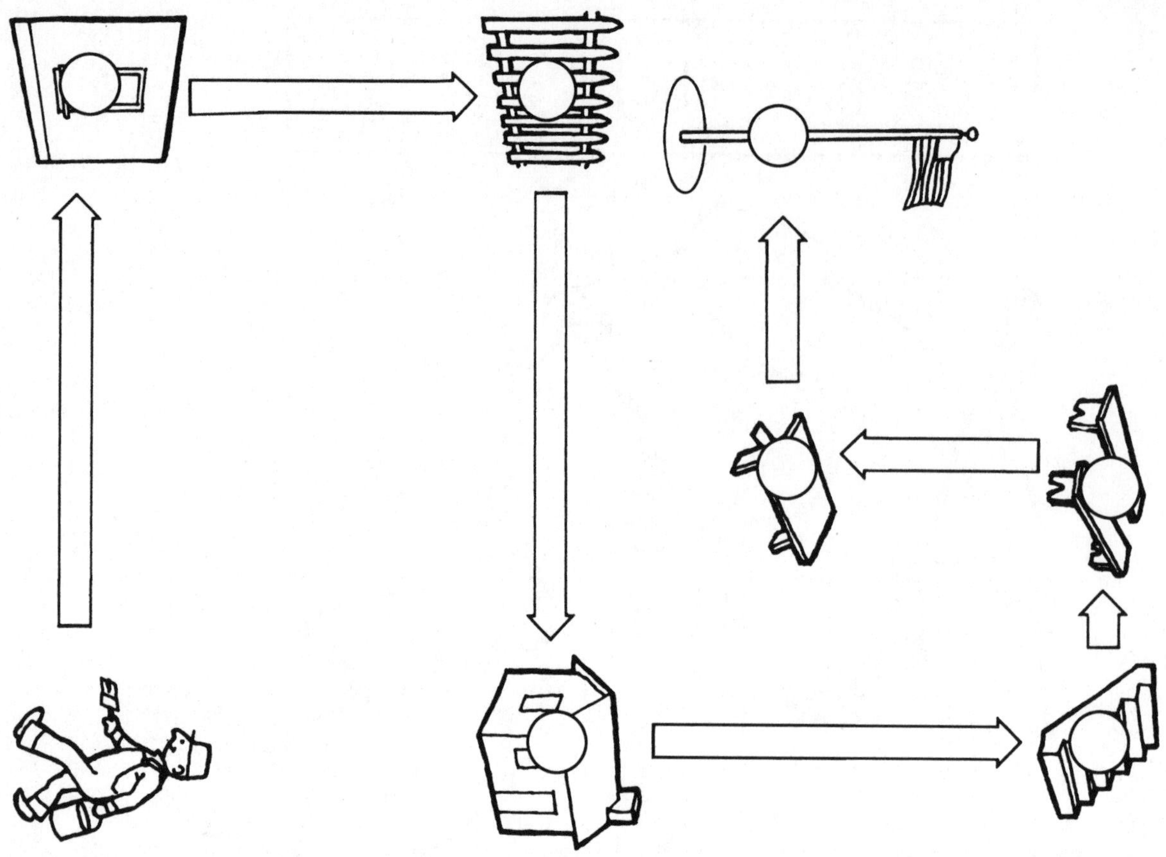

Name ____________________

fish cow car

____

____

____

____

furniture	plants

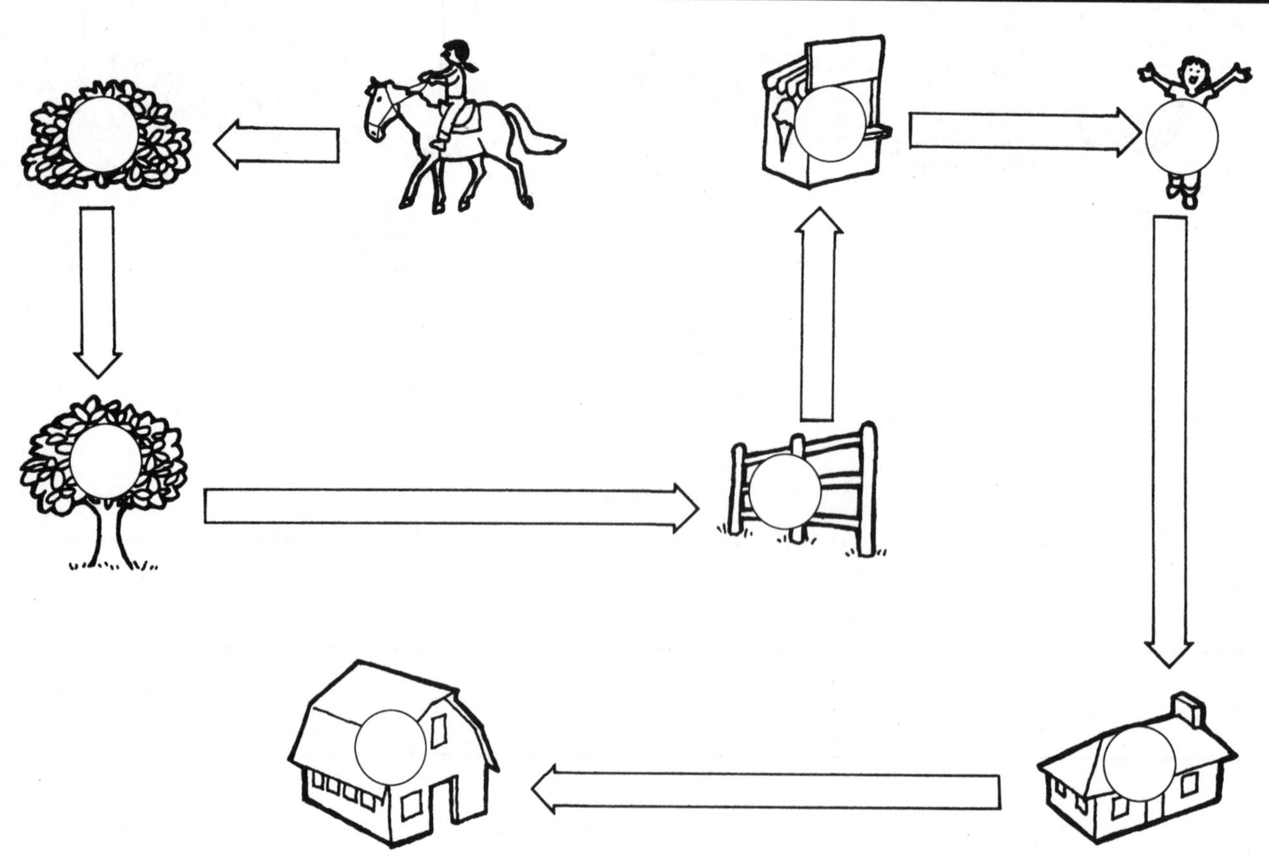

Name ___________________________

bird fly girl

____

____

____

____

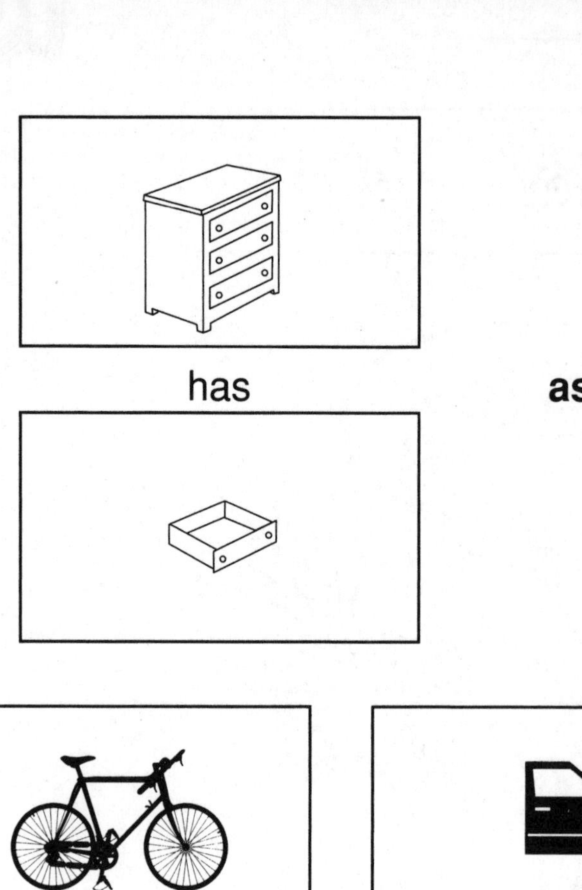

has

as

has

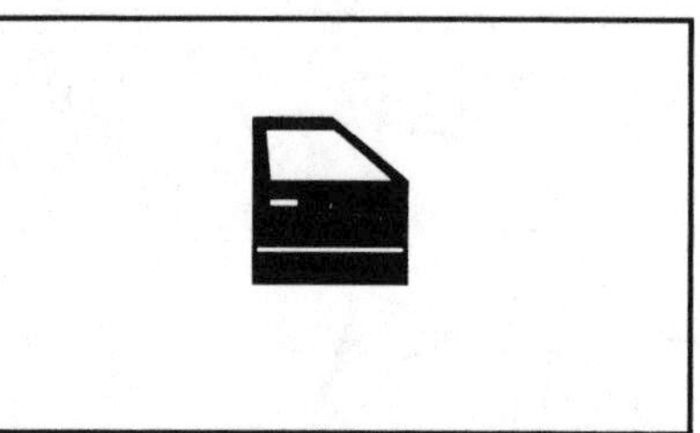

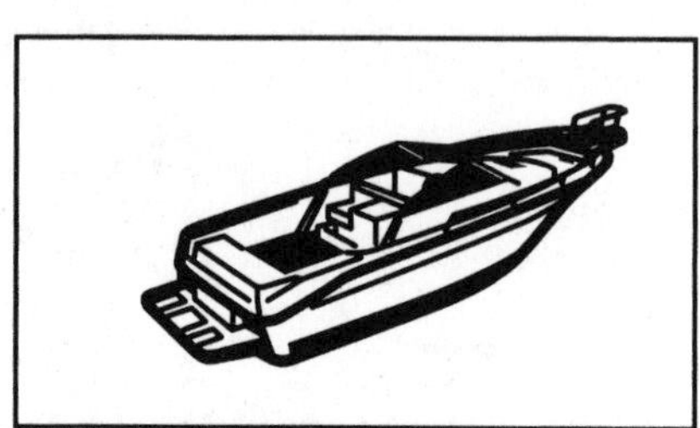

clothing **buildings**

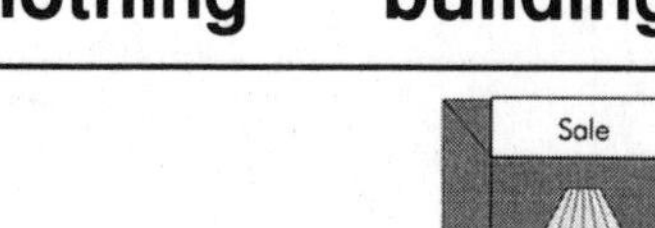

Name ____________________

stop horse fly

____

____

____

____

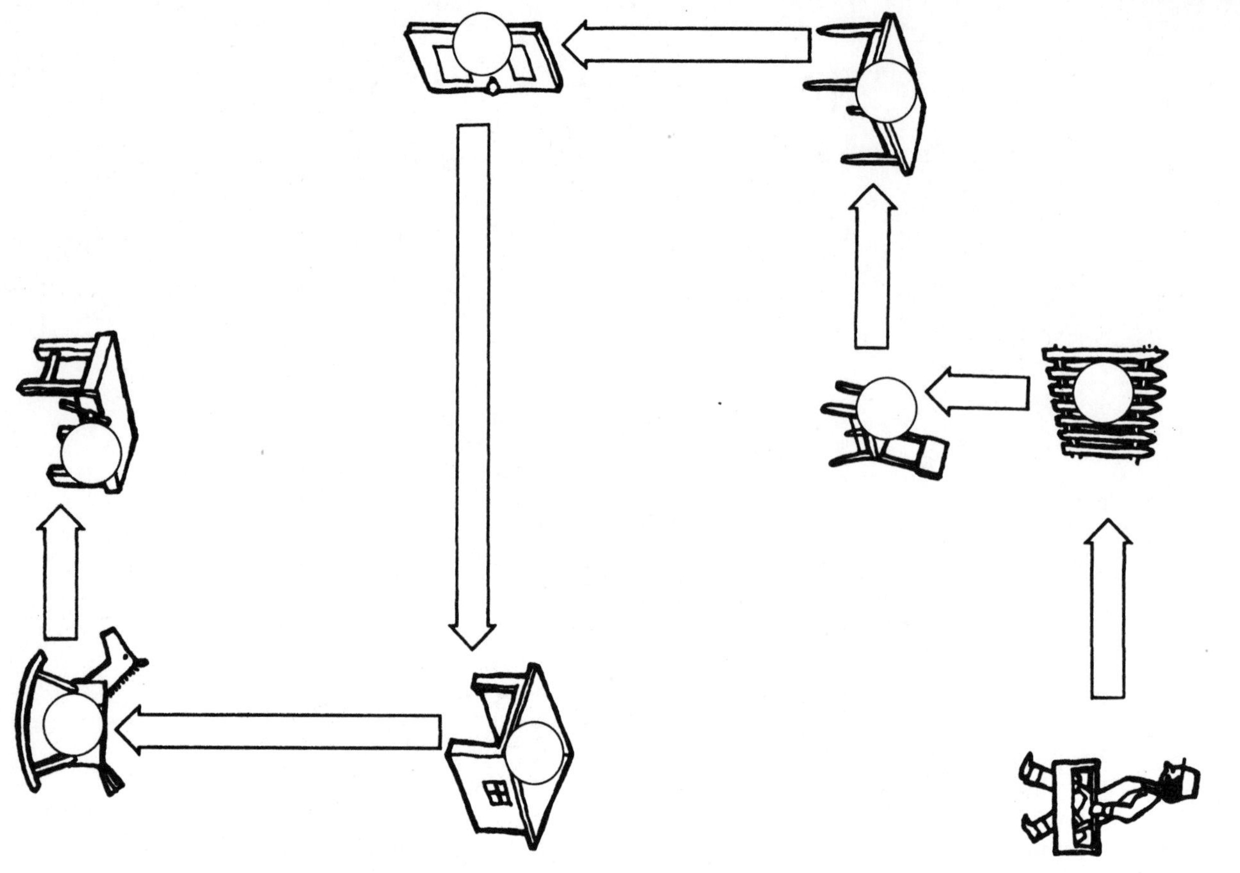

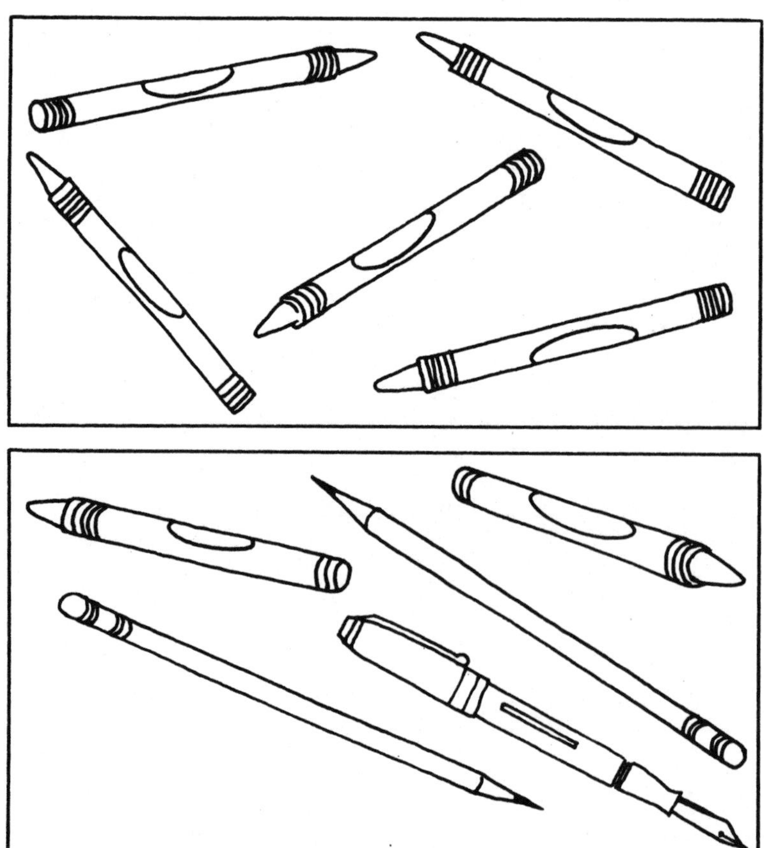

Name ______________________________

mole dig

____

____

____

____

Name ____________________

Name ____________________

cow walk

____

____

____

____

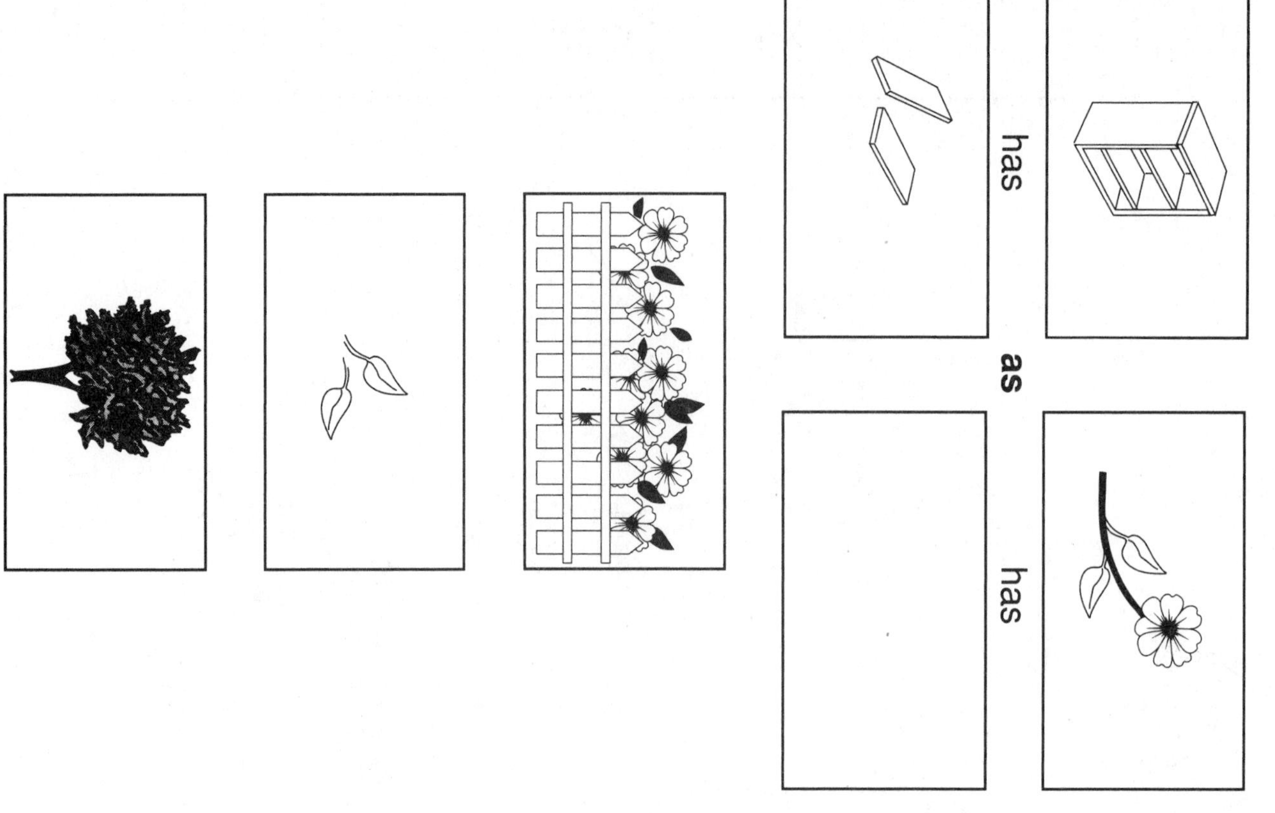
has
as
has

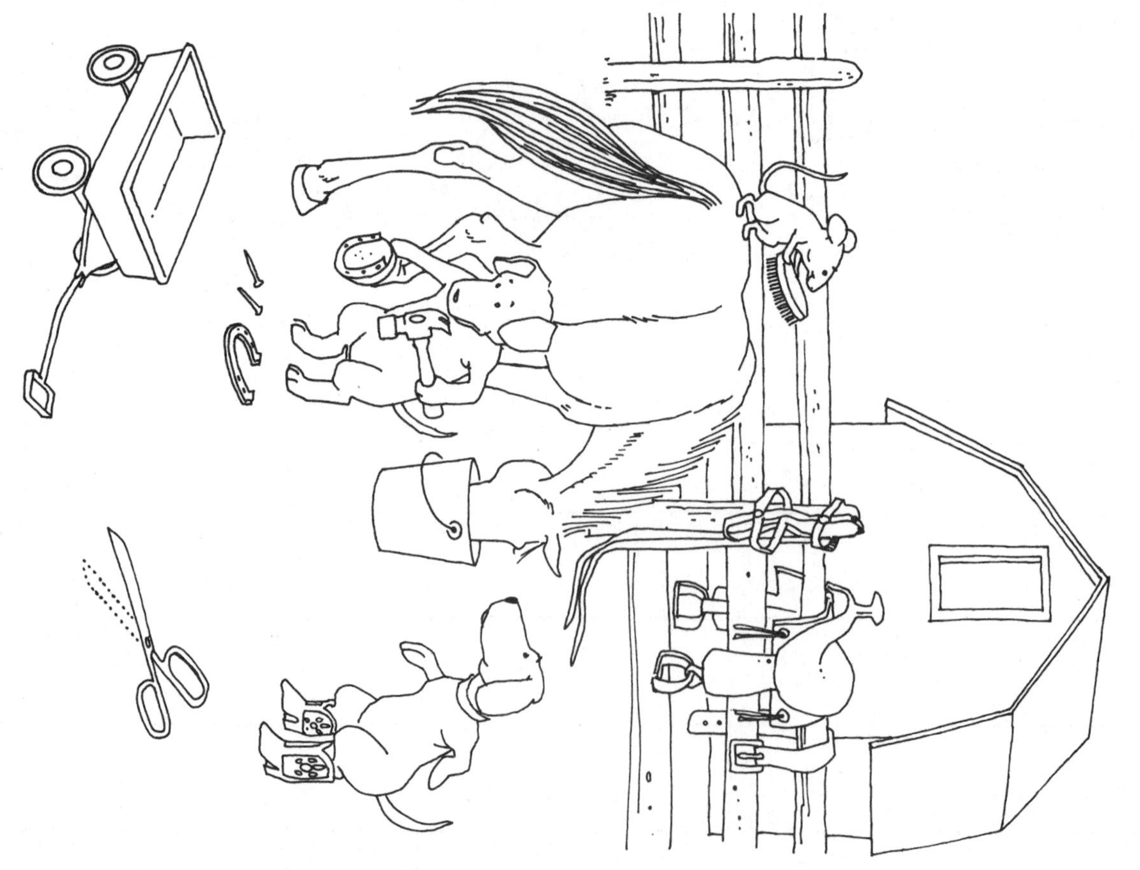

Name ____________________

eat white leaf other

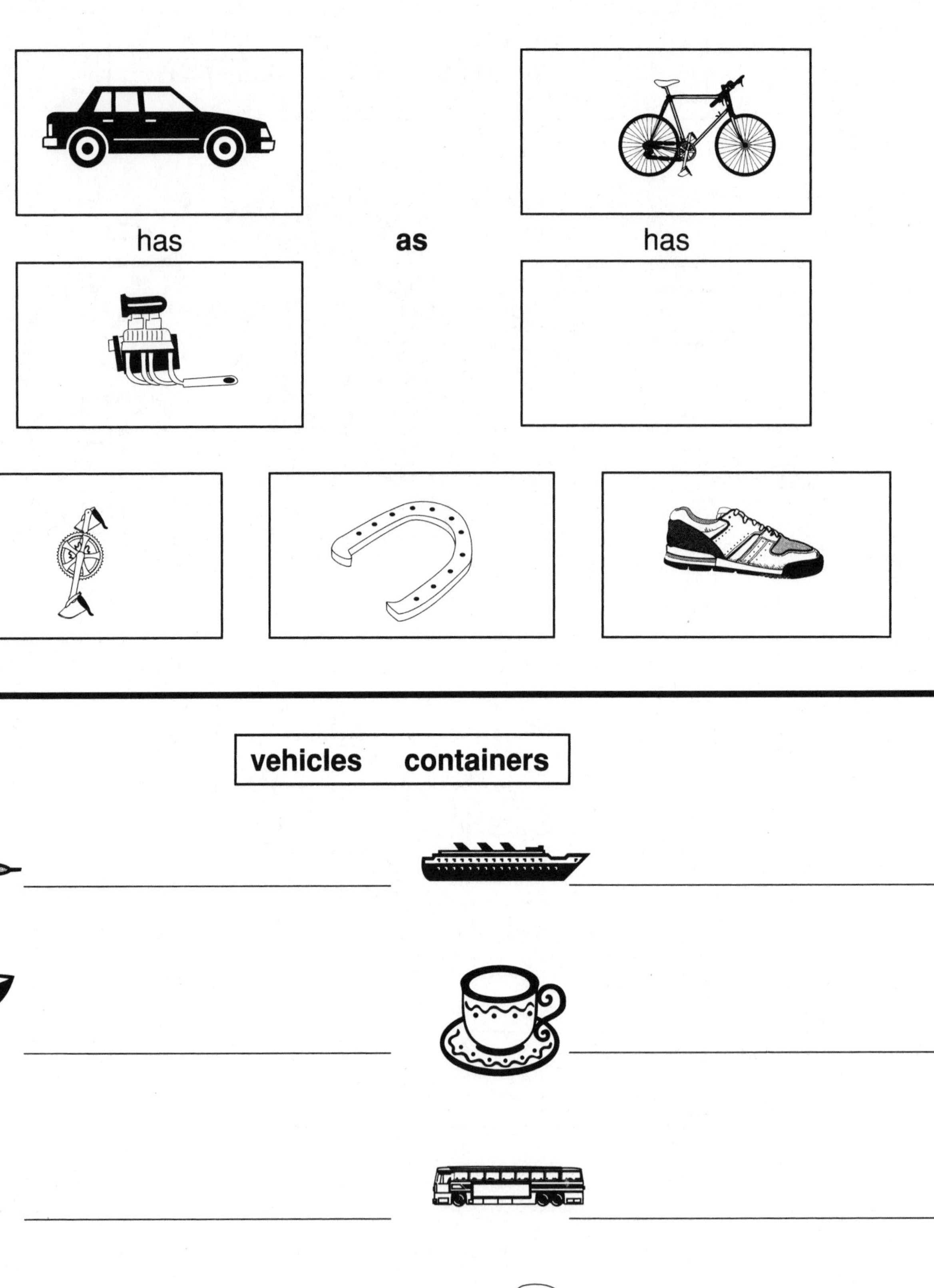
has
as
has
vehicles containers

Name ___________________________

leaf other black

____

____

____

____

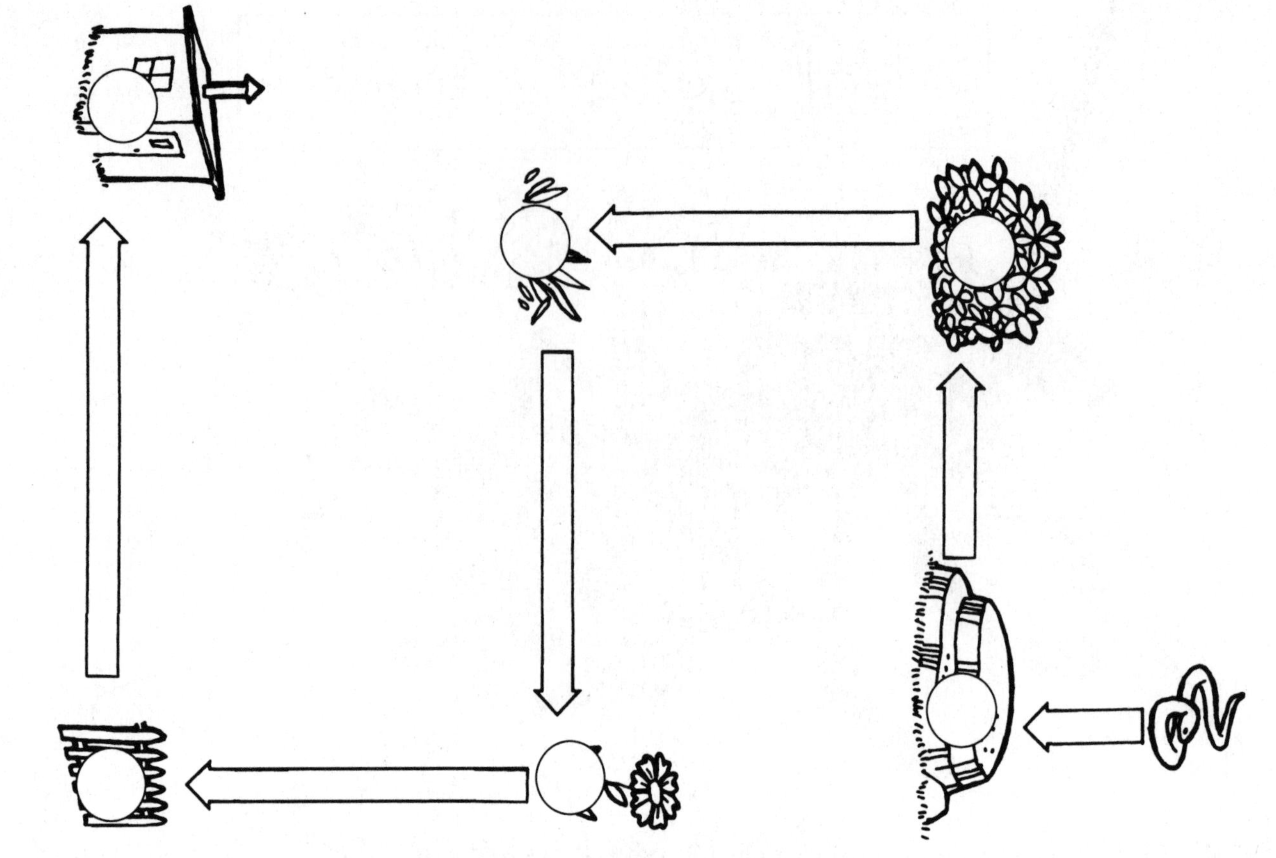

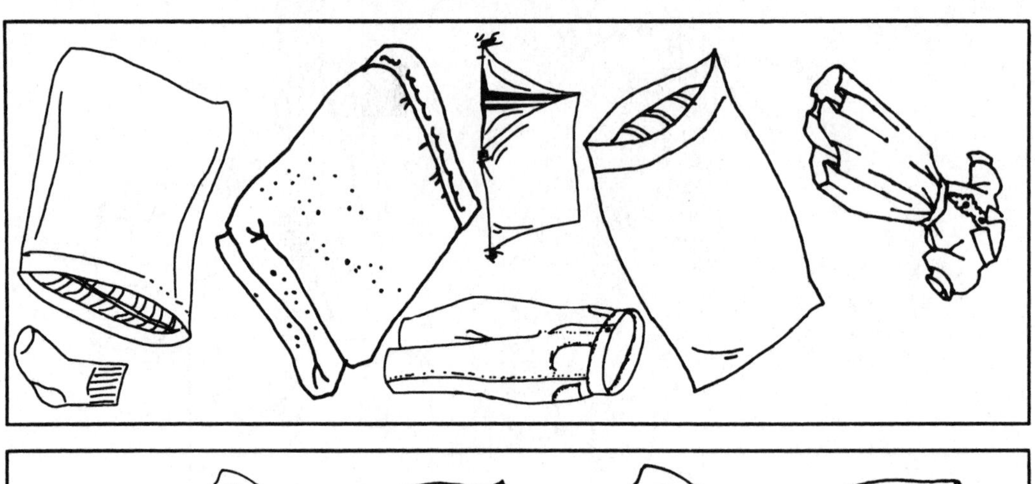

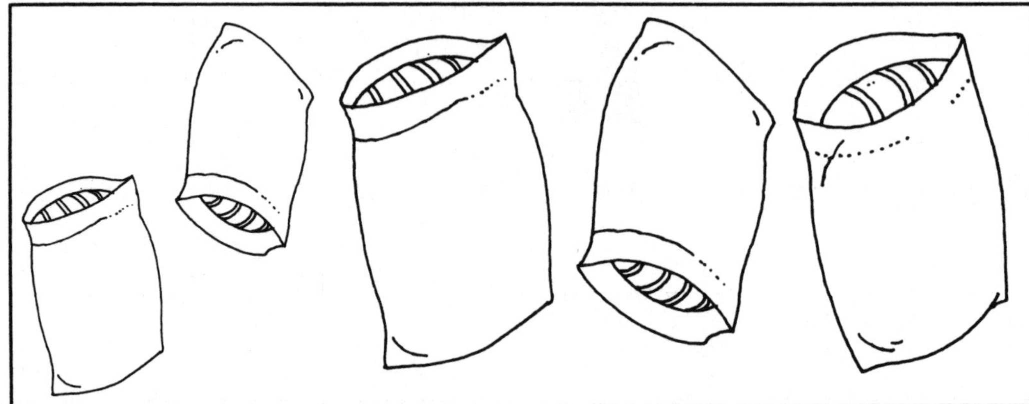

Name ________________________

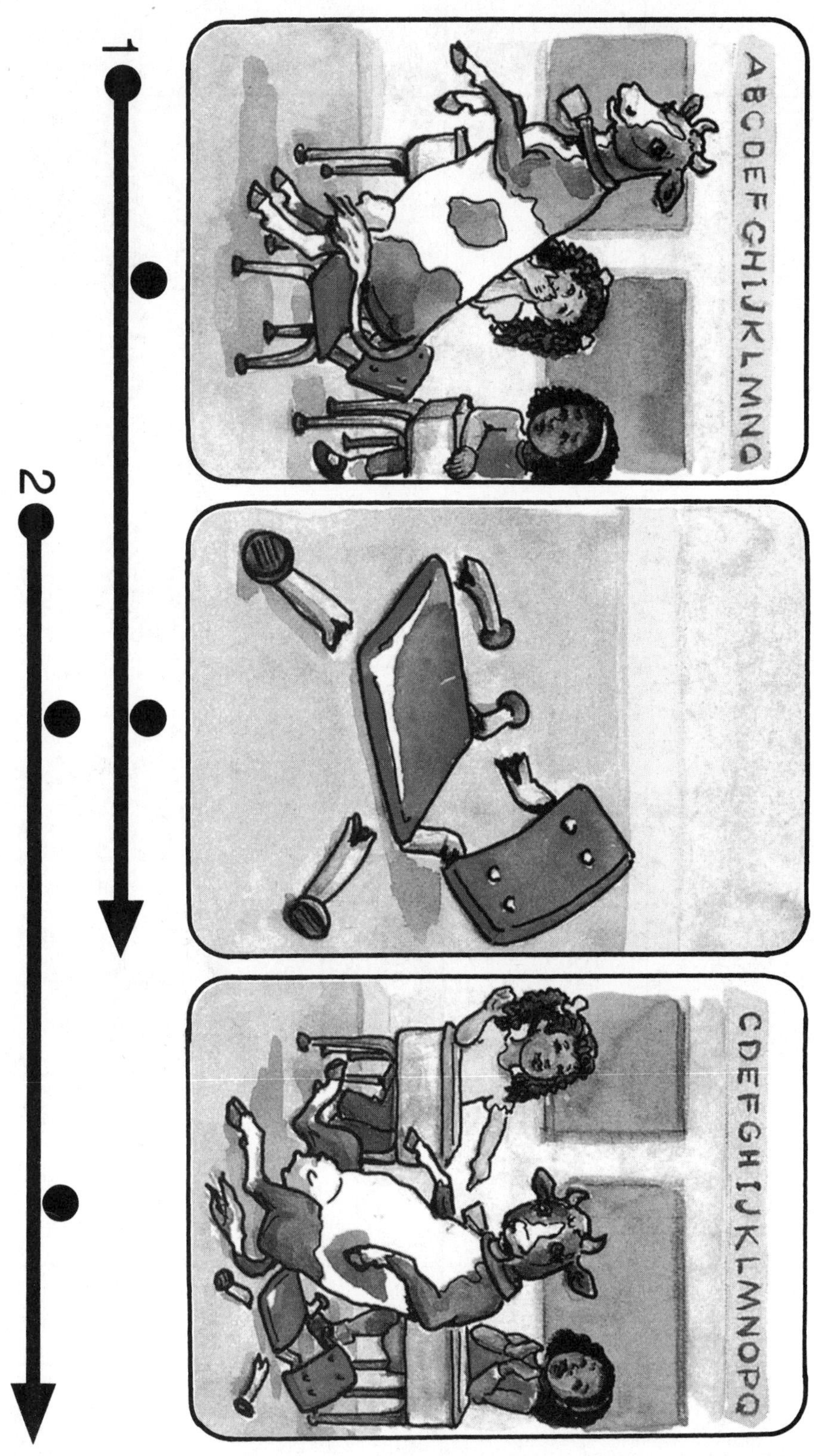

was rope rug

Name ______________________________

Clarabelle	sat on	a hat	Sweetie
Paul	kissed	Molly	a rock
Bleep	painted	a pie	a rat

1. ______________________________

2. ______________________________

3. ______________________________

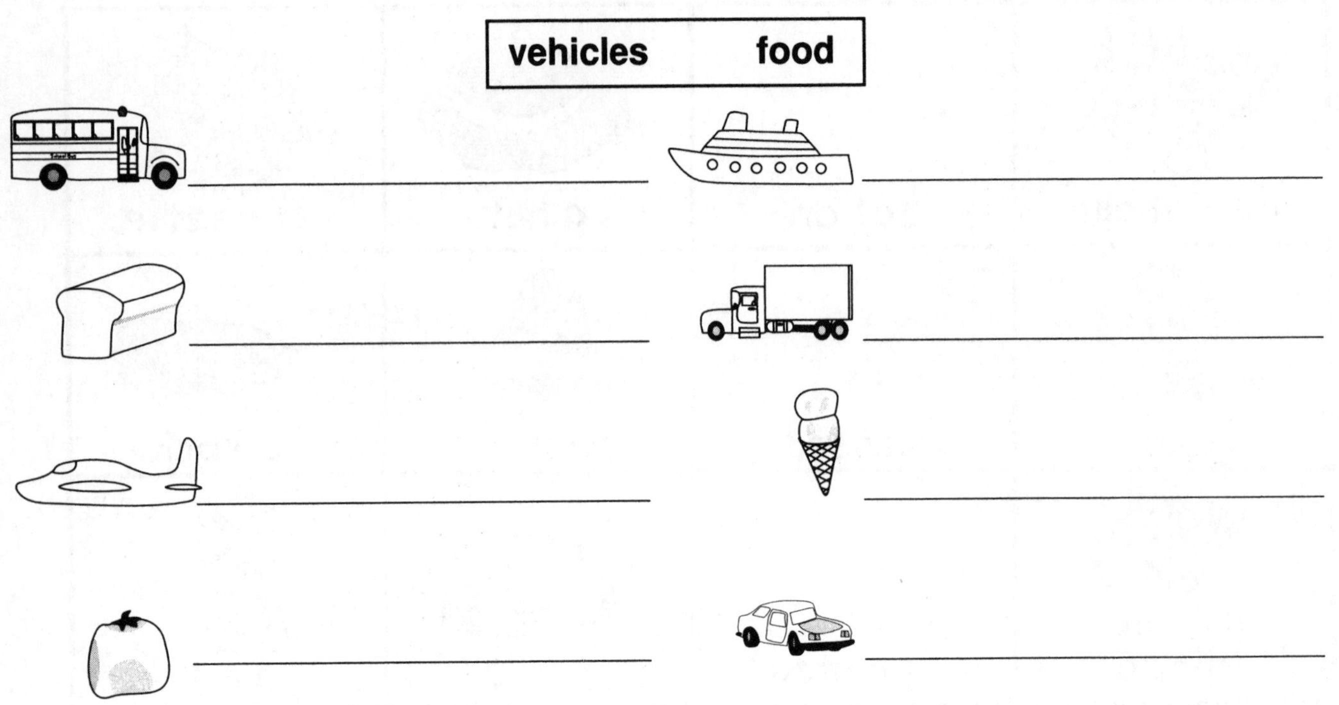
vehicles
food

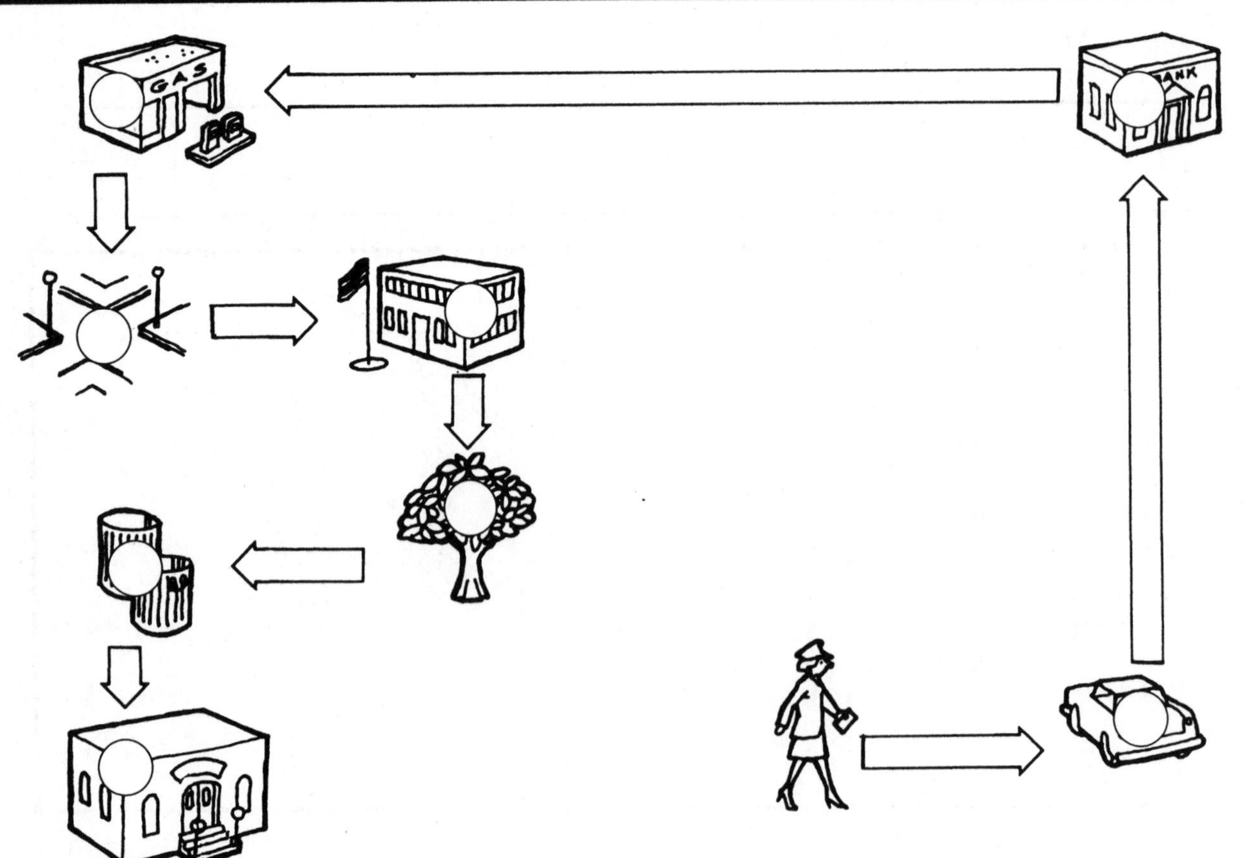
GAS
BANK

Name ______________________________

was	cow	hill

____

____

____

____

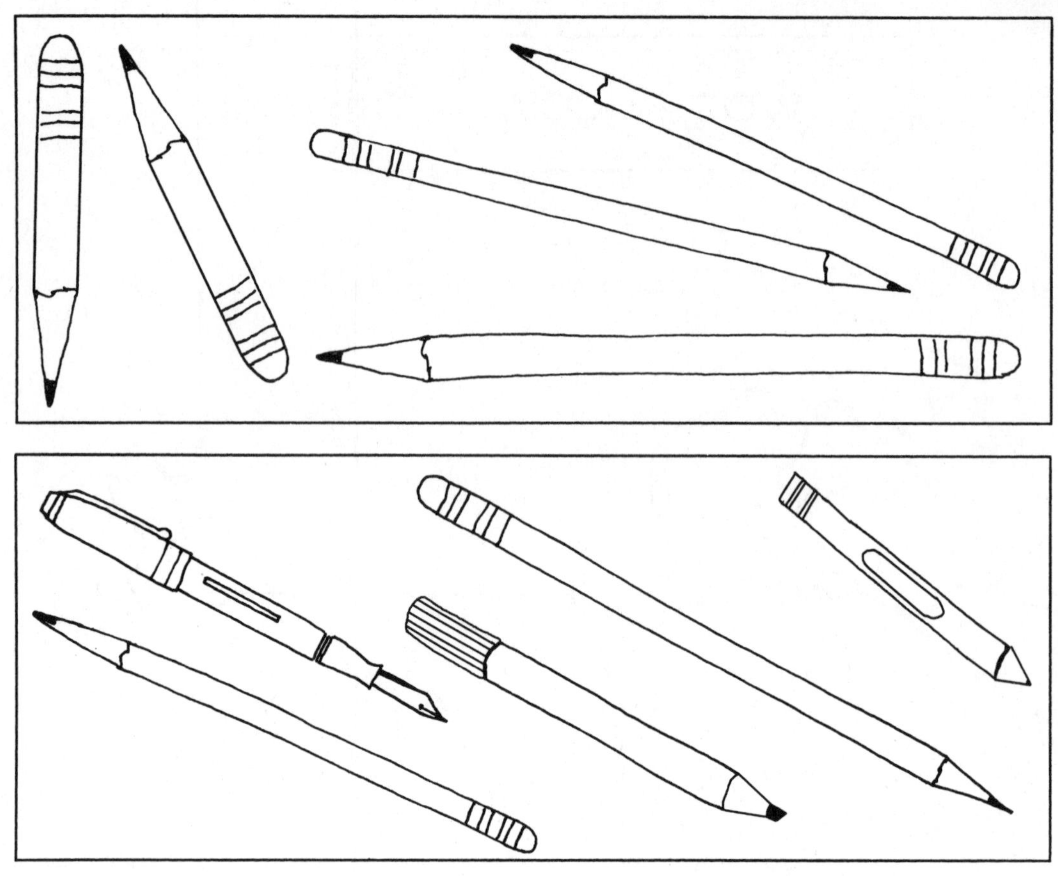

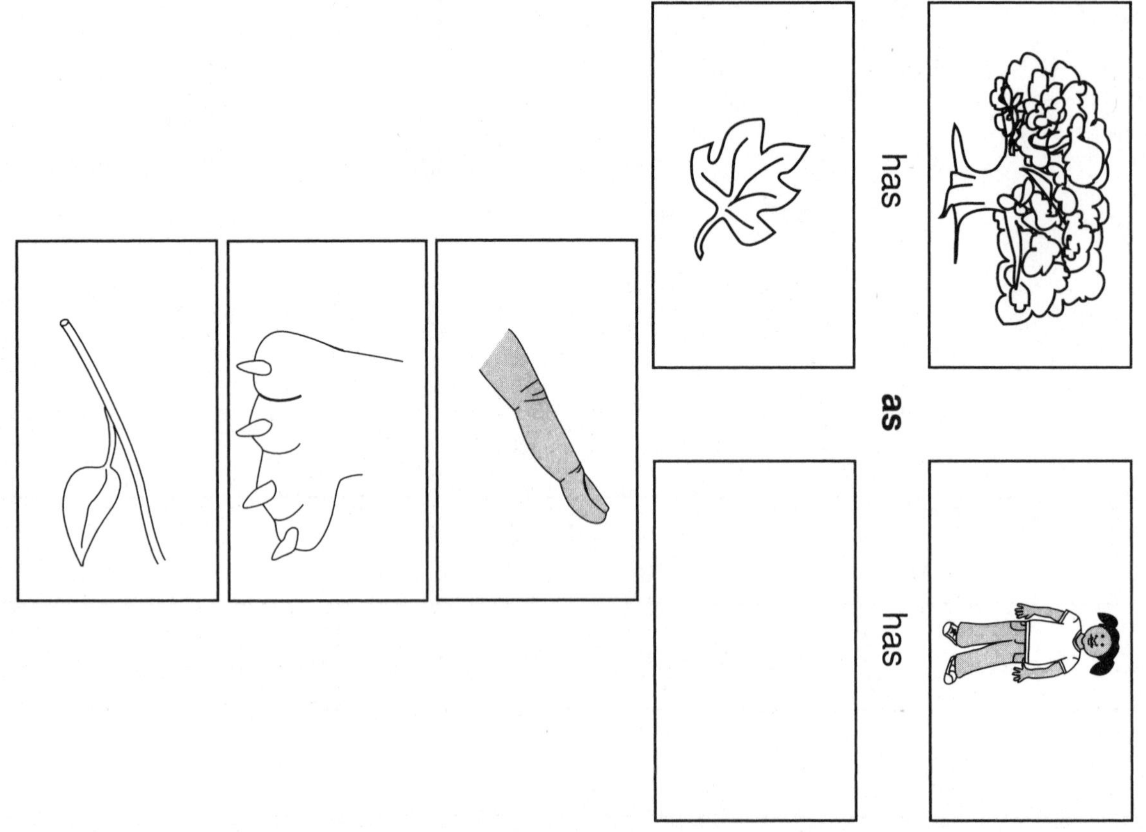
has
as
has

Name ____________________

lake sky kite

rough	tall	old	pull

1. push ______________________

2. young ______________________

3. smooth ______________________

4. short ______________________

---

tools	furniture	plants

______________________ ______________________

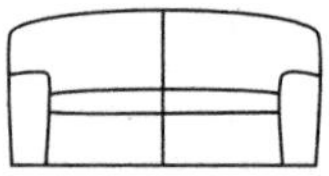

______________________ ______________________

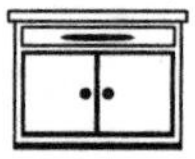

______________________ ______________________

______________________ ______________________

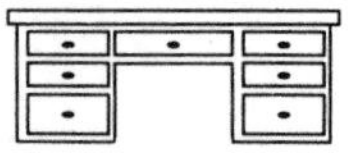

______________________ ______________________

Name ______________________________

was goat dog

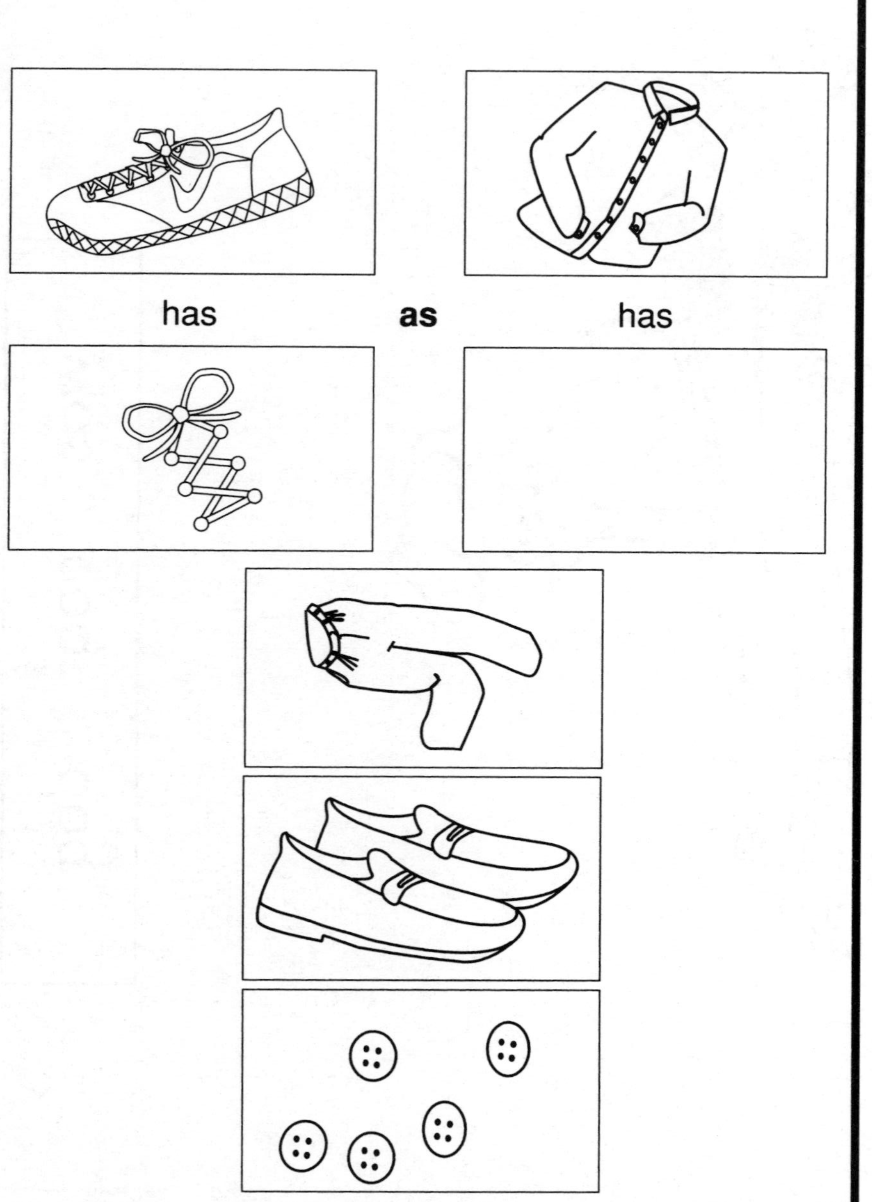

win	dry	short	fast

1. slow ____________
2. lose ____________
3. wet ____________
4. tall ____________

Name ______________________________

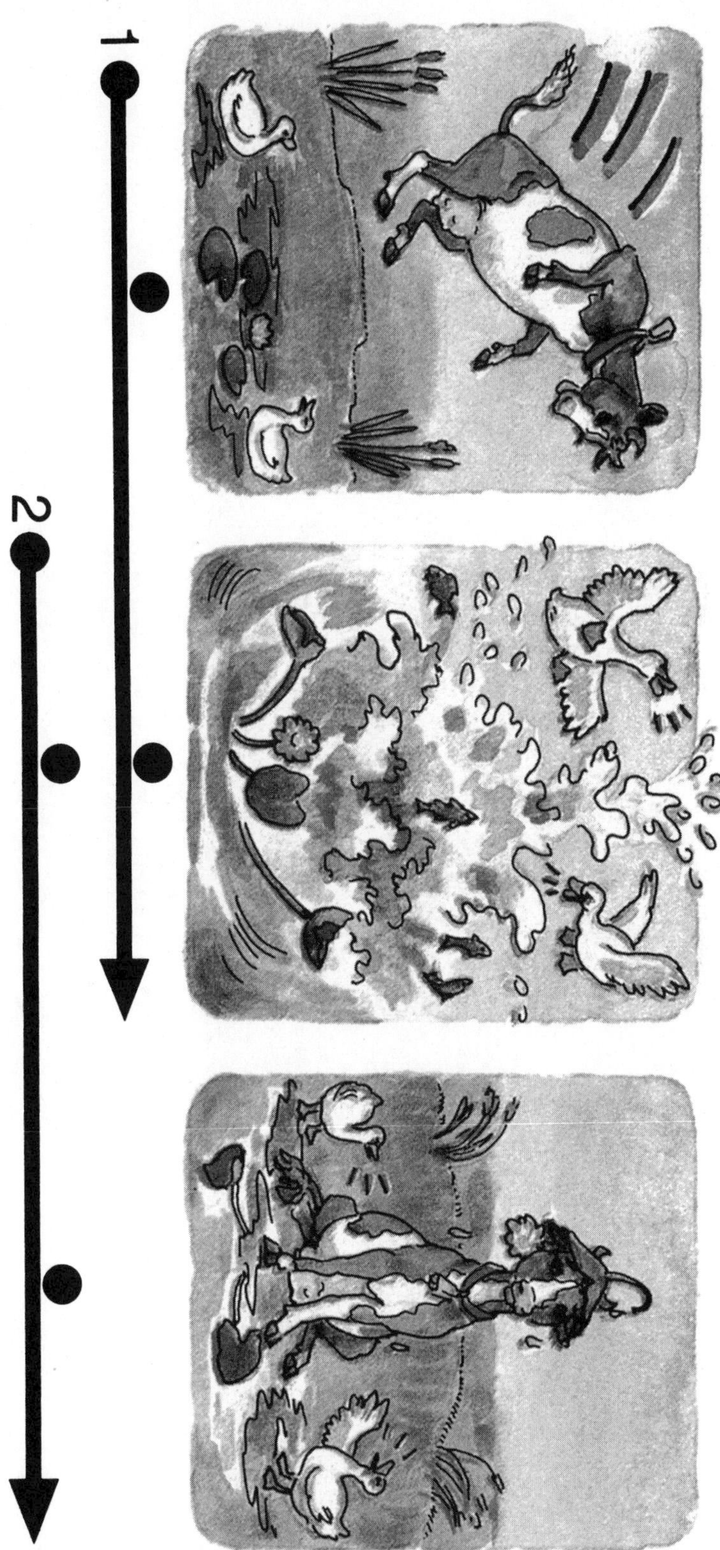

snake

Name ______________________________

1. One day, 16 green frogs were sitting on a log that was floating in a lake. The log was near the shore of the lake, and the frogs were having a very peaceful time, just sitting and sunning and making frog sounds – "Croak, croak."

1

2. Clarabelle was in a field right next to the lake. She saw those happy green frogs all lined up on that floating log and she said to herself, "My, that looks like fun. I would love to sit on that log."

2

3. So she tiptoed into the water and approached one end of the floating log. The frogs saw her coming and said, "Hey, what do you think you're doing? Get out of here. Can't you see that this is a frog log, not a cow log?"

3

4. But when Clarabelle ____________________

____

____

____

____

____

____

____

____

4

Name ___________________________

boy cat girl

____

____

____

____

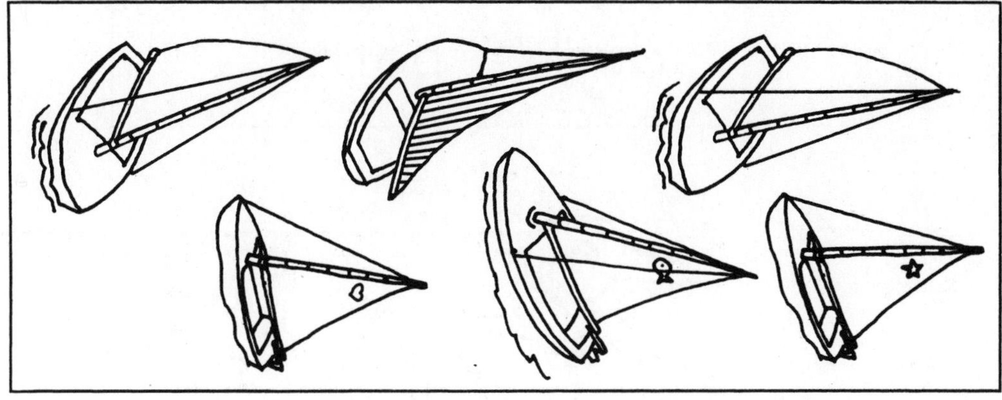

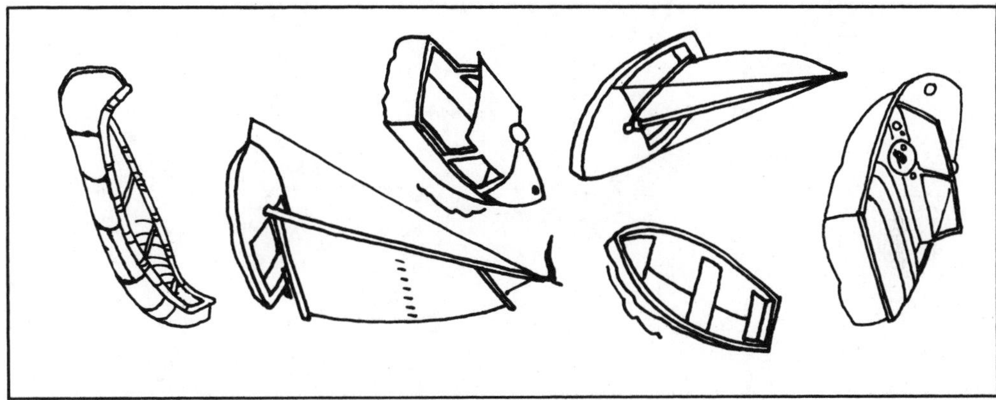

big	win	push	smooth	open

1. rough ________________
2. lose ________________
3. shut ________________
4. pull ________________
5. small ________________

Name ______________________

duck barn

____

____

____

____

vehicles	colors	plants

truck ____________

tree ____________

ship ____________

green ____________

van ____________

weed ____________

pink ____________

yellow ____________

grass ____________

red ____________

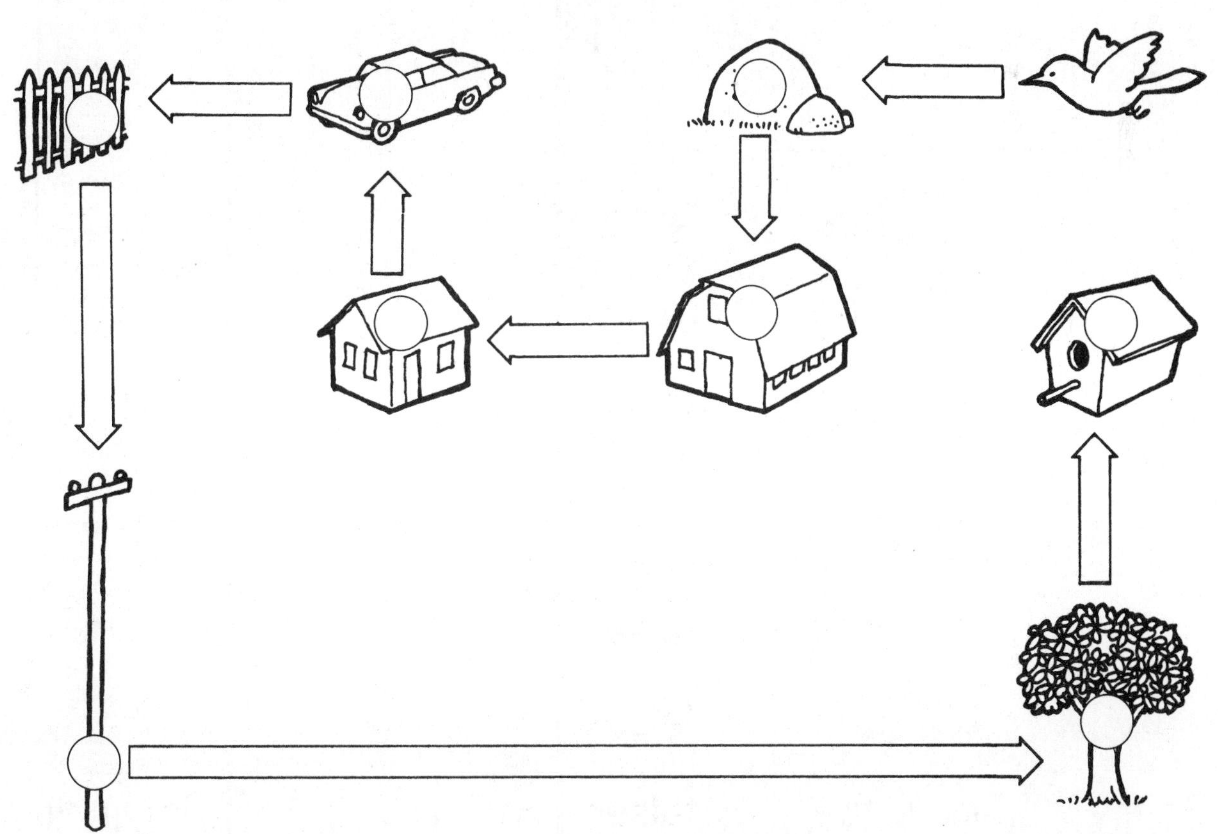

Name ______________________________

1. ______________________________

a. true false

b. true false

c. true false

2. ______________________________

a. true false

b. true false

c. true false

3. ______________________________

a. true false

b. true false

c. true false

4. ______________________________

a. true false

b. true false

c. true false

Roger

Clarabelle

Molly

Paul

Sweetie

Bragging Rat

hole mouse

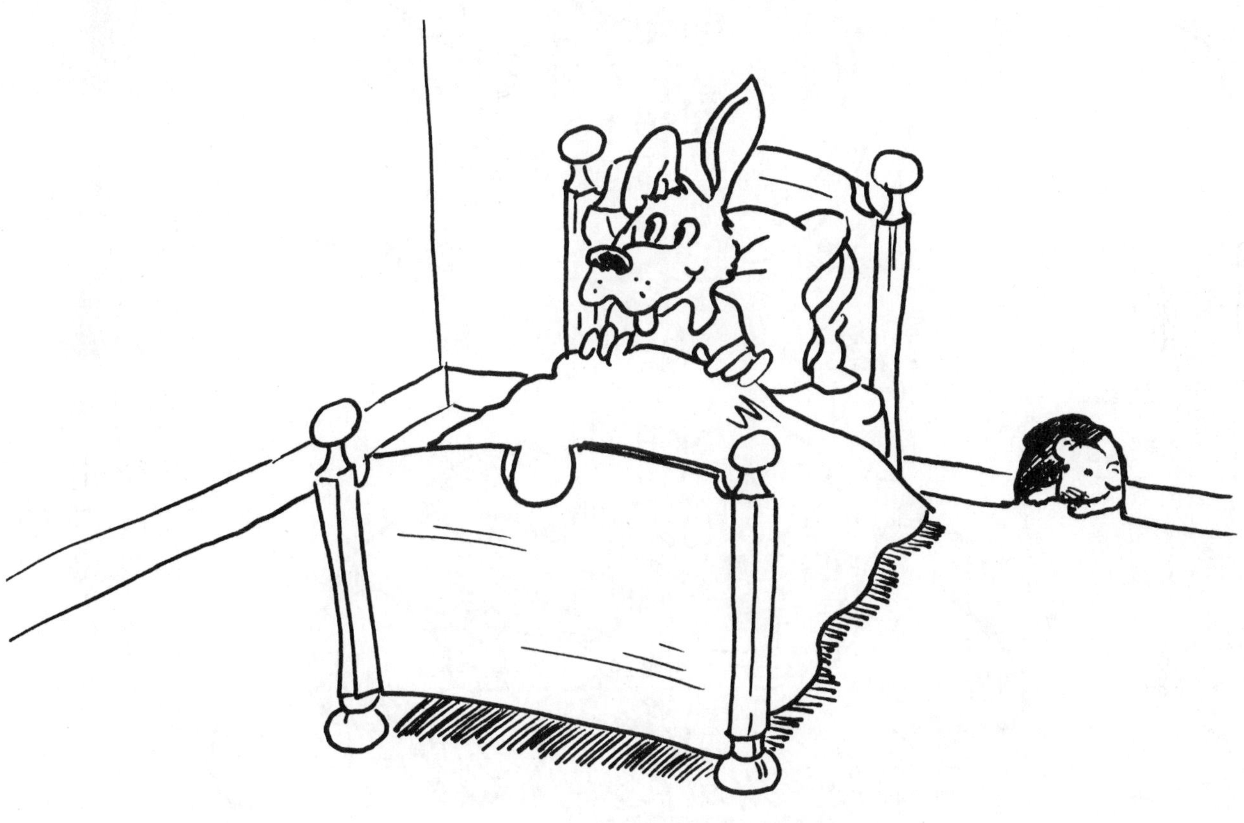

Name ______________________________

will stick turn

____

____

____

____

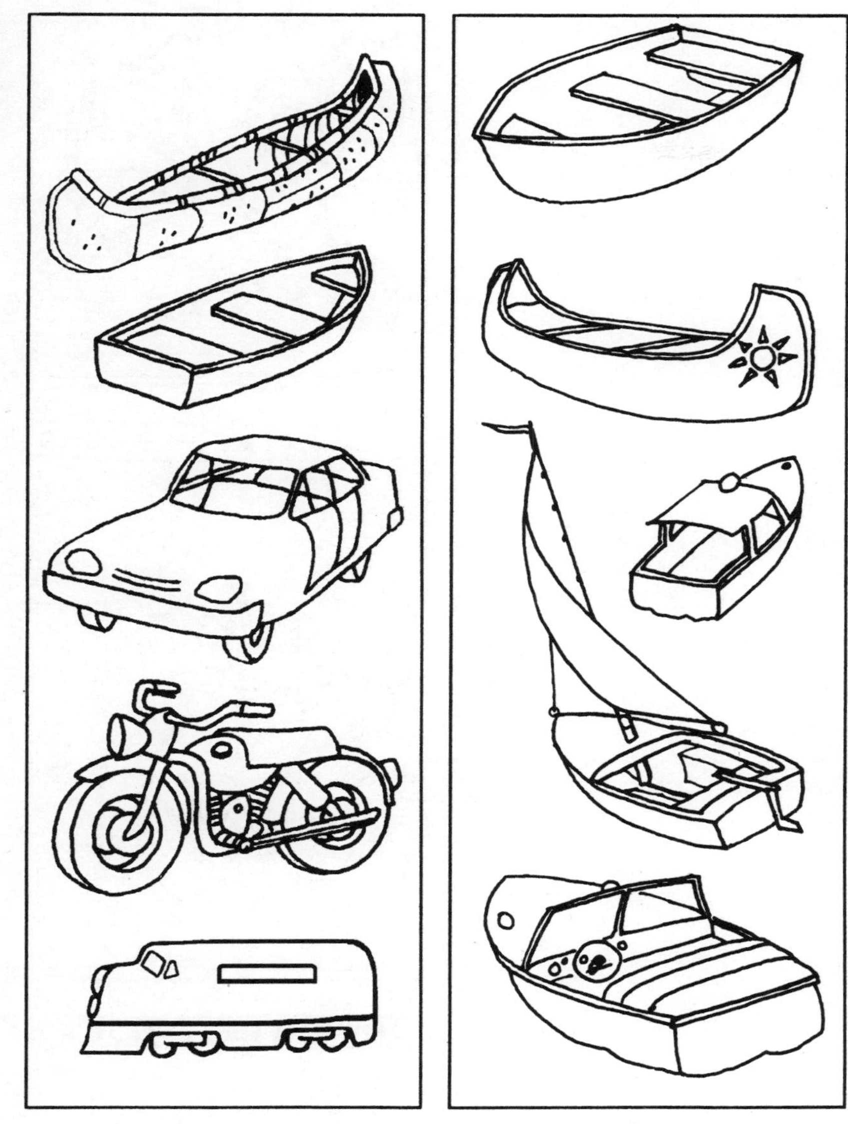

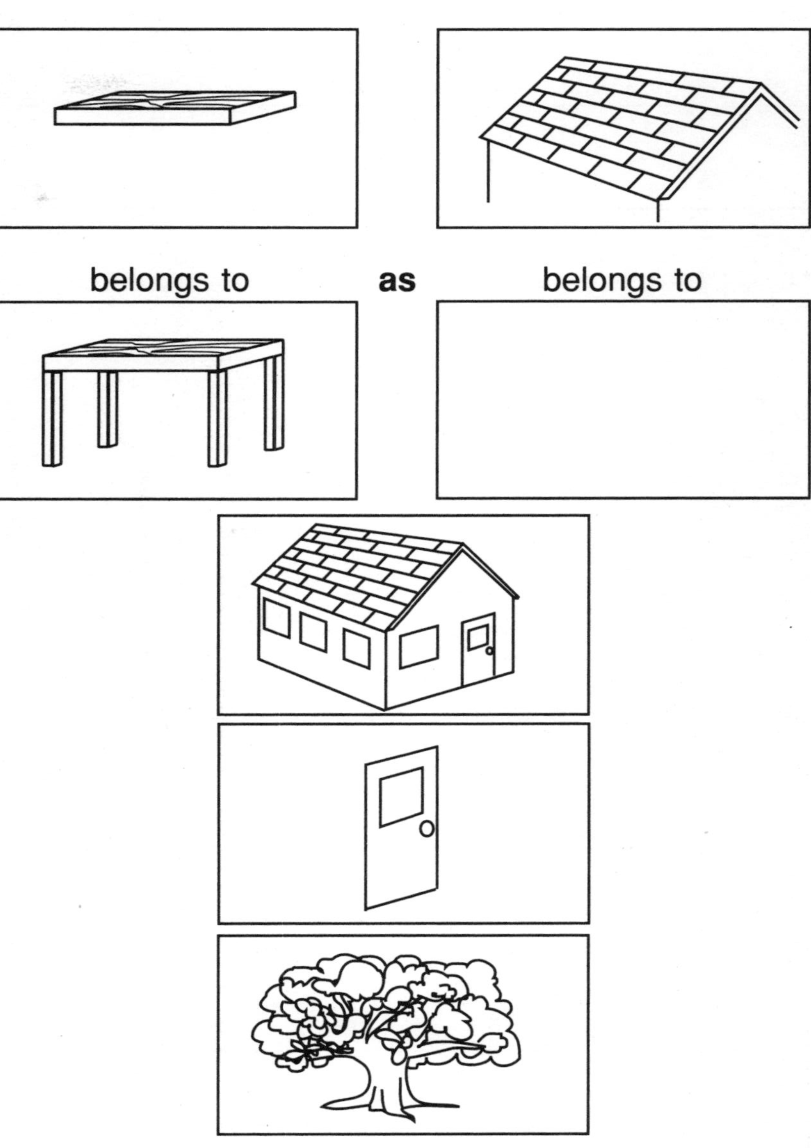
belongs to
as
belongs to

Name ____________

Clarabelle little chair broke

1.

2.

1.

2.

3.

4.

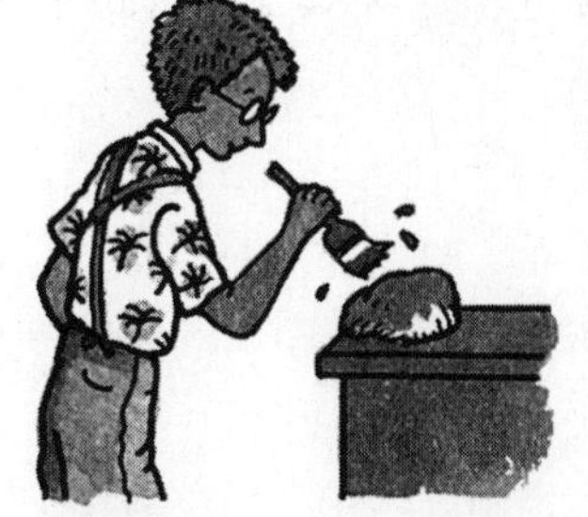

5.

6.

7.

8.

Name ___________________________

near cop

quiet	shallow	cooked	short

1. long ______________________

2. deep ______________________

3. loud ______________________

4. raw ______________________

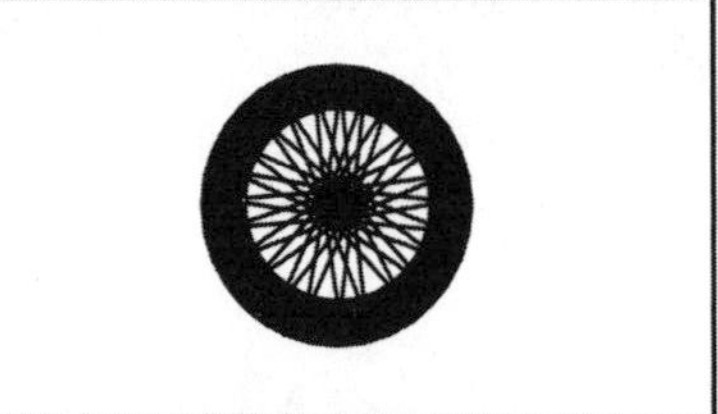

belongs to

as

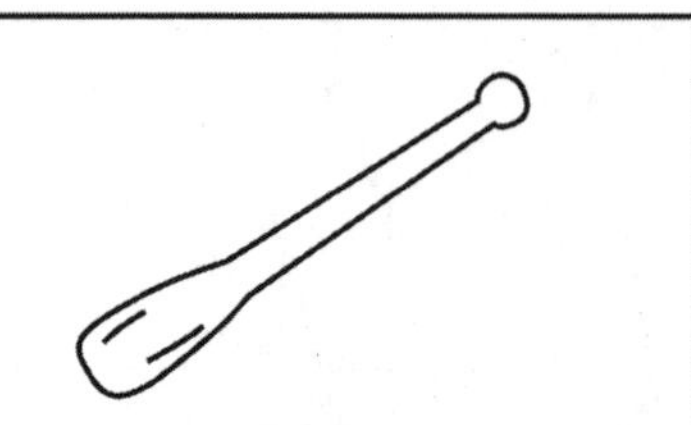

belongs to

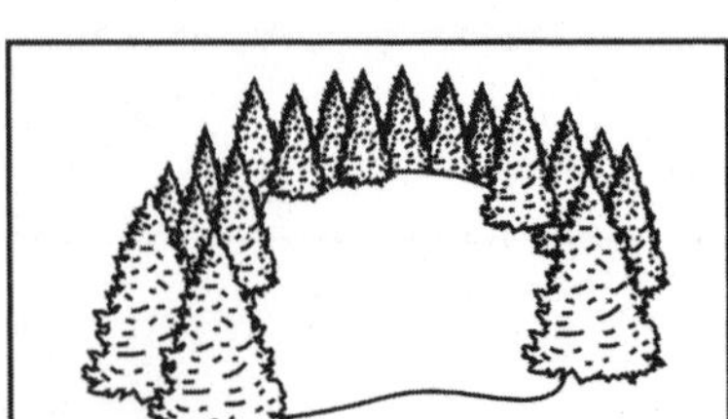

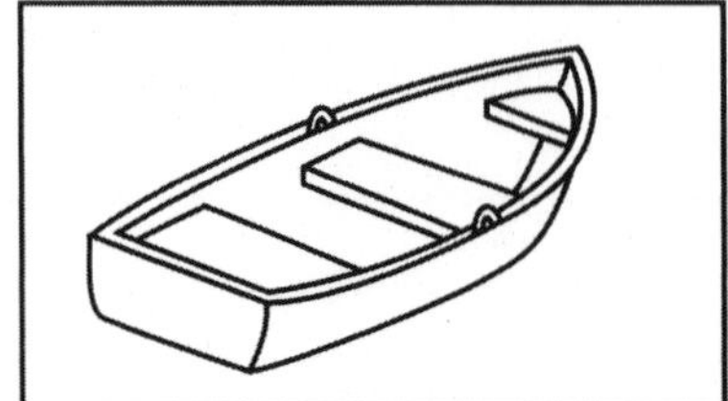

Name ____________________

balls black boat white

____

____

____

____

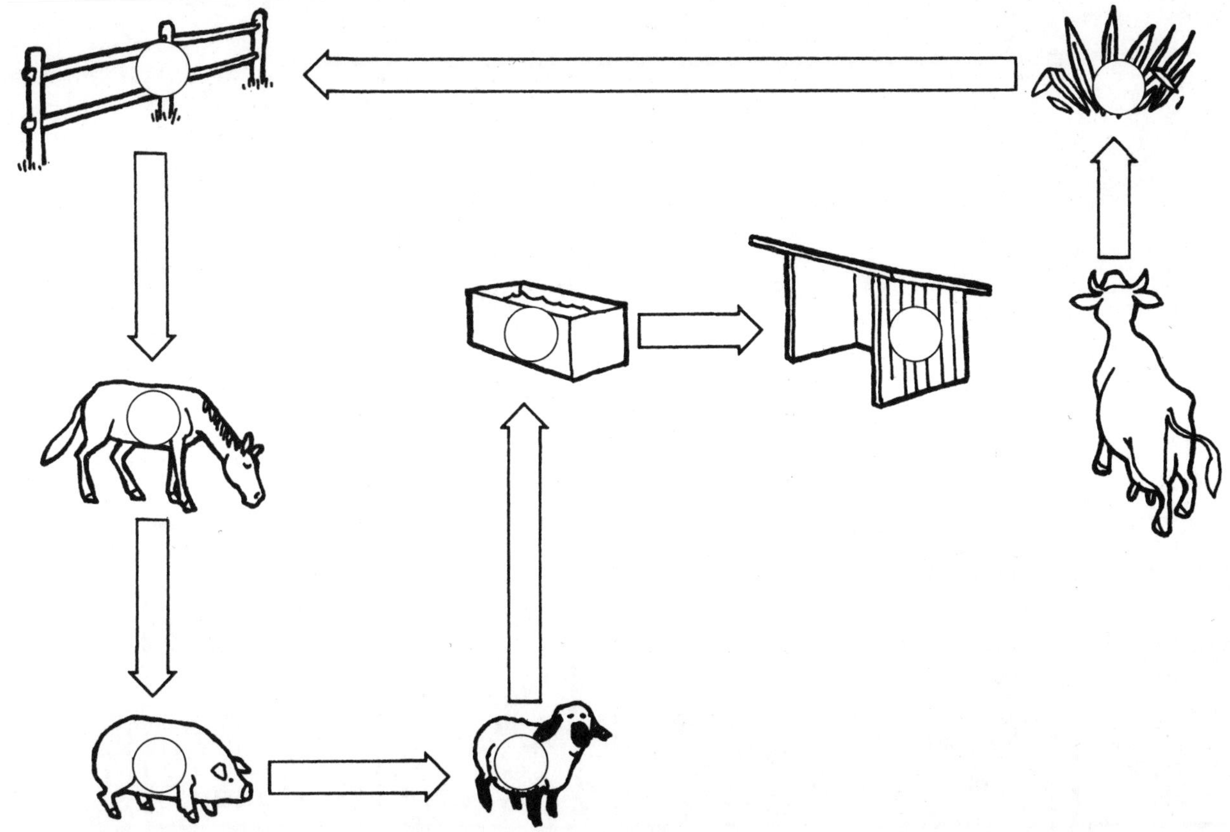

Name ______________________________

number 1	kite	honey	turtle	wrecking yard

a. ______________________________ ☐

b. ______________________________ ☐

c. ______________________________ ☐

d. ______________________________ ☐

e. ______________________________ ☐

f. ______________________

g. ______________________

h. ______________________

i. ______________________

j. ______________________

Name ______________________________

licked ear cow

____

____

____

____

belongs to
as
belongs to

Name ______________________________

Sweetie Andrea Honey bit chased

1.

____

____

2.

____

____

wide **shiny** **pull** **short** **long**

1. tall ________
2. push ________
3. narrow ________
4. dull ________
5. short ________

---

containers **numbers** **tools**

jar ________	six ________
saw ________	bag ________
ten ________	rake ________
cup ________	three ________
mop ________	nine ________

Name ______________________________

black white

cry	short	difficult	wide	dark

1. easy ____________________

2. laugh ____________________

3. light ____________________

4. narrow ____________________

5. tall ____________________

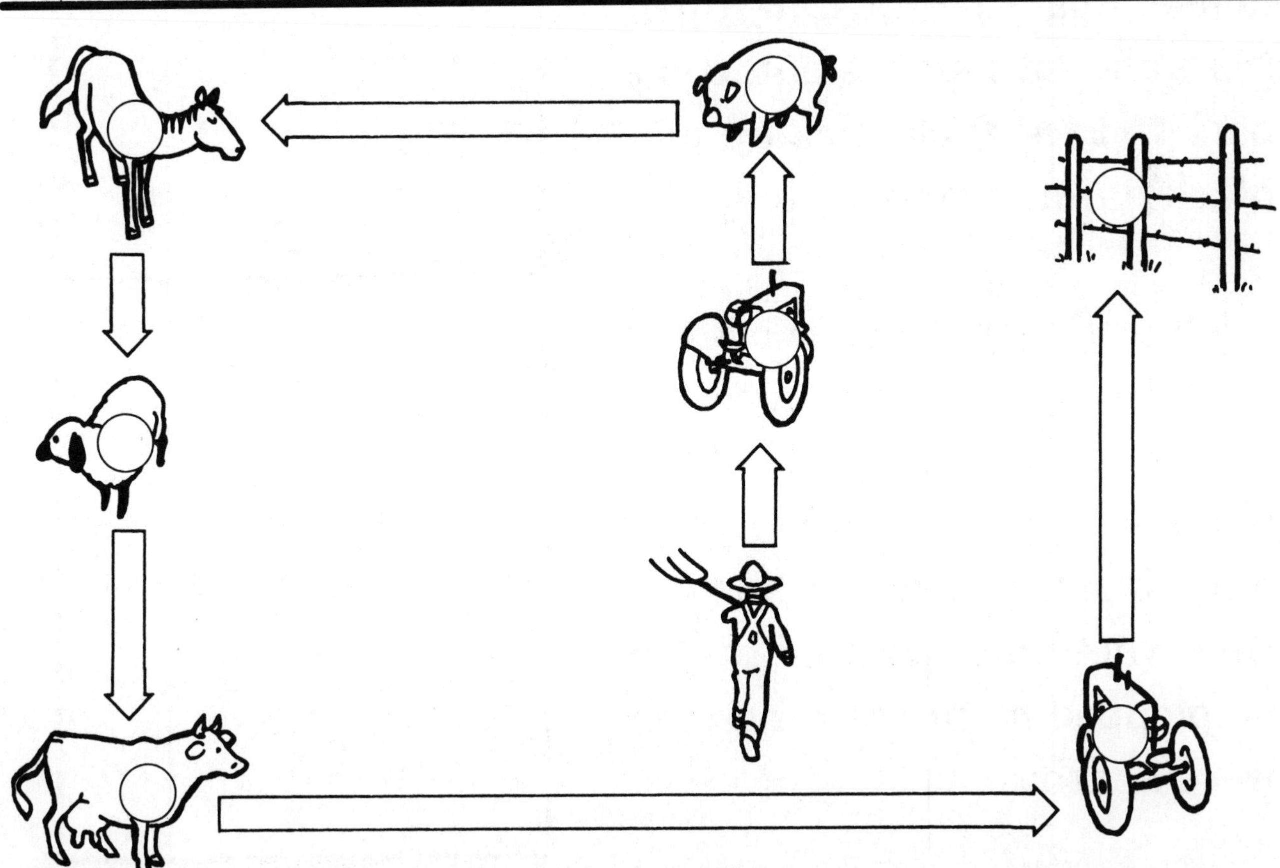

Name ______________________________

1. Roger had many favorite hats. But his most favorite was a big black hat. One day, he put on that hat and went out for a walk. The day was very hot and Roger started to sweat.

2. Roger didn't want to sweat all over his very favorite hat. So he took off his hat and put it under a bench that was next to a house. Roger planned to finish his walk without his hat, come back to the bench, pick up his black hat and go back home.

3. What Roger didn't know was that the bench was next to Paul's house and that Paul planned to paint that bench pink. Roger also didn't know that when Paul painted things, he plopped paint on things that were nearby.

1
2
3

4. So, while Roger was on his walk, Paul came out and

4

Name ______________________________

front of back

____

____

____

____

sad	clean	push	near	dirty

1. dirty ____________________

2. clean ____________________

3. far ____________________

4. happy ____________________

5. pull ____________________

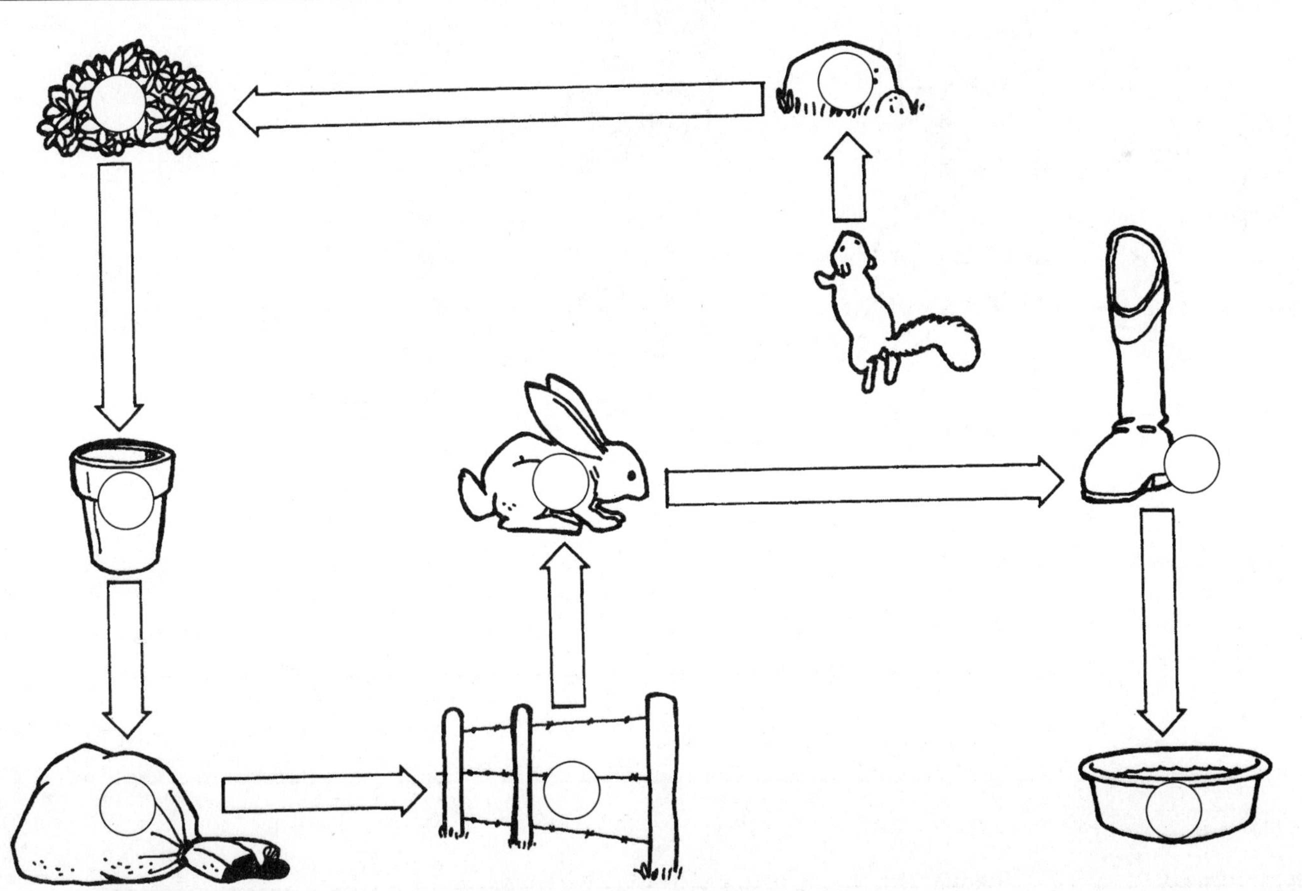

Name ______________________________

tiger front of eagle back

____

____

____

____

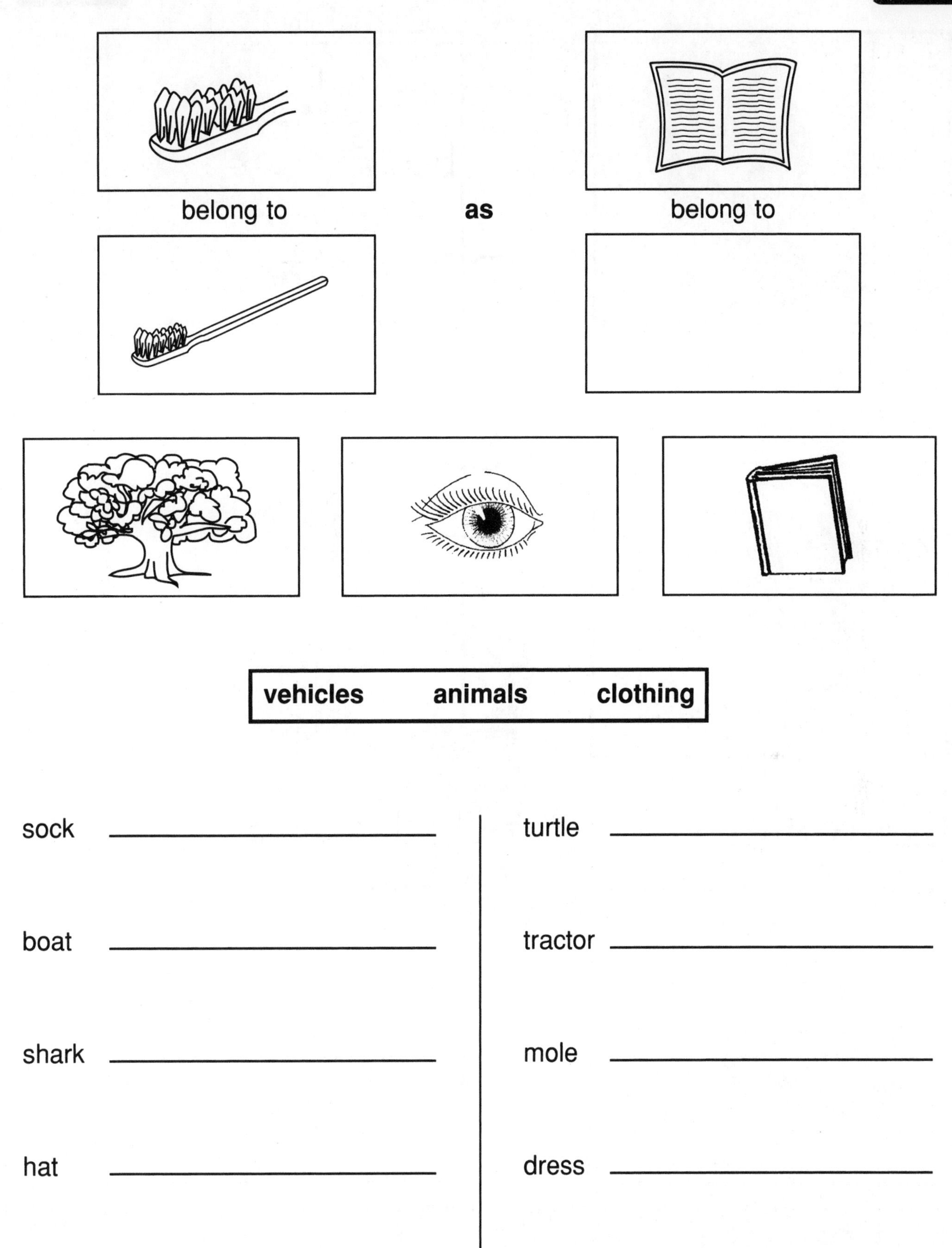

vehicles	animals	clothing

sock ______________

boat ______________

shark ______________

hat ______________

train ______________

turtle ______________

tractor ______________

mole ______________

dress ______________

car ______________

Name ______________________________

☐ Paul

☐ Sweetie

☐ Rolla

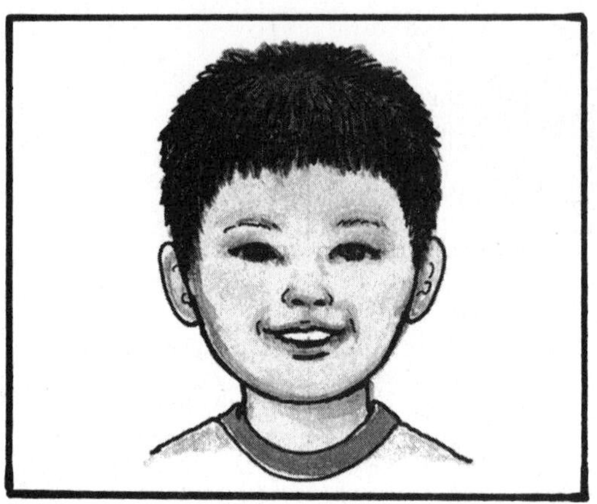

☐ Roger

☐ Honey

☐ Roxie

☐ Bleep and Molly

☐ Clarabelle

☐ Bragging Rats